Lecture Notes in Artificial Intelligence   898

Subseries of Lecture Notes in Computer Science
Edited by J. G. Carbonell and J. Siekmann

Lecture Notes in Computer Science
Edited by G. Goos, J. Hartmanis and J. van Leeuwen

Petra Steffens (Ed.)

Machine Translation and the Lexicon

Third International EAMT Workshop
Heidelberg, Germany, April 26-28, 1993
Proceedings

 Springer

Series Editors

Jaime G. Carbonell
School of Computer Science
Carnegie Mellon University
Pittsburgh, PA 15213-3891, USA

Jörg Siekmann
University of Saarland
German Research Center for Artificial Intelligence (DFKI)
Stuhlsatzenhausweg 3, D-66123 Saarbrücken, Germany

Volume Editor

Petra Steffens
IBM Deutschland Informationssysteme GmbH, European Language Business Unit
Vangerowstrasse 18, D-69115 Heidelberg, Germany

CR Subject Classification (1991): I.2.7

ISBN 3-540-59040-4 Springer-Verlag Berlin Heidelberg New York

CIP data applied for

© Springer-Verlag Berlin Heidelberg 1995
Printed in Germany

Typesetting: Camera ready by author
SPIN: 10485375   45/3140-543210 - Printed on acid-free paper

To Stella Isabel and Victor André,
the joys of my life

Foreword

The European Association is one of three regional associations which together make up the International Association for Machine Translation. The other two are the Association for Machine Translation in the Americas and the Asia-Pacific Association for Machine Translation. Each regional association organises local activities in its own geographical area. The parent association publishes a newsletter, MT News International, which appears three times a year with news of the machine translation scene. The International Association is also the sponsoring body for the Machine Translation Summit, a major meeting held once every two years, rotating through the three areas and organised by each regional association in turn.

All the associations are dedicated to furthering the cause of machine translation. Since this book is the product of a workshop organised under the auspices of the European Association, the standpoint which gives a special flavour to the endeavours of all the associations can most appropriately be illustrated by quoting from the European Association's statutes:

"The Association's purpose shall be to bring together users, developers, researchers and others interested in the field of machine and/or computer assisted translation research, development and use."

In others words, machine translation is perceived as an activity which requires the breaking down of communication barriers between groups which, even though all are concerned with machine translation, are usually considered disparate and which do not enjoy many natural opportunities to come together. Traditionally, the research community meets in academic conferences. Some few users belong to user groups, although many are isolated and feel, sometimes rightly, neglected by both the research community and the developers. System developers can fall into the trap of seeing themselves as the jealous guardians of their own technology, and be reluctant to discuss with either the research community or the users.

Such a situation is good for nobody. If the academic researcher never talks to the manufacturer, he cannot profit from the developers' expertise in order to discover where an investment of his own efforts might lead to the development of better products, with the consequent stimulus to the field which in its turn will benefit both researcher and user. If the manufacturer does not talk to the research worker, he cannot learn what current trends in research might be put to use in the development of improved systems. And both research worker and system manufacturer are ultimately dependent on the user, who will accept or reject the results of their efforts. Thus, both should know and be aware of the users' needs and desires. Finally, the user himself can make optimal use of those tools available to him only if he knows the state of the art and its limitations as well as what the future is likely to hold, information he can only get from the researcher and the developer.

This book is a splendid example of how fruitful discussion between the three communities can be. The workshop on which it was based brought together academics, system developers and users in a friendly and cooperative atmosphere which fostered good contact and good discussion. The results of that discussion are well represented in a book which contains important and illuminating contributions from all three communities and which will, I fell sure, prove a valuable resource for the whole field of machine translation. EAMT is proud to have been a sponsor of the original workshop, and of the book to which it led: we hope to be able to sponsor many more such events in the future.

This foreword cannot conclude without recording EAMT's awareness of the effort needed to bring an enterprise like this to a successful conclusion. Every organisation depends on its members: in this case, they have done us proud.

January 1995   Margaret King
                                                                President of EAMT

Contents

Part III: Describing Lexical Data

Introduction

Petra Steffens

IBM Deutschland Informationssysteme GmbH
Scientific Center Heidelberg
P.O.Box 103069, 69020 Heidelberg
Internet: psteffens at vnet.ibm.com

In April 1993, approximately fifty European experts in the field of Natural Language Processing met at the IBM Scientific Center in Heidelberg to discuss lexical issues which arise in the context of Machine Translation (MT) and Machine–Assisted Translation (MAT). The occasion of their gathering was the *Third Workshop of the European Association for Machine Translation on "Machine Translation and the Lexicon"*. The workshop presentations centered primarily on questions of acquiring, sharing, and managing lexical data, but also addressed aspects of lexical description. One of the main objectives of the workshop was to foster discussion among the developers of M(A)T systems, the researchers who are concerned with the theoretical foundations of such systems, and the actual users of M(A)T systems. The workshop was thus attended by scientists who work in a research–oriented environment, by computational linguists who are involved in the development of commercial M(A)T systems, by translators and other professionals who practise multilingual activities, and by experts engaged in standardisation activities. This book presents a selection of the written versions of the talks that were given at the workshop. In the following discussion, I would like to briefly introduce the topics which the workshop addressed and indicate how the articles included in this volume relate to them.

Considering how labour–intensive it is to compile lexicons for NLP applications manually, substantial efforts have been made to find alternative ways to populate computational lexicons. Traditional dictionaries became the focus of attention for a while in the endeavour to build large computational lexicons semi–automatically. Even though they differ substantially, both in form and in content, from the type of lexical component required by NLP systems, the wealth of lexical knowledge encoded in traditional dictionaries made them an attractive resource for building computational lexicons. Such work takes the machine–readable version of a published dictionary (henceforth referred to as "MRD") as its starting point and, after a more or less comprehensive analysis of the dictionary's macro– and microstructure, seeks to extract and formalise the lexical information that it contains.

Early efforts to exploit MRDs pursued a rather localist approach in that they attempted to extract only certain types of lexical data; they also employed programs for dictionary processing which had been specifically written for a single dictionary (see [10] and [9] for a survey of such projects). In contrast, more recent work aims at developing general methods and tools for processing MRDs. Broadly speaking, such a generic approach to dictionary analysis relies on several things, including utilities to read in the typesetting tapes provided by publishers, a parser for analysing the structure of individual dictionary entries, and a grammar which describes the structure of the entries and drives the parser. This approach has been taken, for example, by the Lexical Systems Group at the IBM T.J. Watson Research Center (see, e.g., [15] and [39]) as well as by the *ELWIS* project at the University of Tübingen ([26]). The tools developed by the Lexical Systems Group at IBM have also been employed in the project *Logic–Programming Based Machine Translation* ([40]) and in the related projected *TransLexis* (the topic of *Brigitte Bläser's* contribution to this volume), where they were used to derive the lexical knowledge required in machine translation from several sources and for several language pairs (see [7]).

Even though the idea of tapping the wealth of lexical information contained in conventional dictionaries and making it available to NLP systems is intriguing, the usefulness of this approach has been widely questioned. The concerns which have been expressed fall into three general categories (see, e.g., [10], [13], and [5]). First, the question of *dictionary coverage* can be problematical: Does the range of lexical items included in a dictionary present a representative selection of the (sub–)language which the dictionary claims to describe, i.e., does the dictionary contain all the relevant vocabulary items while excluding the more "esoteric" ones? How exhaustive is the information provided within a single entry for a given lexical item? For example, does the entry make all the relevant sense distinctions and does it explicate the inter–relations that hold between the different word senses? Does it provide all of the word's collocates? Does it allow the derivation of all of a word's subcategorization characteristics?

Second, the usefulness of a given MRD is closely related to the *reliability* of the information that it contains. Since the production of dictionaries is often not based on a rigorous and explicit classification scheme for lexical items and since computational methods which would have supported the lexicographers in maintaining consistency in the format of the entries were not available in the past, dictionaries often exhibit both descriptive and formal inconsistencies and ambiguities. Errors and inconsistencies in the descriptive content and the format of dictionary entries have been described, for example by Akkerman, as well as by Boguraev and Briscoe, who report on the difficulties encountered in analysing the grammar codes of the Longman Dictionary of Contemporary English (see [2] and [11]), and similarly by Bläser and Wermke, who subjected the Duden Universalwörterbuch of German to a formal analysis ([8]).

Third, dictionaries have traditionally been written for human consumption and thus rely heavily on their users' linguistic background knowledge. Dictionary definitions and examples of usage, for instance, usually presuppose a capability for full linguistic analysis for their understanding. Since what is to be the result of dictionary analysis is thus also a prerequisite for it, the term *bootstrapping* is sometimes used in this context (see [54] as well as the article by Ide and Véronis in this volume).

Considering the inadequacies of existing MRDs, it is clear that substantial effort is required to correct and refine the output of dictionary processing. This raises the question of how economically efficient it is to build lexical databases from MRDs or, more generally, what has been gained and what can be expected from MRD research. It is this general issue of assessing the usefulness of MRD work which *Nancy Ide and Jean Véronis* address in their contribution to this volume. In particular, they make explicit two postulates which seem to underly the work with MRDs: 1) MRDs contain information that is useful for NLP, and 2) this information is relatively easy to extract from MRDs. Through a detailed discussion of these postulates, they are led to the conclusion that MRDs do not appear to be consistent and complete enough to make them a substantial basis for a lexical knowledge base, and that, given the amount of work required to extract the information contained in MRDs, the return on investment is rather low. For Ide and Véronis, however, this does not imply that MRDs cannot contribute to the task of scaling up lexical databases, or that the research devoted to MRDs over the last 15 years has been for naught. Rather, like many other researchers (see, e.g., [6] and [34]), the authors advocate an approach to the construction of NLP lexicons which relies on multiple sources (MRDs, language corpora, etc.) and which recognizes the importance of manual refinement. In addition, they point out several areas of NLP research which have profited greatly from the insights gained from work with MRDs, such as the development of database models for dictionaries and other textual data, the assessment of the kind of knowledge needed for NLP, and the consideration of pure associational information for various NLP tasks. What they view as the most significant contribution of MRD research, however, is the growing insight that a more active collaboration of the NLP community with lexicographers and electronic publishers would be equally beneficial for all.

The requirement for a closer cooperation especially between lexicographers, and computational linguists has also been strongly emphasized by T.Briscoe:

> The future in computational lexicology and lexicography lies not in further conversion and exploitation of MRDs, but rather in active collaboration with lexicographers and dictionary publishers. Most dictionary publishers urgently need to make the transition from separate projects developing printed dictionaries to cumulative and ongoing development of L[exical] D[ata] B[ases]. ([13], p.63)

There are currently several projects in progress which seek to respond to these observations by bringing together lexicographers who work in dictionary publishing with computational linguists, the aim being to design and create lexical databases from which both dictionaries for human use and lexicons for natural language applications can be derived. Examples of such projects are *Genelex* ([3]), *DELIS* ([29], [24]), *Lexic* ([51]), *Hector* ([4]), and the *Cambridge Language Survey*, which is the topic of *Paul Procter's* contribution to this book.

In addition to using dictionaries to acquire lexical data (semi–)automatically, other methods which are based on language data in their original form, for example, methods that utilize the data contained in text corpora, have been investigated more recently. Whereas dictionaries provide a secondary source of linguistic knowledge in that they present the lexicographer's abstraction from real language use, language corpora are supposed to reflect a language in a more direct and unbiased way. Lexical acquisition efforts that exploit textual corpora pertain to various levels of linguistic description. These efforts have been directed, for example, at the generation of bilingual term lists (e.g., [50], [25], [23]), the identification of proper nouns and their semantic characterisation ([20]), the determination of lexically conditioned word associations (e.g., [17], [46], [31], [19]), the extraction of subcategorization information for verbs (e.g., [12], [38], [49], [52]), and the identification of semantic properties such as hyponymy relations among nouns (e.g., [28]) and conceptual similarity among nouns (e.g., [31]). Linguistic knowledge extracted from corpora has been used for a variety of NLP tasks and applications, among them resolution of structural ambiguities (e.g., [32], [53]), word sense disambiguation (e.g., [21], [27]), anaphora resolution (e.g., [22] and [37]), language generation (e.g., [46], [45]), and machine translation, where the use of corpus–based methods is central to the paradigm of statistical MT (e.g., [47], [14]).

The issue of lexical acquisition, both from MRDs and from corpora, is also central to the research on which *Ulrike Schwall and Angelika Storrer* report in this volume. Their work departs from a descriptive account of two types of multiword verb lexemes: verb idioms such as "to kick the bucket", and support verb constructions such as "to set into motion". After a discussion of the morphological, syntactic, and semantic properties which a lexical description should account for in order to enable a successful analysis, transfer, and generation of these constructions in MT systems, the authors report on several feasibility studies which have been undertaken to acquire lexical information on multiword verb lexemes: one employs statistical methods for the exploration of German text corpora and another applies dictionary–based extraction methods to a German monolingual collocation dictionary. They discuss the strengths and weaknesses of each method and point out some of the morphological and syntactic characteristics of German which pose a special challenge for the automatic acquisition of multiword lexemes from corpora. The conclusion they draw from this is that, for the acquisition of lexical information on multiword lexemes, one should employ a combination of corpus– and dictionary–based methods in which machine–readable dictionaries should be considered the primary source of information.

A special problem which arises in the area of lexical acquisition is that of automatically collecting terminology, in particular, differentiating special–language terms from general–language lexical items in text. In his article *The Pragmatics of Terminology: their Role in the Acquisition and Representation of Terminological Data*, *Khurshid Ahmad* proposes an approach to this task which relies on using special–language and general–language corpora comparatively: by determining the relative frequency of occurrence of a term both in a special–language corpus and in a general–language corpus and by computing their co–efficient, an indication of the term's subject–specific nature is obtained — which, in remembrance of Malinowski's ethno–linguistic studies, Ahmad refers to as a term's *co-efficient of weirdness*. He explains how the computation of a term's weirdness, together with other functions for terminology extraction and maintenance is supported by a set of integrated tools called *System Quirk*. In particular, he proposes a way of structuring terminological databases (or "term banks", as they are frequently called), according to certain pragmatic properties, in two parts, one of which contains less familiar and, therefore, frequently–accessed terms and the other of which contains more familiar, and therefore, less frequently–accessed terms. He also describes how System Quirk supports such an organisation.

Not only is there common agreement nowadays that lexical acquisition for NLP applications should rely on both dictionary and corpus data, but dictionary publishers have also realised that the lexicographic process itself would greatly benefit from a working environment in which lexical databases are integrated with online language corpora. As a result, several dictionary publishers are currently engaged in projects in which tools are being developed that support such a corpus–based approach to lexicography; examples are Oxford University Press, which participates in the already–mentioned projects Hector and DELIS, Van Dale Lexicografie, which is one of the DELIS project partners, and Cambridge University Press, which initiated the Cambridge Language Survey (CLS). In his contribution to this volume, *Paul Procter* describes the approach of the *Cambridge Language Survey* to building an integrated system for lexicographic development, or an "Integrated Language Database", as he calls it. Specifically, he explains techniques for syntactic analysis, for sense–tagging, and for identifying collocations which are used within the CLS for analysing corpora and for linking each word of the corpora to its corresponding entry in a dictionary. While the work done within the CLS has focussed on English so far, the objective of the project is to develop monolingual Integrated Language Databases for a number of European languages and to provide the corresponding translation links. This goal is being pursued in cooperation with several partners, among them suppliers of NLP products, in particular of MT and MAT systems, who contribute to the project by articulating their requirements for a lexical database.

A special variant of lexical acquisition from textual data employs methods from Machine Learning, in particular techniques which became known as "memory–based" or "example–based" (see, e.g., [18]; see also [42] and [41] for the use of example–based techniques in MT). These techniques begin with a set of correctly described linguistic data, the "exemplars" or "cases", and, by using similarity metrics, classify new instances of data with reference to the already–known cases. In his contribution to this volume, *Walter Daelemans* describes how methods from memory–based learning can be applied to various lexical acquisition tasks, such as identifying syllable boundaries, converting graphemes to phonemes, assigning word stress and determining part of speech. The approach he takes relies on a similarity–based learning algorithm which belongs to the family of lazy learning techniques (see [1]). Augmented by a method for assigning different degrees of importance to the features which have been used in describing the reference data, the algorithm produces results which, in most cases, are more accurate than those achieved by a connectionist or rule–based approach. Besides the engineering implications that his findings have for lexical acquisition, Daelemans argues that the theoretical relevance of his work lies in a process–oriented view of the lexicon: here, the lexicon is not seen as a static data structure, but as a set of processes by which unseen data can be classified. In this view, the notion of reusability, which will be discussed in the paragraphs that follow, refers to the multiple applicability of the acquisition method rather than the multifunctionality of the acquired lexical data.

Given that from an economic point of view it is hardly justifiable, and given that from a theoretical point of view it is unsatisfactory to start constructing a lexicon from scratch whenever a new application is being developed or whenever new theoretical assumptions are adopted, the sharing or *reusability* of lexical data has become a major concern over the last few years. The idea of sharing and reusing lexical data has been discussed as well under such headings as "the polytheoretic lexicon" (see [48]) and "the multifunctional lexicon" (see [35]). In reviewing the discussion on reuse, Calzolari ([16]) distinguishes two types of reusability:

1. reusability in the sense that already existing resources can be used again for an application other than the original one, and
2. reusability in the sense that new lexical resources are developed in a way that they can be employed for different applications and in different theoretical and methodological frameworks.

Whereas the preceding sections have dealt mainly with questions that arise in connection with reusability in the first sense, the following sections will address issues related to reusability in the second sense. As a major milestone in the discussion on reuse we have to consider the CEC–funded *EUROTRA-7* (ET–7) Study ([30]), which assessed the feasibility of constructing and sharing lexical and terminological resources among NLP projects and applications. In particular, the study surveyed existing sources for lexical acquisition, as well as existing standards, methods, and techniques for developing reusable lexicons, and proposed an architecture for a multifunctional lexicon together with a formalism and a method for the representation of lexical knowledge. In addition, it made recommendations for further short– and medium–term actions to arrive at large–scale, reusable lexical and terminological resources.

Central to the ideas and notions developed within the ET–7 Study is a scenario for the reuse of lexical data which accommodates both aspects of reusability explained above and which may be manifested in either of two ways: as a multifunctional lexical resource which supplies data to different applications ("data pool model"), or as a catalogue of guidelines and standards for lexical description and representation ("data exchange model"). The so–called "reuse scenario" assigns the concepts and activities associated with the two aspects of reusability explained above to three layers of description:

1. *the acquisition layer*: comprises sources for lexical knowledge such as corpora, machine–readable dictionaries, or NLP lexicons together with their respective acquisition tools
2. *the representation layer*: hosts a knowledge source containing lexical data pertaining to different levels of linguistic description (e.g., morphology, syntax, semantics), and usable in different application contexts

3. *the application layer*: embraces different types of NLP applications, which require lexical data of varying format and descriptive content and which obtain these data from the common lexical knowledge source by use of appropriate compiling and filtering tools

Departing from this scenario, an architecture for reusable lexical resources has been proposed within the ET–7 Study, which comprises three levels of lexical representation:

1. *a generic description layer*, which is based on a powerful representation formalism for lexical knowledge, which accommodates tests for determining the minimal observable differences between lexical items, and at which lexical acquisition efforts are targeted (this layer is referred to as the "Common Interface Layer")
2. *an application layer*, which consists of theory– and application–specific lexicons, and which includes a database that contains common lexical knowledge to be provided to the different applications
3. *a compiler/interpreter layer*, which embraces tools that translate between the generic representations and the application–specific ones

One of the recommendations made by the ET–7 Study is to use a formalism based on typed feature logic for the Common Interface Layer ([44]; for a survey of feature logics and their role in grammar writing see [33]; for the use of typed feature structures in formulating grammar and transfer rules, see [55]). This choice is motivated by several aspects: typed feature formalisms have a sound mathematical foundation which can be kept within the boundaries of monotonic logic; they have great expressive power, which, e.g., allows for a class–based treatment of lexical objects, supports the representation and processing of partial information, and provides type–checking mechanisms; and, they are deemed particularly appropriate as an interface to data description languages of object–oriented database systems, which the ET–7 Study proposes using for the storage of lexical data.

In his contribution to this volume, *Hans–Ulrich Krieger* addresses two topics related to the use of typed feature formalisms for the modelling of linguistic knowledge in order to provide a uniform, HPSG–oriented framework for the representation of different levels of linguistic description. Given the fact that finite automata are frequently used as a modelling device for areas of linguistic description like morphophonology and morphosyntax (see, e.g., [43]), he proposes a way of representing and processing them within typed feature formalisms. Similarly, he shows how certain types of logical inferencing, in particular those expressed by DeMorgan's law and by the law of double negation, can be handled within typed feature formalisms, so that logical form simplification becomes part of the parsing process.

As mentioned above, the ET–7 Study set out to prepare the ground for further standardisation efforts in the area of linguistic resources. One of the standardisation initiatives which builds upon the ideas developed within ET–7 is *EAGLES*, the Expert Advisory Group on Language Engineering Standards.

In order to promote the consensus–building process among language researchers, EAGLES was launched in 1993 within the CEC program for Linguistic Research and Engineering (LRE). The overall objective of EAGLES is to accelerate the process of defining standards for developing, exploiting, and evaluating large–scale language resources. The work of EAGLES is concentrated in five areas: text corpora, computational lexicons, grammar formalisms, evaluation and assessment, and spoken language. Each area corresponds to one EAGLES Working Group. In her contribution to this volume, *Nicoletta Calzolari* provides an account of the historical background of EAGLES, its relation to other projects, its general mode of operation, the steps which are being taken to arrive at guidelines in the area of computational lexicons, and some preliminary results which were produced by the Corpus and the Lexicon Working Group in the area of morphosyntax.

It is important to note that the notion of the reuse of lexical data is commonly thought to refer not only to the exchangeability of lexical data between computerised applications, but also to the possibility that the lexical data can be used by both computer systems and human users. In fact, for certain language–related activities, it is indispensable that one and the same lexical resource is of service to humans as well as to NLP applications. As an example, consider a situation where, within the same organisational context and for the same subject area, translation is performed both by humans and by an MT system: only if in either case the same terminological data are accessed, can terminological consistency be guaranteed and maintenance efforts be kept at a minimum. However, while the need for a single terminological resource may seem an obvious requirement, the way things happen in real life is different. As a case in point, take the German software company SAP, which supports its human translators and technical writers with a terminological database accommodating all 13 languages currently in use at the company (SAPterm), and where, in addition to human translation, the MT system METAL is employed for translating software manuals from German to English. In her contribution to this volume, *Katharina Koch* explains the difficulties encountered in keeping SAPterm and the METAL lexicons synchronised, and describes how a translation memory is employed to — at least partially — compensate for the lack of one common terminological resource.

In light of users' needs, suppliers of commercial NLP — and in particular of M(A)T — systems become increasingly aware of the necessity for multifunctional lexicons that can provide lexical and terminological data both to humans and NLP applications. Two papers in this volume bear witness to development efforts that are designed to meet this need. The article by *Daniel Bachut et al.* describes a data model for multilingual lexicons, parts of which have been realised in several multilingual products that were developed by the French Company *Eurolang — Sonovision Itep-Technologies*. The model pays tribute to the reuse concept in that it has been designed to accommodate lexical information for different European languages that can be used both by humans and by MT systems, to represent lexical information in a way that is intended to be theory-neutral, and to account for general vocabulary as well as for subject–specific terminology. In their article, Bachut and his colleagues provide both a detailed account of the model's principal entities and relations, and a discussion of the linguistic and lexicographic motivation underlying its design.

The other article in this volume which exemplifies industrial efforts to develop a multilingual lexicon and terminology management system for human and computer use was contributed by *Brigitte Bläser*. Bläser describes the IBM system *TransLexis*, a system which addresses all three dimensions of the reuse scenario that was described above (see also [7]): it is based on a theoretically–motivated data model, which provides the descriptive apparatus for several European languages and which also accounts for both general vocabulary and terminology ("representation layer"); it serves different MT and MAT systems and provides a graphical user interface for developing, maintaining, and querying lexical and terminological information ("application layer"); and it is interfaced with several dictionaries, which have been employed in the acquisition of lexical knowledge ("acquisition layer").

The issue of multifunctionality is also central to the paper by *Vangelis Karkaletsis et al.*, which is based on research carried out within the CEC–funded LRE–project *Glossasoft*. Geared primarily to the task of software localisation, the authors present a knowledge–based architecture for the representation of linguistic and extra–linguistic terminological information. In particular, the model which they propose accommodates four different types of knowledge: knowledge about the software application to be localised, general knowledge about the given subject domain (e.g., Window Management Systems), language–independent conceptual knowledge, and language–specific linguistic knowledge. The formalism that is used to represent this knowledge supports a class–based treatment of concepts and terms, and provides the corresponding inference mechanisms for property inheritance, subsumption, and consistency checking. To illustrate the reusability of the architecture for different linguistic tasks, and to show how the different types of knowledge are employed in them, the authors outline the use of the model they have proposed for the generation of multilingual messages and for the matching of sentences as required for the implementation of a translation memory.

The integration of terminological data and knowledge of a given subject domain has also been pursued in the CEC–funded **ESPRIT** project *Translator's Workbench* ([36]). This project is aimed at developing a comprehensive set of tools that support different types of users in performing different language–related tasks such as translation and text production in a nonnative language. In particular, one of the objectives was to provide a terminological database which offers the translator or technical writer not only the possibility of maintaining and searching multilingual terminology, but also a way of exploring the subject area to which a given term belongs. In her article *Navigation through Terminological Databases*, *Renate Mayer* explains how this has been achieved: together with linguistic information for a given term, texts are stored that provide further definitional and explanatory information for the term; by methods employed in information retrieval, these texts are indexed and texts relating to the same topic are organised in clusters; based on hypertext techniques, a browser has been implemented, which allows the user to navigate through this network of terms and descriptive texts, thus providing background information on a given subject and on related topics.

While the majority of the papers included in this volume emphasize aspects of acquiring and managing lexical data, the contributions by Folker Caroli, Ulrich Heid, and Nicholas Ostler address primarily issues of lexical description. Like Schwall and Storrer, *Folker Caroli* is concerned with the requirements which multiword lexemes pose for a lexical treatment in NLP systems. He discusses different types of lexical cooccurrences and investigates the problem of how translation equivalents can be found for such units, taking into account their syntactic and semantic structure, as well as their functional, pragmatic, and stylistic properties. From this discussion, he derives a set of descriptive parameters and describes the types of lexical information which must be provided for a computational treatment of multiword lexemes.

Ulrich Heid and Nicholas Ostler both present work from the above–mentioned project *DELIS*. This CEC–funded project, which began in 1993 and is coordinated by the University of Stuttgart, is characterised by a convergence of strands that emanated from the reuse discussion; specifically, it follows up some of the recommendations made within the ET–7 Study. The main objectives of DELIS are to produce monolingual and contrastive lexical descriptions of the syntactic and semantic properties of a selected range of nouns and verbs for several European languages, to formalise these descriptions in a typed feature based representation language, and to build a tool for the interactive, corpus–based acquisition of lexical entries which supports the descriptive methodology adopted. Since the overall goal of DELIS is to contribute to the creation of multifunctional lexical resources, two aspects of the project deserve special mention. One is the project's interdisciplinary nature: the project partners are theoretical linguists, developers of NLP applications and lexicographers; the methods and tools developed within the project will be validated in several different application environments, namely, in dictionary publishing, technical documentation, and machine translation. The other distinguishing feature of the project is its striving for empirical foundation: in order to facilitate the reusability of the lexical data and to motivate the lexicographic decisions that have been made, all lexical descriptions will be related with linguistic phenomena observed in the corpora used in the project. In the first phase of the project, the descriptive work focusses on the syntactic and semantic properties of vocabulary items of perception.

Taking Fillmore's Frame Semantics as a starting point, *Nicholas Ostler* presents some of the linguistic phenomena which a lexical description of perception verbs and nouns of English, Danish, Dutch, Italian, and French must account for. In particular, he analyses the behaviour of these lexical items with regard to intensionality and shows how context determines the semantic status of a verb's arguments, i.e., their having an intensional or extensional interpretation.

The monolingual dictionary fragments which incorporate the results of this analysis are the topic of *Ulrich Heid's* contribution to this volume: he explains their architecture and investigates the possibilities of relating them to build a set of contrastive dictionaries. He claims that the onomasiological approach underlying the construction of the monolingual lexical descriptions in DELIS provides not only a useful framework for building parallel monolingual lexicon fragments, but also makes it possible to relate these, thus facilitating the construction of bilingual lexical entries. As a first attempt at validating the resulting bilingual dictionary fragments, the article explores the feasibility of using the DELIS dictionary entries in an HPSG–based machine translation environment.

Acknowledgements

The following persons have contributed to planning and organising the Third Workshop of the European Association for Machine Translation on "Machine Translation and the Lexicon" through their imagination and their understanding of the subject field: Jakob Hoepelman, Maghi King, Hubert Lehmann, and Ulrike Schwall. For this, I wish to thank them. Several individuals, in particular Ulrich Heid, Susan McCormick, and Angelika Storrer, offered me their advice and editorial comments on the Introduction to this volume, for which I am very grateful. I am most indebted to Jens Hohensee, who, with admirable dedication and organisational skill, helped with all facets of the workshop's organisation. I also wish to thank Birgit Braun, Christel Nahkor, and Christiane Sturm for their administrative help in running the workshop and for their help in recording and writing up the discussions that took place during the workshop. My thanks go also to Michael Hoffmann and to Benno Rölker who, before and during the workshop, provided their expertise for planning the technical logistics and for coping with the conference equipment. I am most indebted to all of the workshop's participants, who shared the results of their work and who, with admirable openness and involvement, contributed to many a stimulating discussion. Last, but certainly not least, I should like to express my gratitude towards IBM Germany, which supported the workshop through generously providing human resources and facilities.

References

1. David Aha, Dennis Kibler, and Marc Albert. Instance–based learning algorithms. *Machine Learning*, 6:37–66, 1991.
2. Eric Akkerman. An independent analysis of the LDOCE grammar coding system. In Bran Boguraev and Ted Briscoe, editors, *Computational Lexicography for Natural Language Processing*, pages 65–83. Longman Group UK Limited, Harlow, GB, 1989.

3. Marie-Hélène Antoni-Lay, Gil Francopoulo, and Laurence Zaysser. A generic model for reuseable lexicons: The Genelex project. *Literary and Linguistic Computing*, 9(1):47–54, 1994.

4. Beryl Atkins. Tools for computer–aided corpus–lexicography: the hector project. In Ferenc Kiefer et al., editor, *Papers in Computational Lexicography — Complex'92*, pages 1–59, Budapest, 1992.

5. Beryl Atkins and Beth Levin. Admitting impediments. In Uri Zernik, editor, *Exploiting On-Line Resources to Build a Lexicon*, pages 233–262. Lawrence Erlbaum Associates, Hillsdale, New Jersey, 1991.

6. Remo Bindi, Nicloletta Calzolari, Monica Monachini, and Antonio Zampolli. Corpora and computational lexica: integration of different methodologies of lexical knowledge acquisition. *Literary and Linguistic Computing*, 9(1):29–46, 1994.

7. Brigitte Bläser, Angelika Storrer, and Ulrike Schwall. A reusable lexical database tool for machine translation. In *Proceedings of the Twelfth International Conference on Computational Linguistics (COLING)*, pages 510–516, Nantes, 1992.

8. Brigitte Bläser and Matthias Wermke. Projekt "Elektronische Wörterbücher und Lexika": Abschlußbericht der Definitionsphase. IWBS-Report 145, IBM Germany, Heidelberg, Stuttgart, 1990.

9. Bran Boguraev. Machine–readable dictionaries and computational linguistics research. Research Report RC 17854, IBM Research Division, Yorktown Heights, New York, 1992.

10. Bran Boguraev and Ted Briscoe. Introduction. In Bran Boguraev and Ted Briscoe, editors, *Computational Lexicography for Natural Language Processing*, pages 1–40. Longman Group UK Limited, Harlow, GB, 1989.

11. Bran Boguraev and Ted Briscoe. Utilising the LDOCE grammar codes. In Bran Boguraev and Ted Briscoe, editors, *Computational Lexicography for Natural Language Processing*, pages 85–116. Longman Group UK Limited, Harlow, GB, 1989.

12. Michael Brent. Automatic acquisition of subcategorization frames from untagged text. In *Proceedings of the 29th Annual Meeting of the Association for Computational Linguistics (ACL)*, pages 209–214, Berkeley, California, 1991.

13. Ted Briscoe. Lexical issues in natural language processing. In Ewan Klein and Frank Veltman, editors, *1991 Symposium Proceedings on Natural Language and Speech*, pages 39–68. Springer–Verlag, Berlin, Heidelberg, 1991.

14. Peter Brown, Vincent Della Pietra, Stephen Della Pietra, and Robert Mercer. The mathematics of statistical machine translation: parameter estimation. *Computational Linguistics*, 19(2):263–311, 1993.

15. Roy Byrd, Nicloletta Calzolari, Martin Chodorow, Judith Klavans, Mary Neff, and Omneya Rizk. Tools and methods for computational lexicology. *Computational Linguistics*, 13(3):219–240, 1987.

16. Nicoletta Calzolari. Lexical databases and textual corpora: perspectives of integration for a lexical knowledge base. In Uri Zernik, editor, *Lexical Acquisition: Exploiting On-Line Resources to Build a Lexicon*, pages 191–208. Lawrence Erlbaum Associates, Hillsdale, New Jersey, 1991.

17. Nicoletta Calzolari and Remo Bindi. Acquisition of lexical information from a large textual Italian corpus. In *Proceedings of the 13th International Conference on Computational Linguistics (COLING)*, pages 54–59, Helsinki, 1990.

18. Clarie Cardie. A case–based approach to knowledge acquisition for domain–specific sentence analysis. In *Proceedings of the AAAI-93 National Conference on Artificial Intelligence*, pages 798–803, 1993.

19. Kenneth Church and Patrick Hanks. Word association norms, mutual information, and lexicography. *Computational Linguistics*, 16(1):22–29, 1990.

20. Sam Coates-Stephens. Automatic lexical acquisition using within–text descriptors of proper nouns. In *Proceedings of the Seventh Annual Conference of the UW Centre for the New OED and Text Research: Using Corpora*, pages 154–166, Waterloo, Ontario, 1991. UW Centre for the New OED and Text Research.

21. Ido Dagan, Alon Itai, and Ulrike Schwall. Two languages are more informative than one. In *Proceedings of the 29th Annual Meeting of the Association for Computational Linguistics (ACL)*, pages 130–137, Berkeley, California, 1991.

22. Ido Dagan, Herbert Leass, John Justeson, Shalom Lappin, and Amnon Ribak. Syntax and lexical statistics in anaphora resolution. *Journal of Applied Artificial Intelligence*, 1995. to appear.

23. Beatrice Daille, Eric Gaussier, and Jean-Marc Langé. Towards automatic extraction of monolingual and bilingual terminology. In *Proceedings of the Thirteenth International Conference on Computational Linguistics (COLING)*, pages 515–521, Kyoto, 1994.

24. Martin Emele and Ulrich Heid. DELIS: tools for corpus–based lexicon building. In Harald Trost, editor, *Proceedings of KONVENS'94 — Verarbeitung natürlicher Sprache*, pages 415–418, Wien, 1994.

25. William Gale and Kenneth Church. Identifying word correspondences in parallel texts. In *Proceedings of the 4th Darpa Workshop on Speech and Natural Language*, pages 152–157, 1991.

26. Ralf Hauser and Angelika Storrer. Dictionary entry parsing using the LexParse system. *Lexicographica*, 9:174–219, 1993.

27. Marti Hearst. Noun homograph disambiguation using local context in large text corpora. In *Proceedings of the Seventh Annual Conference of the UW Centre for the New OED and Text Research: Using Corpora*, pages 1–22, Waterloo, Canada, 1991. UW Centre for the New OED and Text Research.

28. Marti Hearst. Automatic acquisition of hyponyms from large text corpora. In *Proceedings of the Twelfth International Conference on Computational Linguistics (COLING)*, pages 539–545, Nantes, 1992.

29. Ulrich Heid. Relating lexicon and corpus: computational support for corpus–based lexicon building in DELIS. In W. Martin et al., editor, *Proceedings of EURALEX'94*, pages 459–471, Amsterdam, 1994.

30. Ulrich Heid and John McNaught. EUROTRA-7 Study: Feasibility and project definition study on the reusability of lexical and terminological resources in computerized applications. Final report, CEC–DG XIII, Luxemburg, 1991.

31. Donald Hindle. Noun classification from predicate–argument structures. In *Proceedings of the 28th Annual Meeting of the Association for Computational Linguistics (ACL)*, pages 268–275, Pittsburgh, Pennsylvania, 1990.

32. Donald Hindle and Mats Rooth. Structural ambiguity and lexical relations. *Computational Linguistics*, 19(1):102–120, 1993.

33. Bill Keller. *Feature Logics, Infinitary Descriptions and Grammar*, volume 44 of *CSLI Lecture Notes*. Center for the Study of Language and Information, Stanford, California, 1993.

34. Judith Klavans and Evelyne Tzoukermann. Linking bilingual corpora and machine readable dictionaries with the BICORD system. In *Proceedings of the 6th Annual Conference of the UW Centre for the New Oxford English Dictionary and Text Research*, pages 19–29, Waterloo, Ontario, 1990.

35. Eugenie Knops and Gregor Thurmair. Design of a multifunctional lexicon. In Helmi Sonneveld and Kurt Loenig, editors, *Terminology: Applications in Interdisciplinary Communication*, pages 87–110. John Benjamins Publishing Company, Amsterdam and Philadelphia, 1993.

36. Marianne Kugler, Gerhard Heyer, Ralf Kese, Beate von Kleist-Retzow, and Günter Winkelmann. The translator's workbench: an environment for multi–lingual text processing and translation. In *Proceedings of the Third Machine Translation Summit*, pages 81–83, Washington, D.C., 1991.

37. Shalom Lappin and Herbert Leass. An algorithm for pronominal anaphora resolution. *Computational Linguistics*, 1995. to appear.

38. Christopher Manning. Automatic acquisition of a large subcategorization dictionary from corpora. In *Proceedings of the 31st Annual Meeting of the Association for Computational Linguistics (ACL)*, pages 235–242, Columbus, Ohio, 1991.

39. Mary Neff and Bran Boguraev. From machine–readable dictionaries to lexical data bases. Research Report RC 17854, IBM Research Division, Yorktown Heights, New York, 1990.

40. Mary Neff and Michael McCord. Acquiring lexical data from machine–readable dictionary resources for machine translation. In *Proceedings of the 2nd IBM I.T.L. Conference on Natural Language Processing*, pages 235–244, Paris, 1990. Compagnie IBM France.

41. Lee Ruggels. Example–based machine translation advances in Japan. *TechLink: Natural Lanaguage Processing*, March 1994. Supplied by the TechMonitoring Service of SRI International.

42. Satoshi Sato and Makoto Nagao. Toward memory–based translation. In *Proceedings of the 13th International Conference on Computational Linguistics (COLING)*, pages 247–252, Helsinki, 1990.

43. Anne Schiller and Petra Steffens. Morphological processing in the two–level paradigm. In Otthein Herzog and Claus-Rainer Rollinger, editors, *Text Understanding in LILOG*, pages 112–126. Springer–Verlag, Berlin, Heidelberg, 1991.

44. Jörg Schütz and Folker Caroli. An architecture for reusable lexical resources in a multi–theoretical environment, DOC–8 of the EUROTRA–7 study. Technical report, CEC–DG XIII, Luxemburg, 1991.

45. Frank Smadja. Macrocoding the lexicon with co-occurrence knowledge. In Uri Zernik, editor, *Lexical Acquisition: Exploiting On–Line Resources to Build a Lexicon*, pages 165–189. Lawrence Erlbaum Associates, Hillsdale, New Jersey, 1991.

46. Frank Smadja and Kathleen McKeown. Automatically extracting and representing collocations for language generation. In *Proceedings of the 28th Annual Meeting of the Association for Computational Linguistics (ACL)*, pages 252–259, Pittsburgh, Pennsylvania, 1990.

47. Keh-Yih Su and Jing-Shin Chang. Why corpus-based statistics–oriented machine translation. In *Proceedings of the Fourth International Conference on Theoretical and Methodological Issues in Machine Translation (TMI)*, pages 249–262, Montréal, Canada, 1992.

48. Hans Uszkoreit. Toward a polytheoretical lexicon. In *Proceedings of the Workshop on Automating the Lexicon*, Marina di Grosseto, Italy, 1986.

49. Takehito Utsuro, Yuji Matsumoto, and Makoto Nagao. Verbal case frame acquisition from bilingual corpora. In *Proceedings of the 13th International Joint Conference on Artificial Intelligence (IJCAI)*, pages 1150–1156, Chambéry, 1993.

50. Pim van der Eijk. Automating the acquisition of bilingual terminology. In *Proceedings of the Sixth Conference of the European Chapter of the Association for*

Computational Linguistics (EACL), pages 113–119, Utrecht, 1993.

51. Pim van der Eijk, Laura Bloksma, and Mark van der Kraan. Towards developing reusable NLP dictionaries. In *Proceedings of the Twelfth International Conference on Computational Linguistics (COLING)*, pages 53–59, Nantes, 1992.

52. Paola Velardi and Maria Teresa Pazienza. Computer aided interpretation of lexical cooccurrences. In *Proceedings of the 27th Annual Meeting of the Association for Computational Linguistics (ACL)*, pages 185–192, Vancouver, Canada, 1990.

53. Ralph Weischedel, Richard Schwartz, Jeff Palmucci, Marie Meteer, and Lance Ramshaw. Coping with ambiguity and unknown words through probabilistic models. *Computational Linguistics*, 19(2):359–382, 1993.

54. Yorick Wilks, Dan Fass, Cheng–ming Guo, James McDonald, Tony Plate, and Brian Slator. Machine tractable dictionaries as tools and resources for natural language processing. In *Proceedings of the Eleventh International Conference on Computational Linguistics (COLING)*, pages 750–755, Budapest, 1988.

55. Rémi Zajac. Inheritance and constraint–based grammar formalisms. *Computational Linguistics*, 18(2):159–182, 1990.

Part I

Acquiring Lexical Data

Part I

Acquiring Lexical Data

Knowledge Extraction from Machine-Readable Dictionaries: An Evaluation

Nancy Ide and Jean Véronis

Laboratoire Parole et Langage
CNRS & Université de Provence
29, Avenue Robert Schuman
13621 Aix-en-Provence Cedex 1 (France)
e-mail: {ide,veronis}@fraix11.univ-aix.fr

Department of Computer Science
Vassar College
Poughkeepsie, New York 12601 (U.S.A.)
e-mail: {ide,veronis}@cs.vassar.edu

Abstract. Machine-readable versions of everyday dictionaries have been seen as a likely source of information for use in natural language processing because they contain an enormous amount of lexical and semantic knowledge. However, after 15 years of research, the results appear to be disappointing. No comprehensive evaluation of machine-readable dictionaries (MRDs) as a knowledge source has been made to date, although this is necessary to determine what, if anything, can be gained from MRD research. To this end, this paper will first consider the postulates upon which MRD research has been based over the past fifteen years, discuss the validity of these postulates, and evaluate the results of this work. We will then propose possible future directions and applications that may exploit these years of effort, in the light of current directions in not only NLP research, but also fields such as lexicography and electronic publishing.

1 Introduction

The need for robust lexical and semantic information to assist in realistic natural language processing (NLP) applications is well known. Machine-readable versions of everyday dictionaries have been seen as a likely source of information for use in NLP because they contain an enormous amount of lexical and semantic knowledge collected together over years of effort by lexicographers. Considerable research has been devoted to devising methods to extract this information from dictionaries (see, for instance, [1,2,3,4,5,6,7,8,9,10,11]) based on the supposition that it is sufficient to form the kernel of a knowledge base that can be extended by utilizing information from other sources.

Interest in machine-readable dictionaries (MRDs) as a ready-made source of knowledge has waned somewhat in recent years. The number of papers on the topic at computational linguistics conferences and workshops (including the NewOED conference, which is devoted to the topic) is reduced, indicating either that extraction methods are well-established and robust (which is unlikely) or that research has turned to other areas. At the same time, the NLP community has turned its attention to corpora as a source of linguistic knowledge, evident both in the upsurge in the number of papers, journals, workshops, etc. dealing with corpora as a linguistic resource (e.g., the recent issue of *Computational Linguistics*, vol. 19, 1-2, 1993, devoted to corpus-based work, the workshop at ACL'93 on corpora, etc.) and in recent large-scale funding patterns (e.g., the European LRE program for corpora, ARPA's Linguistic Data Consortium in the U.S., etc.). It is clear that MRDs failed to live up to early expectations that they would provide a source of ready-made, comprehensive lexical knowledge. But does this mean that these many years of work on MRDs constitutes wasted effort? Does it mean that MRDs are conclusively unsuitable as a source for automatically building knowledge bases? In fact, while work on MRDs is eclipsed by the recent interest in corpora, no comprehensive evaluation of the value of MRDs as a knowledge source has been made in the light of the past ten or fifteen years' experience. Given the recent trend away from MRDs, as well as a greater understanding of what is needed in knowledge bases for NLP and how partial knowledge can be exploited, such an evaluation is timely in order to determine what may--or may not--be valuable to retrieve from MRD research.

This paper will first consider the postulates upon which MRD research has been based over the past fifteen years, discuss the validity of these postulates, and evaluate the results of this work. We will then propose possible future directions and applications that may exploit these years of effort, in the light of current directions in not only NLP research, but also fields such as lexicography and electronic publishing. We recognize a convergence of interests and goals between NLP and these other communities (cf. [12,13]), which may result in a benefit to all of them.

2 Thesis

MRD research has been based on two implicit postulates:

> **Postulate P1.** MRDs contain information that is useful for NLP.

> **Postulate P2.** This information is relatively easy to extract from MRDs.

The basis for postulate 1 is obvious when one considers a definition like the one for *fork* in Fig. 1, which identifies several semantic relations between *fork* and other lexical items that might be found in a semantic network. Access to this kind of information is often essential for many NLP tasks (sense disambiguation, PP attachment, etc.).

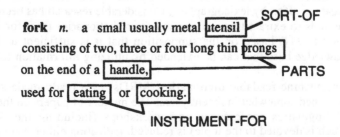

Fig. 1. Semantic information in definitions

Postulate 2, that most of this information is relatively easy to extract, was reinforced by work such as that described in [2] and [3], which proposed simple heuristics for automatically extracting hypernyms. These heurisitics exploit the fact that definitions for nouns typically give a hypernym term as the head of the defining noun phrase, as demonstrated in the following examples from the *Collins English Dictionary (CED)*:

> **dipper** • a *ladle* used for dipping...
> **ladle** • a long-handled *spoon*...
> **spoon** • a metal, wooden, or plastic *utensil*...

The apparent success of extraction strategies such as this led to a flurry of activity in the area and the application of these techniques to various MRDs. Early results in MRD research were promising and led many to feel that MRDs would provide perhaps the most important source of information for building knowledge bases automatically (see, for instance, the position papers by Amsler and Boguraev at TINLAP-3 in 1987 [14, 15]).

3 Antithesis

However, despite early success in using information from machine readable dictionaries, it is still not clear that the results of early studies will scale up to enable automatically building full-scale knowledge bases from MRDs. In fact, the previous ten or fifteen years of work in the field has produced little more than a handful of limited and imperfect taxonomies, which hardly lives up to early expectations. In addition, there have been very few studies assessing the quality and usefulness of information extracted from MRDs, or showing how to systematically extract more complex information from definition texts.

In order to fully assess the value of MRD research to date, it is necessary to reconsider the fundamental postulates underlying this work by asking the following:

(1) How useful is the information in MRDs? In particular, is the information complete, coherent, and comprehensive enough to provide a basis for building knowledge bases? If not, what kind and how much of the information is missing?

(2) Is the extraction of information from MRDs as simple as applying strategies such as that of Chodorow, Byrd, and Heidorn?

3.1 Discussion of postulate P1

Although many studies boasted a high success rate in extracting information from MRDs, it has never been clear that extracted information is coherent or comprehensive enough to form a basis for knowledge bases. This is particularly true for information extracted from definition texts. Ide and Véronis [7] show that even in the most straightforward case (detection of hypernyms for concrete objects, kitchen utensils) 50-70% of the information is garbled in some way in five major English dictionaries. Similarly, it is not clear that the information in dictionaries is precisely what is needed to build knowledge bases. For example, Kilgariff [16] suggests that sense distinctions in the *LDOCE* (one of the most-used dictionaries in MRD research, which, as a learner's dictionary, is also one of the simplest) do not reflect actual use, and therefore may not form a viable basis for building knowledge bases for NLP. In addition, some types of knowledge simply do not exist in dictionaries.

Dictionary information is flawed. It is well known that information in the definition texts of dictionaries is often seriously inconsistent. Since a dictionary is typically the product of several lexicographers' efforts and is constructed, revised, and updated over many years, inconsistencies in the criteria for constructing definition texts necessarily evolve. In addition, space and readability restrictions as well as syntactic restrictions on phrasing may dictate that certain information is unspecified or left to be implied by other parts of the definition.

A pervasive problem in automatically extracted hierarchies is the attachment of terms too high in the hierarchy, which occurs in 21-34% of the definitions in the sample from the five dictionaries cited in [7]. For example, while *pan* and *bottle* are *vessels* in the *CED*, *cup* and *bowl* are simply *containers*, the hypernym of *vessel*. The problem of attachment too high in the hierarchy is compounded by the fact that it occurs relatively randomly within a given dictionary, which is evident in the hierarchies shown in Fig. 2. Because of inconsistencies such as these, semantic networks extracted from different dictionaries look very different, as demonstrated in the same figure.

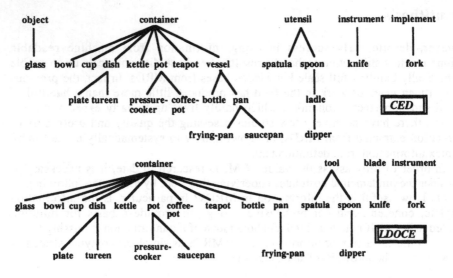

Fig. 2. Hierarchies from different dictionaries

In some cases, information is missing altogether. For example, the definition of *corkscrew* from *Webster's 9th*, "a pointed spiral *piece* of metal...", gives "piece" as the hypernym, which is clearly incorrrect. *Device,* which is the hypernym given in several other dictionaries, is better and should have been given if the dictionary were consistent.

Another pervasive problem with hypernyms generated from MRDs concerns information at the higher levels of the hierarchy, where terms tend to become more general and less clearly defined. For example, most people will agree on whether some object falls into the category *fork* or *spoon,* but there is much less agreement on what objects are *implements* or *utensils*. In addition, at the higher levels some concepts simply lack a term to designate them exactly. This lack of clear-cut terms for higher level concepts generates (at least) two phenomena in dictionary definitions. First, when higher level concepts are being defined, definitions are often circular. For instance, consider these definitions from the *CED*:

tool • an *implement*, such as a hammer...
implement • a piece of *equipment*; *tool* or *utensil*.
utensil • an *implement, tool* or *container*...

Circular definitions yield hierarchies containing loops, which are not usable in knowledge bases. Second, in such cases definitions often give a list of head nouns separated by the conjunction "or", as in the definitions of *implement* and *utensil* above. In most cases none of the three alternatives is a true hypernym of the word being defined. Regarding them as such leads to other problems in the resulting hierarchy (Fig. 3): in the hierarchy produced from the definition of *utensil*, enumerating the paths upwards from *spatula* (defined as a *utensil*) leads to the conclusion that *spatula* is a kind of *container*, which is obviously incorrect. As demonstrated in [7] the introduction of "covert categories", that is, concepts which do not correspond to any particular word, can help to solve this problem, for instance, by introducing a covert category such as INSTRUMENTAL-OBJECT and using it as a hypernym for *tool, utensil, implement,* and *instrument*. However, the detection and creation of covert categories must be done by hand for the most part.

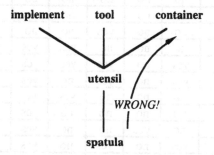

Fig. 3 : Problematic hierarchy

Despite irregularities of this kind, the specification of hypernyms is certainly more consistent in dictionaries than that of other semantic relations (e.g., parts, shape, color, smell, etc.), which is given in a much more random way. For example, in the definitions for *abricot* (apricot) and *pêche* (peach) from three major French dictionaries in Fig. 4, all of the dictionaries indicate that the pit of a peach is hard, but none specifies this property for the pit of the apricot (which is certainly just as hard). Information is given inconsistently even within a given dictionary, as shown when the definitions are presented in tabular form (Fig. 5).

	MICRO-ROBERT	HACHETTE	PETIT LAROUSSE
abricot	Fruit de l'abricotier, à noyau, à chair et peau jaune orangé.	Fruit de l'abricotier, d'une saveur délicate et parfumée, de couleur jaune rosé.	Fruit de l'abricotier, à noyau lisse, à peau et chair jaunes.
pêche	Fruit du pêcher, à noyau très dur et à chair fine.	Fruit comestible du pêcher, au noyau dur, à la chair jaune ou blanche, tendre et sucrée, à la peau rose et duveteuse.	Fruit comestible du pêcher, à chair juteuse et à noyau dur.

Fig. 4. Definitions for *abricot* (apricot) and *pêche* (peach)

	apricot			peach		
Property	MR	HA	PL	MR	HA	PL
sort-of fruit	yes	yes	yes	yes	yes	yes
parent-tree	yes	yes	yes	yes	yes	yes
has a pit	yes	no	yes	yes	yes	yes
form	no	no	no	no	no	no
color	no	no	no	no	no	no
texture	no	no	yes	no	no	no
hardness	no	no	no	yes	yes	yes
has flesh	yes	no	yes	yes	yes	yes
color	yes	no	yes	no	yes	no
texture	no	no	no	yes	no	no
hardness	no	no	no	no	yes	no
taste	no	yes	no	no	yes	no
has skin	yes	no	yes	no	yes	no
color	yes	(yes)	no	no	yes	no
texture	no	no	no	no	yes	no
hardness	no	no	no	no	no	no
etc.						

Fig. 5. Incoherence of properties in definitions

Information may be inappropriate. Some of the information in dictionaries is clearly not what is needed for NLP. For example, Kilgarriff [16] shows that in a sample of 83 words from the LOB corpus, 69 had at least two senses in LDOCE and were therefore ambiguous. However, Kilgarriff found that for 60 of these 69 words (about 87%), there was at least one usage in the LOB corpus which could not with any confidence be classified into a single sense. This occurred because, for example, more than one sense was near the meaning of the word as used in the corpus, or because no sense given in the dictionary applied.

MRD research has assumed for the most part that sense distinctions in dictionaries correspond to sense distinctions that apply in actual use, and therefore could provide the conceptual divisions that should appear in a knowledge base.

However, apart from distinctions between homographs, it is not clear that this assumption holds. The differences in the level of detail and, occasionally, in the ways lines are drawn between senses when one moves from one dictionary to another, already show that sense distinctions in dictionaries are not definitive; studies such as Kilgarriff's bring this fact into focus in relation to real language use, which is obviously the ultimate concern of NLP.

Missing types of information. Some types of information that must be included in a knowledge base are clearly not included in MRDs, in particular, broad contextual or world knowledge. For instance, it is interesting to note that there is no direct connection drawn between *lawn* and *house,* or between *ash* and *tobacco* in the *Collins English Dictionary,* although it is clear that this connection is part of human experience. The sense disambiguation strategy described in [17], which applies a connectionnist approach and relies on such connections between words in definition texts, fails in these cases as a result.

3.2 Discussion of postulate P2

The work of [3] and others made the extraction of semantic information from MRDs appear simple. However, claims of high success rates (often, 98% etc.) were misleading, since "success" (in Chodorow *et al.*'s case [7]) meant finding the *head* of a definition. This did not mean that this head was in fact an appropriate hypernym. In addition, by far the greatest success was achieved for simple semantic information, notably hypernyms. The extraction of other kinds of semantic information proved to be much more problematic due to far greater inconsistencies in the ways it was specified, often demanding relatively sophisticated parsing of the definition text . The following outlines the various sources of difficulty in extracting information from MRDs (see [8, 18, 19, 20]).

Physical formats. MRDs typically come to researchers in unusable formats-- notably, in the form of typesetter tapes from publishers. To make the MRD usable for research, considerable effort was often required, and in fact the translation of MRDs in typesetter format to something more usable has become an area of study in itself. As a result of ambiguities and inconsistencies in typesetter formats, parsing typesetter tapes requires developing a complex grammar of entries (see, for example, [21]). Even with this, problems still arise because conventions are inconsistent. For example, in the *CED*, the entry *Canopic jar, urn* or *vase* must be interpreted as (*Canopic jar*) or (*Canopic urn*) or (*Canopic vase*), whereas the entry *Junggar Pendi, Dzungaria,* or *Zungaria,* which has the same structure, must be interpreted as (*Junggar Pendi*) or (*Dzungaria*) or (*Zungaria*). Because of the inconsistency, fully automated procedures cannot determine the appropriate interpretations.

Most of this work is far outside the realm of NLP research, and in general it is time-consuming and without great intellectual interest. Thus it diverts resources from more central NLP research. As a result, only a handful of dictionaries are available in a usable format, mainly in English. Now that the magnitude of the task is obvious, researchers may be reluctant to start similar work on dictionaries in other languages.

Incoherence of metatext. The difficulty of extracting information arises from inconsistencies in the way information is specified, in particular, variations in definition *metatext* (that is, phrases in definition texts that express semantic relations, such as "used in *V*-ing" for instrument, "consisting of a *N*" for parts, etc.). For example, consider the following from the *CED,* in which the fact that a handle is a part-of a utensil is expressed in vastly different ways:

> **jug** • a vessel...usually <u>having</u> a handle...
> **kettle** • a metal container <u>with</u> a handle...
> **ladle** • a <u>long-handled</u> spoon...
> **corkscrew** • a device...<u>consisting of</u> a pointed metal spiral <u>attached to</u> a handle...
> **fork** • a small usually metal implement <u>consisting of</u> two, three, or four long thin prongs <u>on the end of</u> a handle...
> **knife** • a cutting instrument <u>consisting of</u> a sharp-edged often pointed blade of metal <u>fitted into</u> a handle...
> **basket** • a container...often <u>carried by means of</u> a handle or handles.

This small sample demonstrates that there are often a handful of metatextual phrases signalling particular relations ("having a", "with a", "consisting of", etc.) that can be detected with simple Chodorow-like pattern matching techniques. Even this simple case is problematic; consider

> **lug** • a box or basket for vegetables or fruit <u>with</u> a capacity of 28 to 40 pounds.

where the noun (*N*) in the phrase "with a *N*" is not a part, as it is in the earlier examples.

However, things are rarely even this straightforward. The definitions of *corkscrew, fork, knife,* and *basket* show that there is virtually an open-ended set of metatextual phrases to specify that a handle is a part of some object, for which no pattern can be devised. Bearing in mind that this example shows only a single case (handle) over a handful of definitions in a single dictionary, it is clear that the amount of work required to determine the possible variants could easily exceed that required to construct the corresponding knowledge base by hand.

The bootstrapping problem. It is common in MRD research to use sophisticated syntactic parsers (for example, the Linguistic String Parser as in [22]) to analyze definition texts. But even for the simple examples given above, more than syntactic analysis is required. For example, to determine that a handle is a part-of a basket from the *CED* definition, not only syntactic parsing but also lexical information is needed to differentiate "carried by means of a handle" from "cooked by means of steam". Similarly, in the definition of *ladle,* lexical information would be required in order to determine that the adjective "long-handled" specifies a part of a ladle. In some cases, the resources of a full knowledge base are required to understand the specification. For example, to differentiate "carried by means of a handle" from "carried by means of a wagon", world knowledge is required to determine that "wagon" is not a part of the object carried, although "handle" most likely is.

In addition, in order to create knowledge bases from MRDs, it is necessary to apply sense disambiguation to the words in the dictionary itself as a prior step. Without prior sense disambiguation, automatically extracted hierarchies are necessarily *tangled* [1], because many words are polysemous. For example, in the *CED,* the word *pan* has the following senses (among others):

pan[1] **1.a** a wide metal *vessel*... [CED]
pan[2] **1** the *leaf* of the betel tree... [CED]

The *CED* gives *pan* as the hypernym for *saucepan,* which taken together yields the hierarchy in Fig. 6. The undisambiguated hierarchy is unusable because, following the path upwards from *saucepan,* we find that *saucepan* can be a kind of *leaf,* which is clearly erroneous. Sense disambiguation is a complex task requiring possibly substantial knowledge resources.

All of this means that in order to create resources for use in NLP from MRDs, it is necessary to have full NLP capabilities--including full knowledge bases--already at hand. This is clearly circular, and has led some researchers to attempt MRD analysis using only minimal pre-existing resources that can be constructed by hand, and bootstrapping as MRD analysis proceeds. However, it is becoming clear that the difficulties are so considerable that such methods are unlikely to succeed; indeed, to date, none has been convincingly demonstrated.

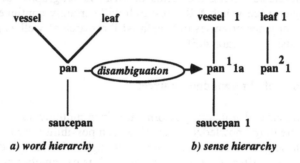

Fig. 6 : Sense-tangled hierarchy

4 Synthesis

The remarks in the preceding sections lead to the conclusion that the two postulates of MRD research were erroneous. The information in MRDs is probably not consistent or complete enough to provide a substantial basis for a knowledge base. In addition, given that the amount of work required to extract the information that does exist in MRDs has now been demonstrated to be extensive (even requiring the existence of the knowledge bases it is intended to create), the return on investment is clearly very low.

Therefore, does the past fifteen years of MRD research constitute wasted effort? If the mostly automatic extraction of near-perfect knowledge is the goal, the answer is certainly "yes". But this assumption reveals a broader postulate than the two cited in section 2 underlying MRD research:

Postulate P0. Large knowledge bases cannot be built by hand.

It is not at all sure that this postulate is valid, given, for example, the work of the CYC project [34], and the fact that lexicographers have been creating knowledge bases by hand for over 200 years. If this broader postulate is abandoned, we can more realistically assess the contribution of MRD research. It is clear that MRDs contain useful data--but most of it is probably usable only with possibly substantial by-hand massaging, requiring human judgement to be incorporated into useful knowledge bases. In addition, it is the trend in NLP research (possibly in part because of the experience with MRDs) to consider that no single source (dictionaries, corpora, etc.) could provide all or even most of the knowledge required for NLP. Therefore, it is now widely recognized that knowledge base construction requires combining information from multiple sources (section 4.1). Clearly, coupled with information from other sources and subjected to by-hand amelioration, information extracted from MRDs is a valuable resource for building knowledge bases.

However, there are other contributions of MRD research that may be less well-recognized. In fact, MRD research has contributed significantly to several areas, in particular, the development of encoding and database models for dictionaries and other textual data (section 4.2), the assessment of the kind of knowledge needed for NLP (section 4.3), and the consideration of pure associational information for various NLP tasks (section 4.4).

Probably the most important contribution of MRD research is the fostering of a convergence of interests among the fields of NLP, lexicography, and electronic publishing--a convergence which MRD research will certainly continue to feed and develop. This convergence promises to benefit NLP research as well as lexicography and electronic publishing (section 4.5).

4.1 Combination of knowledge sources

It is now becoming clear that merging information from multiple sources is essential to the process of creating knowledge bases. One such possibility involves the use of information from several dictionaries, since although information derived from individual dictionaries suffers from incompleteness, it is extremely unlikely that the same information is consistently missing from all dictionaries. It is therefore possible to use information from several dictionaries to fill in information which is missing or faulty in one or more others. For example, in a small experiment, merging multiple dictionaries produced highly encouraging results: in a merged hierarchy created from five English dictionaries, the percentage of problematic cases was reduced from 55-70% to around 5% [7]. By-hand work is still required, but merging can substantially improve the quality of the extracted information.

It is now widely recognized that combining information extracted from MRDs with information provided by corpus analysis is a fruitful means to fill out knowledge bases, since corpora can provide information such as common collocates, proper nouns, role preference information, frequency of use and similar statistics, etc. However, with corpora as with MRDs, fully automatic extraction is not likely.

We foresee that the creation of knowledge bases in the future will be accomplished by giving the human knowledge-base-creator access to multiple resources, including MRDs and corpora, together with tools to extract different kinds of information and combine it more or less by-hand. Indeed, projects to develop workstations for this kind of work are already underway. This information will be widely varied in kind, including both detailed linguistic information as well as statistics, associational links, etc.

4.2 Physical organization of dictionaries

MRD research has necessarily involved considerable work on rendering dictionaries into a usable format for extraction of information. To this end, an encoding format for MRDs has been developed under the aegis of the Text Encoding Initiative (see [23, 24, 25, 26]) which can be applied across mono- and bi-lingual western dictionaries. Such a format must necessarily be both general enough to be applicable across different dictionaries, whose structures often vary widely, and at the same time capture the fundamental structural principles (e.g., hierarchical structure, factoring of information) that underlie dictionaries. A common encoding format enables the application of common software and hence the reusability of MRDs, and is extremely useful in the publishing industry for rendering in-house data in common formats which are directly suitable for typesetting, generation of dictionaries in different forms (e.g., concise, learner's), etc.

The development of an encoding format suitable for MRDs demands identification of the dicionary entry's constituent elements as well as a deep understanding of the structural principles underlying dictionaries. Thus a related problem is the determination of a database model suitable for representing the information in MRDs. Lexical data, as is obvious in any dictionary entry, is much more complex than the kind of data (suppliers and parts, employees' records, etc.) that has provided the impetus for most database research. Therefore, classical data models (for example, relational models) do not apply very well to lexical data, although several attempts have been made (see for example [6, 27]). Ide, Véronis, and Le Maitre [28] have proposed an alternative feature-based model for lexical databases, which allows for a full representation of sense nesting and defines an inheritance mechanism that enables the elimination of redundant information. The model has been implemented in an object-oriented DBMS [29]. This and other similar work continues to feed the development of database models to represent lexical data and textual information, which is becoming an increasingly active area of research in database design.

4.3 Assessment of the needs of NLP

MRD research to date has provided the basis of an assessment of the kind of knowledge that is needed in NLP. In particular, in comprehensively examining the information presented by lexicographers who had no conscious intention to provide a fully systematic set of semantic specifications, numerous subtleties concerning semantic distinction and semantic relations have become more clear. The covert category problem and the attendant thinking about overlapping meanings, circularity, etc., described in section 3.1.1 provides one simple example.

The exact nature and kind of information required for various NLP tasks has not been fully explored. For example, even in the case of taxonomies, it is not always clear what must be included: for instance, we know that some inheritance mechanisms are needed for parsing (e.g., for successful PP attachment in "I ate a trout with bones", it is necessary that *trout* inherits the feature *has-bones* from *vertebrate*)--but are there cases where more precise or different kinds of information are necessary? Is the broad semantic information in a dictionary sufficient? Too much? It is difficult to draw a precise taxonomy in many cases (e.g., it is very difficult to determine whether a given item is a *pot*, a *pan,* or both), and yet humans easily understand sentences containing words for which the taxonomic relations are unclear. This suggests that the kind of precision NLP researchers have traditionally sought in knowledge bases may be unnecessary in some cases. We can ask if very different kinds and amounts of information required for different NLP tasks, and if so, it will be essential to precisely identify these differences. Some studies have attempted to assess in detail the kinds of knowledge required for given NLP tasks (see, for example, [30]); such studies provide a start, but it is clear that more consideration of the exact requirements of various NLP tasks needs to be done.

4.4 Exploitation of associational information

Work on extracting semantic information from definition texts involves an attempt to identify not only which words are related, but also the nature of the relationship. However, several researchers have used MRDs as a source of *associational* information indicating which words are related, without regard for the nature of the relationship, to perform tasks such as sense disambiguation, topic identification, etc. The fundamental assumption underlying these studies is that words in a definition are closely related semantically to the defined word. Such studies have identified senses by counting overlaps between words in the definition texts of different senses and surrounding words in context [31, 9] and generated lists of topic or key words by extracting the not only the most frequent words in a text, but also the most frequent words in their definitions [32]. Other studies have employed the same principle by building associational networks on the basis of the implicit association between headword and words in the definition text for sense disambiguation ([17, 33]).

The work which has utilised the word associations implicit in a dictionary's structure has shown considerable success, although like much NLP research these studies have typically involved small-sized experiments, and it is not clear that the methods will scale up to real-size data. However, at the very least, this work demonstrates that the associational information in MRDs--which is trivial to extract since no complex processing is required--is potentially valuable for use in NLP.

4.5 Synergy among NLP, lexicography, electronic publishing

One of the most promising possibilities for the future of MRD research results from a merging of interests among NLP researchers, lexicographers, and electronic publishers. Lexicographers, possibly as a result of MRD research, are increasingly interested in creating lexical data bases containing the kinds of information that NLP research had hoped to extract from MRDs; some lexicographers are explicitly concerned with creating NLP-like knowledge bases [12, 13]. Creation of such databases would in turn provide NLP with more of the resources it needs. In addition, electronic publishing has made possible the creation of commercially available, hypertext-like dictionaries which would include information and facilities well beyond that of print dictionaries. This sort of product is likely to explode on the market in the near future, and in fact a few such dictionaries (Sony Data Discman, Larousse, etc.) already exist.

So far, computerization has been applied to lexicography in only limited ways; the COBUILD project [35] was one of the first to utilize computers to exploit corpora in the creation of lexical entries, and most dictionary publishers now create dictionaries by first creating in-house databases--although such databases typically contain only gross distinctions among information fields (orthographic form, pronunciation, part-of-speech, etymology, definition text, etc.). Almost no work has been done to improve definition texts themselves or to systematize semantic information (apart from occasional attempts such as the *LDOCE* semantic codes).

Computerization of dictionary-making at the semantic level could involve the following:

(1) *the creation of explicit semantic links* (hypernym, part, color, etc.) between words or entries. This would be especially useful for creating electronic (hypertextual) dictionaries. Such links could lead to the development of precise templates for classes of objects, etc. (e.g., Fig. 7).

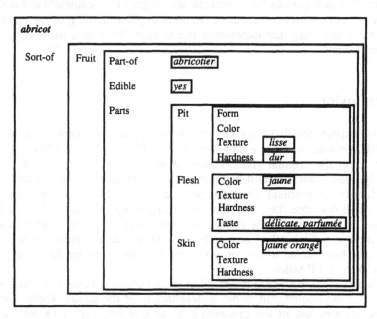

Fig. 7. Template for dictionary entries (fruits)

So far, navigation and query in electronic dictionaries is rather limited and relies on user's judgement and understanding of definitions to be usable. However, an explicit semantic net underlying the dictionary could be very useful for nativation and query. For example, we can envision display to varying levels of detail, depending on user preference, of the information in the template for *fruit*, and even user navigation within the template (click on PARTS-OF "apricot" and get "pit," "flesh," "skin," etc.; click on "pit" and get the properties of apricot pit, etc.). Information could be linked to images and sounds, and displayed in template form; or definitions and sub-definitions could be generated in natural language, in any form (concise, learner's version, full, etc.).

(2) *ensuring consistency of the content of entries*. The templates created for different classes of concepts could be used to ensure that the information given for each entry when it is appropriate to do so. This could eliminate the kinds of inconsistencies demonstrated in the entries for *apricot* and *peach* given in section 3.1.1.

(3) *ensuring consistency of metatext*. As outlined above in section 3.2.2, MRD research has revealed that metatext in dictionaries is highly variable and relatively inconsistent, and, by compiling lists of metatextual specifications for various relations, has identified both the sources and potential solutions to the problem of

inconsistency. We can even imagine that metatext could be automatically generated from templates of the type described above.

(4) *ensuring consistency of sense division.* Lexicographers have sought means to remove the arbitrariness of sense divisions. Computerization has already been helpful, for example, by automatizing and systematizing the use of corpora as a source of information about word senses. Knowledge bases could take this systematization even farther. For instance, a dictionary might define *cup* as "**1.** a container for liquid... **2.** its content", *bowl* as "**1.** a container...; its content", but *glass* only as "**1.** a container...", which ignores the metonymic use of glass ("its content") and is therefore inconsistent. An electronic database containing explicit marking of metonymic links could enable checking that metonymic use is specified where necessary, and in a consistent format.

5 Conclusion

The false expectation that large knowledge bases could be generated automatically from MRDs has led to a perception that the past fifteen years of MRD research has failed to meet the original goals. Indeed, it seems to be the case that large-scale knowledge bases will be built using information from multiple sources, and will require human involvement. From this perspective, it is clear that while they are not the exclusive resource they may have been originally thought to be, MRDs have something to contribute to the creation of knowledge bases. In some instances that contribution is not what had originally been expected, as evident in the fact that MRDs have been found to contain a vast bank of associational information that is useful in many NLP tasks.

It is also clear that MRD research has in fact contributed to other NLP goals. In particular, it has contributed to our understanding of the nature, kinds, and role of semantic information in the processing of natural languages, as well as to the increasingly obvious idea that widely varying types of information--several in addition to the traditionally accepted set--are needed for NLP. This may in turn lead to more systematic assessment of the needs of various NLP tasks, an area which deserves serious attention.

The most promising avenue of activity, however, involves collaboration between the NLP community and lexicographers and electronic publishers. The two communities are already beginning to work with one another; one clear example is a recent survey sent to NLP researchers from Longman publishers, asking for their input in devising new database versions of the *LDOCE*. Obviously, collaboration--both in terms of shared information and shared effort--can benefit both communities. The result could be better dictionaries and exciting new possibilities for electronic, hypertextual dictionary databases, as well as a wealth of material useful for NLP.

References

1.   R. A. Amsler: The structure of the Merriam-Webster Pocket Dictionary. Ph. D. Dissertation, University of Texas at Austin, (1980)
2.   N. Calzolari: Detecting patterns in a lexical data base. Proceedings of the 10th International Conference on Computational Linguistics, COLING'84, 170-173 (1984).

3. M. S. Chodorow, R.J. Byrd, G. E. Heidorn: Extracting semantic hierarchies from a large on-line dictionary. Proceedings of the 23rd Annual Conference of the Association for Computational Linguistics, Chicago, 299-304 (1985).

4. J. Markowitz, T. Ahlswede, M. Evens: Semantically significant patterns in dictionary definitions. Proceedings of the 24th Annual Conference of the Association for Computational Linguistics, New York, 112-119 (1986).

5. R.J. Byrd, N. Calzolari, M.S. Chodorow, J.L. Klavans, M.S. Neff, O. Rizk: Tools and methods for computational linguistics. Computational Linguistics, 13, 3/4, 219-240 (1987).

6. J. Nakamura, M. Nagao: Extraction of semantic information from an ordinary English dictionary and its evaluation. Proceedings of the 13th International Conference on Computational Linguistics, COLING'88, 459-464 (1988).

7. N. Ide, J.Véronis: Refining taxonomies extracted from machine-readable dictionaries. In: S. Hockey, N. Ide (eds.): Research in Humanities Computing 2. Oxford University Press (in press).

8. J. Klavans, M. Chodorow, N. Wacholder: From dictionary to knowledge base via taxonomy. Proceedings of the 6th Conference of the UW Centre for the New OED, Waterloo, 110-132 (1990).

9. Y. Wilks, D. Fass, C. Guo, J. MacDonald, T. Plate, B. Slator: Providing machine tractable dictionary tools. Machine Translation 5, 99-154 (1990).

10. F. Pigamo: Outils de traitement sémantique du langage naturel. Thèse de l'Ecole Nationale Supérieure des Télécommunications, Paris, 242pp. (1990).

11. A. Alonge: Analysing dictionary definitions of motion verbs. Proceedings of the 15th International Conference on Computational Linguistics, COLING'92 1315-1319 (1992),.

12. R. Martin: Inférences et définition lexicographique. Colloque "Lexique et Inférences", Metz, (1991).

13. P. Procter: Cambridge Language Survey: The development of a non-language specific semantic coding system using multiple inheritance. Paper presented at International Workshop of the European Association of Machine Translation, "Machine Translation and the Lexicon", Heidelberg, 26-28 (April 1993).

14. R.A. Amsler: Words and worlds. Proceedings of the Third Workshop on Theoretical Issues in Natural Language Processing (TINLAP-3). Las Cruces, NM (1987).

15. B.K. Boguraev: The definitional power of words. Proceedings of the Third Workshop on Theoretical Issues in Natural Language Processing (TINLAP-3). Las Cruces, NM, 11-15 (1987).

16. A. Kilgarriff: Dictionary word sense distinctions: An enquiry into their nature. Computers and the Humanities, 26 (5-6), 365-388 (1993).

17. J. Véronis, N.M. Ide: Word sense disambiguation with very large neural networks extracted from machine readable dictionaries. Proceedings of the 14th International Conference on Computational Linguistics, COLING'90, Helsinki, 2, 389-394 (1990).

18. K. Jensen, J.-L. Binot: Disambiguating prepositional phrase attachements by using on-line dictionary definitions. Computational Linguistics 13, 3-4, 251-260 (1987).

19. S. Montemagni, L. Vanderwende: Structural patterns vs. string patterns for extracting semantic information from dictionaries. Proceedings of the 15th International Conference on Computational Linguistics, COLING'92, 546-552 (1992).

20. Y. Ravin: Disambiguating and interpreting verb definitions. Proceedings of the 28th Annual Conference of the Association for Computational Linguistics, Pittsburgh, 260-267 (1990).

21. M.S. Neff, B.K. Boguraev: Dictionaries, dictionary grammars and dictionary entry parsing. Proceedings of the 27rd Annual Conference of the Association for Computational Linguistics, Vancouver, 91-101 (1989).

22. T. Ahlswede, M. Evens, K. Rossi: Building a lexical database by parsing Webster's Seventh Collegiate Dictionary. Proceedings of the 2nd Annual Conference of the UW Centre for the NewOED, Waterloo, Canada, 65-76 (1985).

23. R.A. Amsler, F.W. Tompa: An SGML-based standard for English monolingual dictionaries. Proceedings of the 4th Annual Conference of the UW Centre for the New Oxford English Dictionary, Waterloo, Ontario, 61-80 (1988).

24. N. Ide, J. Véronis: Print dictionaries, TEI Working Paper AI5 D17, Distributed by the Text Encoding Initiative. Compter Center, University of Illinois at Chicago, 60pp. (1992).

25. N. Ide, J. Veronis, S. Warwick-Armstrong, N. Calzolari: Principles for encoding machine readable dictionaries, EURALEX'92 Proceedings, H. Tommola, K. Varantola, T. Salmi-Tolonen, Y. Schopp, eds., in Studia Translatologica, Ser. a, 2, Tampere, Finland, 239-246 (1992).

26. N. Ide, J. Véronis: Encoding dictionaries. Computers and the Humanities 29, 1-3 (to appear).

27. M.S. Neff, R.J. Byrd, O.A. Rizk: Creating and querying lexical databases. Proceedings of the Association for Computational Linguistics Second Applied Conference on Natural Language Processing. Austin, Texas 84-92 (1988),.

28. N. Ide, J. Le Maitre, J. Veronis: Outline of a model for lexical databases. Information Processing and Managment 29, 2, 159-186 (1993).

29. J. Le Maitre, N. Ide, J. Véronis: Deux modèles pour la représentation des données lexicales et leur implémentation orientée-objet. Actes des 9èmes Journées Bases de Données Avancées, Toulouse, 312-331 (1993).

30. S.W. McRoy: Using multiple knowledge sources for word sense discrimination. Computational Linguistics 18, 1, 1-30 (1992).

31. M. Lesk: Automated sense disambiguation using machine-readable dictionaries: How to tell a pine cone from an ice cream cone. Proceedings of the 1986 SIGDOC Conference (1986).

32. N. Ide, J. Véronis: Caught in the web of words: Using networks generated from dictionaries for content analysis. Paper presented at ACH/ALLC'91 Joint International Conference, Tempe, Arizona (1991).

33. N. Ide, J. Véronis: Very large neural networks for word-sense disambiguation. 9th European Conference on Arfificial Intelligence, ECAI'90, Stockholm, 366-368 (1990).

34. D.B. Lenat, M. Prakash, M. Shepherd: CYC: Using common sense knowledge to overcome brittleness and knowledge acquisition bottlenecks. AI Magazine 7 (4), 65-85 (1986).

35. J.M. Sinclair: An account of the COBUILD project. London: Collins ELT 1987.

Description and Acquisition of Multiword Lexemes

Angelika Storrer[1] and Ulrike Schwall[2]

[1] University of Tübingen (Germany)
[2] Sietec, München (Germany)

Abstract. This paper deals with multiword lexemes (MWLs), focussing on two types of verbal MWLs: verbal idioms and support verb constructions. We discuss the characteristic properties of MWLs, namely non-standard compositionality, restricted substitutability of components, and restricted morpho-syntactic flexibility, and we show how these properties may cause serious problems during the analysis, generation, and transfer steps of machine translation systems. In order to cope with these problems, MT lexicons need to provide detailed descriptions of MWL properties. We list the types of information which we consider the necessary minimum for a successful processing of MWLs, and report on some feasibility studies aimed at the automatic extraction of German verbal multiword lexemes from text corpora and machine-readable dictionaries.

1 Introduction

The treatment of multiword lexemes (MWLs) has always been a challenge for natural language processing (NLP) in general and for machine translation (MT) in particular. Most problems are caused by the fact that MWLs differ considerably from analogous free s yntagmatic constructions with respect to semantic compositionality, substitutability of components, and morpho-syntactic flexibility.

In this paper, we first give examples of the morpho-syntactic and semantic peculiarities of MWLs and we explain how these may pose problems for the analysis, generation, and transfer steps of machine translation systems. We then compile a list of those t ypes of information regarding MWL properties which have to be included in lexicons for NLP applications to enable a successful processing of the various MWL types. Finally, we report on some feasibility studies carried out as part of the ELWIS project at the University of Tübingen[3] with the aim to extract German verbal MWLs from text corpora and machine-readable dictionaries. The studies show that statistical methods which have proved to be successful in regard to English text corpora cannot simply be applied to German, and that a combination of corpus and dicti onary-based methods is a more favourable approach towards the automatic acquisition of MWLs provided that machine-readable dictionaries of high quality are available.

---

[3] ELWIS is a project on corpus-based development of Lexical Knowledge Bases carried out at the university of Tübingen (cf. [18]); the project is funded by the ministry of Science and Research of Baden-Württemberg.

2 Types and Properties of Multiword Lexemes

We use the following working definition for the term *multiword lexeme*:

Multiword lexemes are units of a language's lexical system (lexemes)
composed of several words.

This definition sets out two important properties of MWLs. The first property
is lexeme status, which implies that MWLs, in contrast to free syntagmatic
constructions, are stored and retrieved as complex units of the (mental) lexicon.
The second property, to be composed of several words, distinguishes MWLs from
simplex words.[4]

Given this definition, the term *multiword lexeme* covers quite a heteroge-
neous group of lexical units such as idiomatic expressions, lexicalized support
verb constructions, lexicalized multiword compounds, phrasal verbs, and polylexical technical terms (cf. [5]). In the following section, we shall focus on verbal
multiword lexemes, because this is the most interesting group characterized by
a wide range of morpho-syntactic and semantic peculiarities. We use the term
verbal multiword lexeme (VMWL) as a generic term, encompassing both verbal
idioms and support verb constructions:

- Verbal idioms, such as (1) and (2),

  (1) to kick the bucket
  (2) to spill the beans

  have the structure of a verb phrase. However, the meaning of verbal idioms is
  not a compositional result of the idiom-external meaning of its constituents.
  Compared to free VP constructions, the idiomatic construction is subject
  to various morpho-syntactic constraints. Like other idioms, verbal idioms
  belong to informal or colloquial registers and express an affective evaluation
  of the things they denote.
  Prototypical idioms often involve metaphors or another form of figuration.
  As a consequence, sentences such as (3) and (4),

  (3) John kicked the bucket.
  (4) John spilled the beans.

  have, aside from their idiomatic reading, an alternative non-idiomatic reading, which may, to a more or lesser degree, be plausible in a given context.

- Support verb constructions (SVC), as (5) and (6),

  (5) to take into consideration
  (6) to raise an objection

  consist of a support verb (SV) and a predicative noun (Npred), which is,
  typically, a nominalization of an abstract verb or adjective.[5] The support

---

[4] From an NLP point of view we consider words as strings between blank spaces,
although we are aware that this is a very simplistic conception from a linguistic
point of view.

[5] We have adopted the term *predicative noun* from French research, cf. [4] and [7].

verb mainly contributes grammatical features such as person, tense, and mode, but influences the denotative meaning of the SVC only to a small degree. Compared to the basic simplex verb, in our examples *to take* and *to raise*, it has lost most of its semantic content. It is rather the function of the Npred to determine the denotative meaning and the argument structure of the construction as a whole. The arguments are normally inherited from the basis of the nominalization: the argument of the SVC in (6), for instance, realized as a prepositional phrase with the preposition *against*, is inherited from the argument of the basic verb *to object against*.

SVCs expand the range of expression of a verbal system: they can be used to make the process expressed by the Npred passive (*to receive praise*) or causative (*to set in motion*) and they can alter the aspectual dimension (*to get/to be/to keep in touch*).[6]

The borderline between verbal idioms and SVCs seems to be quite clear-cut for prototypical cases. In other cases, however, the distinction is difficult to draw and different possibilities of classification exist, depending on the criteria used.[7] What verbal idioms and SVCs have in common is that they differ from free syntagmatic constructions with regard to semantic compositionality, substitutability of components, and morpho-syntactic flexibility. In the following sections, we will describe these properties in more detail.

2.1 Non-standard Compositionality

The principle of semantic compositionality implies that the meaning of an expression is a function of the meaning of its parts and the syntactic rules by which they are combined.

Although it is still controversial whether idioms can be processed compositionally (cf. [19], [14]), there is general agreement that they cannot be analyzed in the same way as their non-idiomatic counterparts. Instead, different strategies have to be provided for three distinct cases of non-standard compositionality:

1. Verbal idioms like *to kick the bucket* have one single undecomposable idiomatic reading, assigned by convention to the expression as a whole. Approaches to treat these idioms compositionally lead to analyses which do not conform to linguistic intuition.

2. Verbal idioms like *to cast pearls before swine* can be broken up into their individual components, the meaning of which is motivated by conventionalized metaphors (*pearls* = something of value; *swine* = unworthy person). Based on the respective metaphorical links, idioms of this type may be compositionally analyzed, although the meaning of the idiomatic construction as a whole is still a matter of convention.[8]

---

[6] Cf. [16] for a contrastive account of the semantic-functional contribution of SVCs.
[7] An overview of possible criteria is given in [12] and [3].
[8] The relationship of metaphoric contents and compositionality is discussed in [19].

3. Some verbal idioms contain components which retain their normal MWL-external meaning: the noun *Streit* in the example (7)

```
(7)  einen Streit vom Zaun brechen
Lit.: a quarrel from fence break
Engl.: to suddenly start a quarrel
```

is a lexically fixed component, i.e., it cannot be substituted by a semantically close lexeme. Nevertheless, the idiom-internal meaning of *Streit* is identical to its idiom-external meaning.

SVCs may be compositionally analyzed to a certain extent, because the SVC-internal meaning of the Npred is identical to its SVC-external meaning. The meaning of the SV, however, does not correspond to the meaning of the respective simplex verb, but is reduced to grammatical features such as aspect, passive, and causative.

2.2 Non-standard Substitutability

Synonyms, i.e., words denoting the same type of objects, may replace one another in a complex expression without changing the semantic value of the expression as a whole. In verbal idioms like *to kick the bucket*, however, the noun *bucket* cannot be replaced by the noun *pail*, even though the two nouns are synonymous in non-idiomatic contexts. Non-standard substitutability, like non-standard compositionality, is a consequence of the fact that many idiom chunks do not refer to objects in the usual way, so that meaning postulates, which are usually valid, cannot be applied.

Some verbal idioms, however, have a component which can be lexicalized by several different lexemes, e.g., *to take a bow/curtain*. The choice of one lexeme or the other will not affect the denotative meaning of the idiom, even though style and frequency of usage may be different. These cases have to be distinguished from cases such as *to be on good/bad terms with*, where the antonyms *good* and *bad* contribute in their regular way to the meaning of the idiom, thus leading to two antonymous idiom variants.

In comparison to idiom components, SVC components are substitutable to a certain extent. A particular Npred, however, cannot be combined with an arbitrary SV which has the required grammatical characteristics. For example, the verbs *bringen (zur Verzweiflung bringen[9])* and *setzen (in Bewegung setzen[10])* both have the features causative/inchoative. The Npred *Brand*, nevertheless, can be combined only with *setzen (in Brand setzen[11])*, and the Npred *Anwendung* only with *bringen (zur Anwendung bringen[12])*. It is obviously the Npred, which selects the appropriate support verb; a phenomenon, which causes severe problems for natural language generation.

---

[9] Engl.: to drive sb to despair.
[10] Engl.: to set in motion.
[11] Engl.: to start a fire.
[12] Engl.: to apply.

2.3 Non-standard Morpho-syntactic Properties

Grammars for NLP systems generally reduce the number of permissible syntactic structures to a limited amount of basic patterns on which a number of syntactic operations are defined. MWLs, specifically VMWLs, provide critical data for NLP grammars, because their morpho-syntactic properties differ from those of compositional expressions in various ways: a certain amount of MWLs represents morpho-syntactic irregularities, because their constructions do not conform to regular syntactic patterns. In (8),

(8) **Sie ist nicht ohne.**
Lit.: **She is not without.**
Engl.: **She is quite something.**

the preposition *ohne* occurs in isolation, i.e., without a dependent NP. In (9) and (10),

(9) **Sie bewahrt ruhig Blut.**
Lit.: **She retains quiet blood.**
Engl.: **She remains calm.**

(10) **Sie ist gut Freund mit ihm.**
Lit.: **She is good friend with him.**
Engl.: **She is good friends with him.**

there is no morphological adjective-noun agreement within the noun phrases *ruhig Blut* and *gut Freund*. In these cases of morpho-syntactic irregularities, the conventional grammatical patterns for compositional expressions are too restrictive to accomodate the MWLs.

In most cases, however, the grammatical patterns specified for compositional expressions are too permissive, because MWLs are subject to various types of morpho-syntactic constraints:[13]

- The number and determiner of noun phrases may be morpho-syntactically fixed. In (11),

  (11) **She has thrown in the towel.**

  any number or determiner variation would cause the phrase to lose its idiomatic meaning, as in (11').

  (11') **She has thrown in a towel/towels.**

- The possibilities of modifying an NP within an VMWL are also quite restricted. Any modification of the NP *the towel* by an adjective or a genitive NP causes the sentence (11) to lose its idiomatic meaning, as can be demostrated by (11").

---

[13] A detailed investigation of various types of constraints is given in [5].

(11'') He has thrown in a blue towel / Peter's towel.

- There are various constraints on the syntactic operations which can be applied to MWL constituents. Due to their complex internal structure, VMWLs are the most interesting group in this regard. In German, the constraints affect operations such as passivization, topicalization, clefting, wh-questioning, scrambling, and coordination (cf. [9]).

However, not every VMWL is subject to all types of restriction. There is a large number of VMWLs which behave more or less identical to their corresponding free syntagmatic constructions. Which syntactic operations and which modifications are possible depends on the referential properties of the MWL constituents involved (cf. [19]).

The relationship between the internal semantic structure of MWLs and their morpho-syntactic properties is still requiring further research, which should be based on examining text corpora.[14] A particular problem for corpus-based MWL research is caused by the fact that, especially in literary and newspaper texts, verbal idioms may be de-idiomatized in various ways in order to intend a pun. Along with the process of de-idiomatisation, all types of the above–described constraints can be intentionally ignored.[15] It is, however, important to note that these constraints are an essential prerequisite for the rhetorical effect which is intended by these puns.

3 Multiword Lexemes as a Problem for Machine Translation

The morpho-syntactic and semantic peculiarities of MWLs discussed in Section 2 pose various types of problems for the analysis, generation and transfer steps of machine translation systems. The following collection of problems is not claiming to be complete. It rather has the function of motivating our proposal for describing MWL properties in NLP lexicons (cf. Section 4).

3.1 Multiword Lexemes in Analysis

The main difficulty in analyzing MWLs is to recognize MWLs as such. Verbal idioms are more difficult to identify if an idiomatic and a literal reading are both possible, as in (12):

(12) John kicked the bucket.

Knowledge of morpho-syntactic constraints on verbal idioms can be used to resolve such ambiguities. For example, a detailed description of the morpho-syntactic properties of the verbal idiom *to kick the bucket* would enable us to determine that (13) and (14)

---

[14] Empirical research on these questions is discussed in, e.g., [13], [15], and [9].
[15] Cf. [21] and [20].

```
(13) The bucket was kicked by John.
(14) John kicked the empty bucket.
```

can only be analyzed in a literal sense. In addition, preference rules can be used in cases where one of the readings is more plausible or more frequent (like the idiomatic reading in *He will bite the dust.*). However, there are cases in which ambiguity can only be resolved by means of discourse, as in the German sentence (15):

```
(15)  Er nahm das Kind auf den Arm.
Lit.: He took the child on the arm.
```

Depending on the context, (15) has either an idiomatic reading (*He pulled the child's leg.*) or a literal reading (*He picked up the child.*). A complex problem even for human translators are puns based on the ambiguity between a literal and an idiomatic reading of a construction (cf. [21] for examples). Such cases are likely to remain beyond the capacity of machine translation for some time.

3.2 Multiword Lexemes in Transfer

The complexity of transfer difficulties caused by MWLs depends on the degree of structural and lexical correspondence between a MWL and its equivalent in the target language. The following cases have to be distinguished:[16]

- There are cases of total lexical and structural correspondence as in (16):

  ```
  (16) die Katze aus dem Sack lassen  <->
          to let the cat out of the bag
  ```

  in which, from an NLP point of view, the verbal idiom does not need to be identified as such, as long as selectional restrictions are not violated.

- Other VMWL equivalents display an analogous internal structure but lexical differences, which are usually motivated by different figurations:

  ```
  (17) einen Frosch im Hals haben <-> avoir un chat dans la gorge
  (18) zwei Fliegen mit einer Klappe schlagen <->
          to hit two birds with one stone
  ```

  In (17) and (18), the verbal idioms must be identified as such but can be translated in a straightforward way, provided that the lexical correspondences between idiom chunks of source and target language are defined in the transfer lexicon. The transfer lexicon entries may then contain surprising entries, particularly when the equivalents cast a different perspective on the same event, as in (19):

  ```
  (19) sich das Leben nehmen <-> se donner la mort
  ```

---

[16] Cf. [5] for a detailed typology of MWL translation equivalence.

in which the German words *Leben (life)* und *nehmen (take)* are translated into the French words *mort (death)* and *donner (give)* respectively.

– Problems increase if MWL equivalents differ with respect to both internal structure and lexical components, as in (20) and (21):

(20) jdm. einen Baeren aufbinden <-> to take sb. for a ride
(21) unter dem Pantoffel stehen <-> to be hen-pecked

When MWLs of this type are modified, the target MWL must often be restructured in a complex way. Sentences such as (22),

(22) Er stand unter dem Pantoffel seiner Chefin.

have to be paraphrased rather than translated, because the English equivalent offers no possibility of reproducing the modifier *seiner Chefin (his boss)*. Complex restructuring processes may also be necessary if an MWL in the source language corresponds with a simplex verb in the target language, as in (23):

(23) Nutzen ziehen aus <-> to benefit from

If the nominal component of such a construction is modified by an adjective, as in (23'), the adjectival modifier has to be transformed into an adverb:

(23') grossen Nutzen ziehen aus <-> to benefit largely from

– Similar problems arise if MWL equivalents are modified in a different way: the nominal part of the English SVC *to take into consideration*, for instance, can be modified by an adjective. The corresponding German construction *in Betracht ziehen*, in contrast, only allows for adverbial modification of the whole construction:

(24) He took his objections into careful consideration.
(24') Er zog seine Bedenken sorgfaeltig in Betracht.

Therefore, the adjective modifier of the Npred in the English sentence (24) must be realized as an adverbial modifier in the German translation (24').

3.3 Multiword Lexemes in Generation

In the generation step of MT the structure of the target multiword lexeme has to be generated and correctly embedded in the target sentence. To fulfil this purpose the system needs detailed specifications of the morpho-syntactic constraints on MWL constructions. The handling of syntactic irregularities implies particular problems: sentences such as (8), (9), and (10) have to be generated, although they do not conform to regular syntactic patterns. In the analysis step, such irregular constructions may be handled using robust analysis techniques. In the generation step, however, mechanisms must be provided to handle irregular structures which occur only in particular MWLs. Highly inflected languages are greatly affected by this problem, since such irregularities often have to do with inflection features.

4 Description of Multiword Lexemes in NLP Lexicons

In this section, we list those types of information which should be included in NLP lexicons as the neccessary minimum.[17] In Section 5, we will use this list to evaluate different methods of lexical acquisition by checking it against the set of information types which can automatically be extracted. This will help us to identify those types of informatio n which must be specified manually in the course of NLP lexicon development.

NLP lexicons should include the following types of information on SVCs:

1. Morpho-syntactic formation of the Npred.
2. Morpho-syntactic formation of SVC arguments.
3. Adverbial vs. attributive modifiability.
4. Semantic contribution of the SV.

NLP lexicons should include the following types of information on idioms:

1. Part of speech of the idiom.
2. Internal syntactic structure of the idiom.
3. Lexical components of the idiom.
4. Idiom-external arguments.
5. Internal semantic structure of the idiom.
6. Lexical variability of the idiom chunks.
7. Morpho-syntactic variability of the idiom chunks.
8. Modifiability of the idiom chunks.
9. Restrictions on syntactic operations applicable to the idiom.

With regard to the complexity of the information, the use of intelligent lexicon formalisms with deduction components which support default inheritance would be of great benefit. This way, only information which cannot be derived from general principles must be specified directly. Sensible default assumptions are, for instance, that verbal idioms are lexically and morpho-syntactically fixed, that noun components should not be modified, and that only those syntactic operations may be applied to idiom chunks, which may also be applied to other types of non-referential expressions (e.g., expletive *it*; cf. [15], [9]). The general principles governing the passivization of verbal idioms still need to be investigated in greater depth, as does the influence of metaphoric contents on the morpho-syntactic flexibility of idiom chunks.

5 Acquisition of Multiword Lexemes from Text Corpora and from Machine–Readable Dictionaries

In the previous section, we saw that NLP lexicons must contain complex information on MWLs and their properties. Since the development of complex MWL

---

[17] A more detailed list, which takes different types of translation equivalence into account, can be found in [5].

descriptions is a time-consuming and laborious enterprise, it is sensible to check first whether existing machine-readable lexical resources can facilitate the task. In the following section, we shall report on several feasibility studies carried out at the University of Tübingen with the aim of automatically extracting information on German MWLs from text corpora and machine-readable dictionaries.

5.1 Corpus-based Acquisition of Support Verb Constructions

One feasibility study, carried out by E. Breidt (cf. [1]), uses text corpora and statistical methods for the extraction of German SVCs and noun-verb collocations.[18] In this study, the Mannheimer Korpus 1 (MK1)[19] was used as text corpus together with tools which calculate two statistical measurements on the basis of bigram tables:[20]

- **Mutual information (MI):** Compares the joint probability p(x,y) that two words, x and y, occur together in the corpus within a predefined distance with the independent probabilities, p(x) and p(y), that x and y occur independently.
  The probability p(x) of x is calculated by dividing the total number of occurrences f(x) of the word x by the total number of word tokens occurring in the corpus. Mutual information values can give an estimate of the degree of association existing between pairs of words.
- **T-score:** A significance measure, which estimates the significance of the word associations relative to the corpus being used.

In the study, the infinitive forms of 16 German support verbs were taken as key words. MI and t-score measurements were taken in a six word window to the left of the respective key-words for bigrams with a frequency of at least three occurrences. Precision was calculated for the set of all word pairs with a t-score greater than 0.6. The precision varied from 57 to 91 percent, the average precision being 72.7 percent.[21] These results are not as convincing as the results achieved in studies which used similar methods to extract English collocations. This is due to characteristic properties of the German language which make the task of extracting interesting collocations from text corpora more difficult than for English:

---

[18] Noun-verb collocations, such as *to pay attention to*, are habitual associations of verbs and. nouns which cannot be predicted by the rules of the language system. Both the verb and noun have lexeme status and are therefore not MWLs according to our definition.

[19] The MK1 was made available to the University of Tübingen by the "Institut für deutsche Sprache" in Mannheim. It is a mixed corpus and contains about 2.7 million word tokens deriving from fiction, scientific texts, newpapers, and magazines.

[20] A detailed specification of the two measurements is given in [6].

[21] Precision was defined as the percentage of word pairs which are noun-verb-collocations or SVCs relative to the set of all word pairs detected with this method. The figures refer to the study reported in [1]; additional studies simulating lemmatized and part-of-speech-tagged corpora are described in [2]; the best ave rage precision in these studies was 87.6 percent.

- **Inflection**: German is a highly inflected language: the inflection paradigm of a strong verb with stem alternation like *kommen* includes three stem forms and in total 24 different word forms. The paradigm of a noun like *Haus* includes two stem forms and in total five word forms. Thus, in contrast to less inflected languages like English, one German word form only covers a small part of the complete inflectional paradigm of the searched lemma. To compensate for this drawback, the availability of a lemmati zed corpus would be of great benefit for the exploitation of German corpora.

- **Word Order**: In German sentences, the Npred and the SV of an SVC can appear in different positions and may be separated from each other by an unpredictable number of words:

  (25) Sie kommen mit keinen Menschen in Beruehrung.
  (26) In Beruehrung mit Menschen kommen sie nicht.
  (27) Sie kommen mit Menschen, die ...., nicht in Beruehrung.
  (28) In Beruehrung mit Menschen, die ...., kommen sie nicht.
  (29) weil sie mit Menschen nie in Beruehrung kommen.
  (30) weil sie nie in Beruehrung mit Menschen kommen.
  (31) weil sie in Beruehrung mit Menschen, die ..., kommen.

  The constituent order SV–Npred, as in (25), is unmarked in main clauses; but the order Npred–SV is also possible, as illustrated in (26). Examples (27) and (28) demonstrate that the distance between the SV and the Npred may be unpredictably long if the argument of the SVC (in our examples the PP *mit Menschen*) is further modified, e.g., by a relative clause. It is therefore obvious that rules such as *Semantic agent is used before the verb; semantic object after.* (cf. [17]), which were successfully used for English corpora cannot simply be applied to German.

  German subordinate clauses, however, demand the fixed constituent order Npred–SV, as illustrated in the examples (29)-(31). This explains why search windows to the left of the verb yield much better results than search windows to the right. But even in subordinate clauses, Npred and SV may be separated from each other by an SVC argument, as in (30), which may be extended by argument modifiers, as in (31).

  To overcome these problems caused by German word order, the availability of parsed corpora is a prerequisite.

In addition to these language-specific problems, corpus-based statistical methods have general limitations: they may detect SVCs, but they do not reveal their internal structure nor will they reveal the morpho-syntactic properties of their constituents. As a consequence, all relevant types of information on SVCs, given in Section 4, will have to be added by the NLP lexicographer.

5.2 Dictionary-based Acquisition of Support Verb Constructions

The dictionary resource used in our feasibility studies on dictionary-based methods was the Duden-Stilwörterbuch (Duden-2, cf. [8]). Duden-2 is a German monolingual collocation dictionary containing descriptions of the combinatory potential of words in syntactic constructions and a well elaborated phraseological part. Parts of this dictionary were made available to us in machine-readable form for research purposes within the ELWIS project. The printsetting tapes were transformed into a lexical database by the dictionary entry parser Lex-Parse (cf. [10]), so that the relevant phraseological items could be queried and accessed directly.

A quantitative comparison of dictionary and corpus results, as carried out for the verbs *kommen, setzen,* and *stellen,* showed that all SVCs and noun-verb-collocations which were detected in the MK1 by using statistical methods are also listed in the Duden-2. From a quantitative point of view, the dictionary is obviously a richer resource than the corpus. However, one should not conclude from this result that the use of text corpora is superfluous: the use of larger corpora than the MK1 might bring up some new collocations which are not recorded in the dictionary. In addition, corpus research offers the opportunity of deciding which collocations occur most frequently in a given text type. Thus, a combination of corpus and dictionary-based methods should produce good results, as long as the internal structure and components of the SVCs are specified in the dictionary.

However, the Duden-2 does not specify all types of information which are neccessary for an NLP treatment of SVCs: information about morpho-syntactic properties of the SVC, number and type of SVC arguments, and the semantic contribution of the SV is not explicitly accounted for. Moreover, there are inconsistencies with respect to the dictionary entry structure, which make it difficult to retrieve SVCs and noun-verb collocations automatically:

- In most cases, SVCs and noun-verb-collocations are not listed under the dictionary entry of the verb, but rather under the entry of the Npred. This is in line with metalexicographic claims (cf. [11]), which advise that collocations are to be included in the entry of the base component (which is the Npred) and not in the entry of the collocate part (which is the SV). Unfortunately, this strategy has not been followed consistently. As a consequence, one has to check the complete lexical database in order to retrieve all SVCs for a given SV.
- SVCs are to be found in different positions of the dictionary's microstructure: they may be part of the example group, part of the group on proverbial expressions, or they appear in the phraseological part. Systematic principles for the placement of SVCs and noun-verb-collocations within the dictionary entries would considerably facilitate their automatic extraction.

5.3 Acquisition of Verbal Idioms

We pointed out in Section 2 that verbal idioms quite often belong to informal and colloquial registers. This is most likely the reason why they do not appear frequently in a corpus of written language, such as the MK1. We made a KWIC (keyword-in-context) search for the headword *Kopf (head)* in the MK1 and found examples for only 30 of the 74 idioms given in the Duden-2. 17 idioms with *Teufel (devil)* as a component are in the dictionary, but only four of them were found with the help of KWIC analyses in our corpus. As a consequence of the low frequency of instances, the overall result obtained by statistical methods is very unsatisfactory.

There are not only quantitative, but above all qualitative arguments in favour of the dictionary as the primary source: dictionaries contain explicit and implicit information on the internal and external structure of idiomatic expressions, which may, to a certain extent, be extracted by using pattern-matching methods. Another feasibility study was carried out using the Duden-2 to give an initial impression of the opportunities and limitations offered by such methods. The study showed that the following types of lexical information may be extracted (semi-)automatically:

- Argument slots are represented by indefinite pronouns like *jemandem* (abbreviated as *jdm.* and meaning *somebody*) and *etwas* (meaning *something*), which have the function of argument indicators carrying information on the case marking and the semantic type of the argument slot fillers. The argument indicator *jdm.* in the idiom description in (32)

  (32) jdm. ueber den Kopf wachsen
  Lit.: sb. over the head grow
  Engl.: to outgrow sb.

  indicates that the idiom has an argument slot filled by a noun phrase in dative case which denotes a living being. The idiom description in (33)

  (33) jdm. etwas auf den Kopf zusagen
  Lit.: sb. sth. to the head tell
  Engl.: to say sth. to sb.'s face

  indicates a dative slot for a living being (=*jdm.*) and an accusative slot for a non-living thing (=*etwas*). The argument indicators can be used to automatically extract information on the arguments of verbal idioms.

- The lexical components of idioms can be obtained if the argument indicators are removed from the idiom description. By removing the indicators *jdm.* and *etwas* from the idiom description in (33), one obtains the internal lexical components of the idiom in their canonical form, namely *auf den Kopf zusagen*.

- Morpho-syntactic flexibility can be inferred by the rule that no variation is possible unless specified otherwise. Possibilities of number and determiner variation are explicitly specified:

  (34) in [des] Teufels Kueche kommen
  Lit.: in the devil's kitchen come
  Engl.: to get into the hell of a mess

In (34), the brackets around *des* indicate that the definite article of the noun phrase *des Teufels* is optional and can also be omitted.

- For <u>lexical variation</u> a similar rule applies: lexical variation is not possible unless specified otherwise. It would, however, be helpful if two different types of lexical variants were explicitly differentiated:

  - Purely **idiom-internal variants** as in (35),

    (35)   sich an den Kopf fassen/greifen
    Lit.: o.s. on the head grasp/seize
    Engl.: to throw one's hands up in despair

    in which the choice of the verbs *fassen* or *greifen* does not affect the denotative meaning of the idiom.

  - **Semantic variants** as in (36),

    (36) Kopf und Kragen riskieren/verlieren
    Lit.: head and collar risk/lose
    Engl.: to risk/lose one's head

    in which the verbs *riskieren* and *verlieren* make distinct semantic contributions to the meaning of the idiom.

  Both types of variants are separated by the same structure indicator, namely the slash. For MT purposes, however, the distinction is essential and has to be made explicit.

- Information on the <u>modifiability of idiom components</u> is implicitly given if one follows the rule "components cannot be modified unless specified otherwise" as a rule of thumb. However, the study showed that that the possibilities of component modification are not systematically accounted for in the Duden-2 and are not very reliable.

There are important types of information on verbal idioms which are not included in the dictionary at all:

The <u>part of speech</u> of idiomatic expressions is not explicitly specified nor can it be inferred from the part of speech of the headword of the dictionary entry in which the idiomatic expression is listed. This is due to the fact that an idiomatic expression is always listed in the dictionary entry of the first noun in its citation form or, if there is no noun, in the dictionary entry of the first content word. Thus, the verbal idiom *zwei Fliegen mit einer Klappe schlagen* is listed in the dictionary under the entry for the noun *Fliege*; and the adverbial idiom *mit Mann und Maus* is listed in the dictionary under the entry for the noun *Mann*.

No information is given on the <u>syntactic operations</u> which may or may not be applied. This information, like the information on part of speech, must be added manually relying on a theory concerning the syntactic and semantic properties of idioms.

6 Conclusion

The machine processing of MWLs requires detailed specifications of their morpho-syntactic properties in the lexicon. The task of drawing up such specifications is laborious and time-consuming, but is indispensable in view of the frequency of MWLs. We showed that the information on MWL properties which has to be encoded in the lexicon is quite complex. To manage this complexity the use of intelligent lexicon formalisms with deduction components supporting default inheritance would be of great benefit. This way, only information which cannot be derived from general principles must be specified explicitly. In order to take full advantage of the options offered by such formalisms, the general relationships between semantic structure, metaphoric content and morpho–syntactic flexibility should be further investigated.

The specifications of MWLs should be based on corpus-based research. However, the feasibility studies discussed in this paper showed that statistical corpus-based methods provide only partial information on SVCs and yield only poor results when applied to verbal idioms. The results demonstrate that statistical methods for extracting verbal MWLs which have proved successful for English cannot simply be applied to German.

If machine-readable dictionaries are available, the combination of corpus- and dictionary-based methods should produce better results than using just one type of source. From the quantitative and qualitative comparison of the Duden-2 dictionary and the MK 1 text corpus, we come to the conclusion that a dictionary, provided that it is of high quality, should be considered as the primary source for acquiring lexical knowledge.

A feasibility study using the Duden-2 has shown, however, that the information given on MWLs is neither extensive nor explicit enough to fully meet the requirements of NLP applications. Nevertheless, partial information on the morpho-syntactic properties of MWLs can be extracted and may then be completed by the MT lexicographer.

References

1. Breidt, E.: Extraktion von Verb-Nomen-Verbindungen aus dem Mannheimer Korpus I. SfS-Report 03-93, University of Tübingen, 1993
2. Breidt, E.: Extraction of V-N-collocations from text corpora: A feasibility study for German. First workshop on very large corpora, Ohio State University, Columbus Ohio, June 1993
3. Breidt, E.: Definition and classification criteria for verbal multiword lexemes. SfS Report, University of Tübingen, (to appear 1994)
4. Bresson, D.: Classification des verbes support (Funktionsverben) de l'allemand. In: Cahiers d'Etudes Germaniques 15, (1988) 53-65
5. Brundage, J., Kresse, M., Schwall, U., Storrer, A.: Multiword Lexemes: A monolingual and contrastive typology for NLP and MT. IWBS Report 232, IBM Institute for Knowledge Based Systems, Stuttgart 1992
6. Church, K., Gale, W., Hanks, P., Hindle, D.: Using statistics in lexical analysis. In: Zernik, U. (ed.): Lexical Acquisition. New York 1991

50

7. Danlos, L.: Support Verb Constructions. Linguistic properties, representation, translation. In: Journal of French Linguistic Study, Vol.2, No. 1 (1992), 1-32

8. Duden-2: Duden Stilwörterbuch der deutschen Sprache (ed. by G. Drosdowski, G.). 7th edition, Mannheim 1988

9. Engelke, S.: Eigenschaften von Phraseolexemen: Eine Untersuchung zu Möglichkeiten der Transformation und internen Modifizierbarkeit von somatischen verbalen Phraseolexemen. M.A. dissertation, University of Tübingen, 1994

10. Hauser, R., Storrer, A.: Dictionary entry parsing using the LexParse system. In: Lexicographica 9 (1993), Tübingen 1994, 174-219

11. Hausmann, F.K.: Kollokationen im Deutschen Wörterbuch. Ein Beitrag zur Theorie des lexikographischen Beispiels. In: Bergenholtz, H., Mugdan, J.(ed.): Lexikographie und Grammatik. Akten des Essener Kolloquiums 1984. Tübingen 1985, 118-129

12. Krenn, B., Volk, M.: DiTo Datenbank Datendokumentation zu Funktionsverbgefügen und Relativsätzen. DFKI-Document D-93-24, Deutsches Forschungszentrum für Künstliche Intelligenz, Saarbrücken 1993

13. Nicolas, T.: Internal modification of English V-NP-idioms. In: Everaert et al. (ed.): Proceedings of the Second Tilburg Workshop on Idioms 1992. Tilburg 1992, 85-96

14. Nunberg, G., Sag, I., Wasow, T.: Idioms. Manuscript, Stanford 1993 (to appear in Language 1994)

15. Schenk, A.: The syntactic behaviour of idioms. In: Everaert et al. (ed.): Proceedings of the Second Tilburg Workshop on Idioms 1992. Tilburg 1992, 97-110

16. Schwall, U.: Aspektualität - Eine semantisch-funktionelle Kategorie. Tübinger Beiträge zur Linguistik 344, Tübingen 1991

17. Smadja, F.A.: Macrocoding the lexicon with co–occurence knowledge. In: Zernik, U. (ed.): Lexical Acquisition: exploring on–line resources to build a lexicon. Hillsdale, NJ 1991

18. Storrer, A., Feldweg, H., Hinrichs, E.W.: Korpusunterstützte Entwicklung lexikalischer Wissensbasen. In: Sprache und Datenverarbeitung 17 (1993), Bonn 1994, 59-72

19. Van der Linden, E.-J.: A categorial, computational theory of idioms. OTS dissertation series, Rijksuniversiteit Utrecht 1993

20. Wiegand, H.E.: Kritische Lanze für das Fackelredensartenwörterbuch. Bericht und Diskussion zu einem Workshop in der österreichischen Akademie der Wissenschaften am 14.2.1994. In: Lexicographica 9, (1993), 1994

21. Wotjak, B: Verbale Phraseolexeme in System und Text. Tübingen 1992

Pragmatics of Specialist Terms: The Acquisition and Representation of Terminology

Khurshid Ahmad

Artificial Intelligence Group, Department of Mathematical and Computing Sciences, University of Surrey, Guildford, Surrey, GU2 5XH.

Abstract. The compilation of specialist terminology requires an understanding of how specialists coin and use terms of their specialisms. We show how an exploitation of the pragmatic features of specialist terms will help in the semi-automatic extraction of terms and in the organisation of terms in terminology data banks.

1 Introduction

The word *terminology* has at least two senses. According to the first, the more popular definition, terminology refers to a systematically collected and organised vocabulary of technical terms used in a particular field, subject or science. In the second, and perhaps less well-known definition, terminology is *the* study of nomenclature or *the* science of terms. This science deals with the coinage, establishment, collection, usage and obsolescence of terms of specialist domains. The coinage-to-obsolescence cycle can be construed as a life-cycle, involving stages of inception, growth, maturity and the ultimate redundancy of a term or indeed collections of terms. Terminology science is the study of this life-cycle.

The terms of a specialist domain are one of the domain's key resources: a resource which has to be nurtured and conserved, a resource which has to be *managed*. The management of terminology deals with practical questions related to the entire life-cycle of terms of a specialist domain, involving a critique of methods, tools and techniques used in the identification, collection, verification/validation, standardisation, and storage in, as well as retrieval from, a specially designed data management system - a *terminology data bank* or *term bank*[1].

The major bottleneck in acquiring terminology is the dependence of the terminologist on the availability of articulate specialists; the terminologist's ability to find and comprehend the written output of a growing plethora of highly specialised domains is being increasingly taxed. This output is perhaps the single most important resource for identifying and elaborating specialist terms. Specialists rely heavily on written text for describing new ideas, consolidating current theory and practice, and censoring *outdated* concepts and traditions. The uses and abuses of ideas, practice, theories and traditions are almost always related to the uses and abuses of terms of the domain.

The claim that terminology is a science of terms can be challenged by semanticists, epistemologists, information scientists, grammarians, lexicographers and text linguists. Semanticists would argue that since terminology deals with the semantics of linguistic expressions, then it really is a branch of semantics dealing with *semantic fields* in restricted domains. Epistemologists can argue that since terminology deals with issues of knowledge primitives, then it really is a part of epistemology. Information scientists can claim that their forays into classification are really what terminology is all about. Grammarians, such as Zellig Harris (1990), have discussed issues related to terminology under the rubric of *sublanguages*. Harris, together with Kittredge and Lehrberger (1982), argues that the collocation patterns observed in scientific discourse, including compound terms and idiosyncratic clauses and sentences, can be understood in the structuralist paradigm pioneered by Harris.

Lexicographers will argue that terminology is really dealing with pragmatics: terms are used by an identifiable discourse community, much like a dialect used in a geographically identifiable area or a sociolect used by a socially identifiable group of people, and, provided we can systematically keep track of the pragmatic data, problems of terminology are almost indistinguishable from those of lexicography. Last but not least, work in text linguistics, particularly that by de Beaugrande and Dressler (1981), includes a spirited discussion of terminological issues.

Michael Halliday has used the notions he has developed in systemic linguistics together with his predications about language as a 'social semiotic' (Halliday 1978), to explore the historical relationships between science, language and literature (Halliday and Martin 1993). Halliday's explorations are of significant import for terminology science in that he has commented on the language used by scientists and has argued that technical terms play an important role in the creation of 'a discourse of organised knowledge'. Focusing on the language of science text books used in schools, and with one eye on what Halliday and Martin perceive as the 'alienating' and 'anti-democratic' nature of twentieth century science, these authors have looked at scientific discourse from the times of Chaucer, through Newton, right up to the language of modern-day science, with exemplars from non-linear dynamics (popularly known as *chaos theory*), cognitive psychology, material sciences, geography and biology. For Halliday et al. the uniqueness of scientific language lies in the 'lexicogrammar' or *wording* of the language.

The scientist adapts and innovates upon the lexicogrammatical resources of his or her first language, or that of the second (or third) language if he or she does not use the first language for scientific writing, for expressing abstract and concrete ideas, for simplifying and summarising complex facts, for explicating and exemplifying, for contradicting and reinforcing, for categorising and stating exceptions to rules. And, in the execution of all these complex tasks - tasks which are executed through the medium of written text - scientists coin new terms, suppress the use of some extant terms, restrict or expand the scope of terms, borrow from other disciplines and from other languages. Terminology, as a collection of vocabulary items and as a science of terms, plays a central role in scientific endeavour.

Given the strategic importance of terminology in technical and scientific documentation and in human and machine translation, it must be gratifying for terminologists that semanticists, philosophers, text and systemic linguists, lexicographers, and information scientists are also interested in terminology. However, while the concerns of a terminologist are similar to those of all the above, the terminologist also has practical considerations of terminology management to address[2].

We would like to argue that terminology management can be regarded as a study of special languages from the point of view of the users, especially of the choices they make, the constraints they encounter in using such a variety of language, and the effect their language use has on the other participants in an act of communication. The definition of terminology management adopted here is a paraphrase of Crystal's definition of pragmatics (1992:217). The central problem of terminology management is to understand and deal with the pragmatics of specialist terms and the pragmatics of specialist texts. But what of terminology management now?

Much of the business of terminology management revolves around the maintenance of terminology data banks. There are international standards (ISO R/1087, 1969), national guidelines (BSI, DIN etc.), and company policies on how to collect and organise data about terms that are already in possession of terminology data bank managers. Terms in existing data banks are stored using a template *record format*. Typically, the record format, a format developed by the standards organisations or autonomous enterprises, specifies slot names for the data related to a typical term; some of these slots are mandatory and others are optional. A record format can have as few as 20 such slots or as many as 60. Essentially, these slots can be grouped under four major groupings, each group referring to one aspect of the terminology life cycle: acquisition, representation, deployment and dissemination (Table 1):

Slot Group	Exemplar Slots
Acquisitional	headword, terminologist's name, date of entry
Representational	grammar, foreign language, equivalent, language variety
Deployment	definition, contextual example
Dissemination	synonyms, antonyms

Table 1. Slots used in terminology record formats

Existing term banks do not as a matter of course focus on usage-related data. However, such data would not only be of help to many users of term banks, but would also help in the efficient organisation of term banks. Terminology entries in a typical term bank do contain deprecated terms, and categories like *currency, frequency of use, regional or geographic variation* and *style* are generally avoided. The absence of such information is usually due to the terminologist's concern about the introduction of polysemy in term banks by the consideration of these pragmatic categories. But more of this later.

By contrast, general-language dictionaries usually contain some pragmatic data. More recently, the methods and techniques of computer-based corpus-oriented lexicography have allowed lexicographers to compute frequency and variance data, for instance, with a speed and accuracy that was not possible only a decade ago (Sinclair 1987, 1991). Landau (1989) has outlined usage categories in general-language dictionaries devised for providing pragmatic information together with the typical values associated with each of the categories (see Table 2).

Usage categories	Typical dictionary labels
1. Currency or temporality	Archaic, obsolete, current
2. Frequency of use	Rare
3. Regional or geographic variation	E.g., Am. English, British English, etc.
4. Tech. or specialised terminology	Astronomy, Chemistry, Physics, etc.
5. Restricted or taboo usage	Vulgar, obscene
6. Insult	Offensive, disparaging, contemptuous
7. Slang	Slang
8. Style, functional variety or register	Informal, colloq.,literary, poetic, humorous
9. Status or cultural level	Non-standard, substandard, illiterate

Table 2: Landau's pragmatic categories and their possible values for dictionary entries

In this paper, it will be shown that the pragmatic categories are relevant to terminology management, like currency, frequency of use, regional or geographic variation. Whilst others, including style (functional variety or register) and status (items 8 and 9 in Table 2) are to be defined more precisely for specialist terms. The 'slang' category is relevant to terminology in that slangs of specialist terms are used in describing complex artefacts, particularly in populist use like advertisements and reportage in mass-circulation print media and in conversations on the factory floor. 'Restricted' and 'insult' categories are not directly applicable to specialist texts. Nevertheless, one can trace the development of a (scientific) theory sometimes by the censorship applied by a specialist domain community and the ways in which certain terms are used in a rather pejorative manner.

The prevalent situation in terminology, as far as pragmatic issues are concerned, can be summed up as follows. Terminologists are concerned with ensuring that scientists and technologists are able to communicate amongst themselves, and with others, in as unambiguous a manner as possible. Much of the discussion in prescriptive terminology is focused on the establishment of monosemy with mononymy and a reduction in polysemy and the elimination of synonymy. As far as a terminologist is concerned, once a term has been coined in a *natural language*, then all regional and societal varieties of that language should endeavour to use the same term. The frequency of usage is not relevant to some in the terminology community, rooted as they are in the traditions of the standards/normative organisations, in that a scientific term, for them, is approved or rejected by standards organisations. The question of whether a certain discourse (domain) community uses a term frequently, rarely, or never, is not really an issue for them. Deprecated terms are entered in traditional term banks usually to persuade a translator, technical writer or other members of a specialist group that these terms are to be avoided, if possible.

The two major areas of terminology management which we claim can benefit from exploring and exploiting pragmatic features are term identification, and the organisation/dissemination of terms. In the area of *term identification*, the pragmatic features can be used for identifying *new* terms, or neologisms, of a specialism from the text archives of the specialism, including learned journals, books, popular articles, newspaper reportage and advertisement material associated with the specialism. A concordance of the specialist archive is produced together with the frequency of all words in the archive. The results of this concordance are compared with a diachronically compatible corpus of general-language texts. Such a contrast is a very simple way of identifying terms as we will show later, and the concordancing of terms is by far the quickest way of establishing its potential lexicogrammatical characteristics. Such a procedure expedites the identification and elaboration of neologisms. Considering that building a term bank is a complex and labour intensive task, that each term can cost up to £10.00 to identify and elaborate, and that a typical domain in science and engineering may require its community to be familiar and fluent with around 2500 to 4000 terms, any saving in term identification will make the difference between having a good quality term bank and having no term bank at all!

In the area of *terminology organisation and dissemination*, pragmatic features can be used to organise and disseminate the terminology of the domain, particularly by partitioning a term bank into a mother term bank, containing, for example, frequent terms, terms in the national variety of the documentor's/translator's language, and daughter term banks that may contain, for instance, less frequent terms, other regional varieties, lesser-used synonyms, and so on. The expectation here is that the documentor or translator will probably be familiar with terms in the mother term bank, but less familiar with the terms in the daughter term bank. We have estimated that a fully elaborated term bank of, say, 4000 terms can demand over 50MB of data; thus a pragmatic partitioning of term banks will make their availability on smaller computer systems more feasible.

Sections 2 and 3 of this paper deal with the acquisition of terms, Section 4 with the representation of terms using pragmatic criteria. Section 5 concludes the paper.

Section 2 contains a discussion of the quantitative difference between specialist texts of a given domain and a representative sample of general-language texts: these differences are crucial for our methodology for semi-automatically acquiring terms from a corpora of specialist texts. Problems related to the design of special-language corpora are discussed in the light of the fact that these texts, like learned journals, books, advertisements, etc., are written for different audience groups. Section 3 describes how the methodology has been effected through the use of a corpus-based terminology (and lexicography) management system - System Quirk. The exploration of the pragmatics of specialist texts will help in the acquisition of terms. Section 4 describes how the pragmatic features of a term can be exploited to partition terms on the basis of an empirical notion of how familiar a typical term bank user may be with a given term.

2 Terminology in Text and its Acquisition

The inextricable link between knowledge and language, a source of continual and heated philosophical debate, is of considerable import to terminology science and practice, particularly in view of the rapid and massive increase in the volume of literature related to science and technology. This increase has been accompanied by a new *genre* of writing, *specialist writing*, a genre that uses and adapts and innovates on the general language to create the special-language literature[3].

Exemplars of specialist writing include the familiar learned-journal text type, the text-book and technical manual texts. But specialist writing also includes the popular science and hobby magazine text types and the newspaper feature and specialist reportage. Furthermore, as most specialisms are involved in trading goods and services, then texts such as advertisements and brochures are also a part of the text archive of a domain.

2.1 The 'Weirdness' of Special-language Texts

A distinctive feature of specialist writing is the profusion of scientific terms in this genre. These are single words or multi-word phrases and are usually coined to express an idea, a fact, or a phenomenon with a view on the part of the person coining the term to the new term being adopted by his or her peers. Scientists show considerable dexterity in coining terms, borrowing sometimes from the dominant language of science and technology, for example, depending on the historical time, from Latin, Greek, Arabic (for example, *atom, nucleus, vitality, chemistry, zero*) and now English. Sometimes acronyms are created (cf. *laser* - acronym for light amplification through stimulated energy radiation), whilst at other times scientists draw upon contemporary literature (for instance, *quarks* in James Joyce's *Finnegans Wake* have found their way into elementary particle physics).

Once a term has been accepted, the scientific community enforces its use with considerable vigour and with equal vigour censors certain terms. Recent literature in linguistics, c. 1960-70, avoided the use of the terms *behaviour, reinforcement*, etc. and instead gave preference to *language acquisition device, transformation*, and so on.

The coinage and the subsequent use of terminology involves Platonist conceptualisations on the one hand and the use of Aristotelian sense-related data on the other[4]: scientific writing is an archive of such conceptualisations and sense-related data. And, if we were to understand the mechanisms and processes that contribute to good scientific writing, we would not only be able to communicate better, but also be able to discuss deeper questions related to knowledge in a more objective manner[5].

At the linguistic level, scientific writing can be distinguished not only by the profusion of scientific terms, a large majority of which can be classified as nominal expressions, but by the preponderance of agentless passives (Svartvik 1966), the marked nominalisation of verbs (Halliday and Martin 1993:64), and by the very low frequency of personal pronouns. It is at the lexical level that the text types in this genre can be distinguished from other text types in general language, like newspaper editorials, short stories and novels, personal letters, and so on.

The most frequently-occurring words in any text belong to the closed-class category. Closed-class words have a largely or wholly grammatical role and include articles, pronouns, prepositions, auxiliary and modal verbs, and conjunctions. The membership of the closed-class word-family is fixed or limited; neologisms are not normally added. The open-class category, on the other hand, comprises words whose membership is in principle indefinite or unlimited. New words and senses are continually being added to this set as new inventions, ideas, and so on, emerge. But there are differences in the distribution of these categories in general language and special language texts.

A comparison of the word frequency between a general-language corpus, say, for example, the Lancaster/Oslo Bergen (LOB) Corpus of British English (c.1961), and a specialist corpus of automotive engineering texts compiled at the University of Surrey (see Section 2.3 for details), shows the difference in behaviour of open-class items in the two corpora (see Table 3). The six most frequent words in both corpora are the same closed-class words, comprising over 15% of the total words in each corpus. The first ten words in both corpora are still closed-class words and comprise just under 25% of the total words of each corpus: this, indeed, is a large number, about 1/4 million for the LOB corpus and about 90,000 words for the Surrey corpus.

Surrey's automotive engineering corpus 369,751 words				Lancaster /Oslo-Bergen corpus 1,013,737 words			
Word Form	Rank	Relative Frequency (%)	Word Class	Word Form	Rank	Relative Frequency (%)	Word Class
the	1	7.15	closed	the	1	6.74	closed
of	2	3.34	closed	of	2	3.53	closed
and	3	2.36	closed	and	3	2.75	closed
to	4	2.23	closed	to	4	2.64	closed
in	5	2.10	closed	a	5	2.23	closed
a	6	1.92	closed	in	6	2.10	closed
is	7	1.33	closed	that	7	1.12	closed
for	8	1.09	closed	is	8	1.10	closed
with	9	0.86	closed	was	9	1.05	closed
on	10	0.75	closed	it	10	1.04	closed
as	11	0.68	closed	for	11	0.92	closed
be	12	0.66	closed	he	12	0.89	closed
are	13	0.64	closed	I	13	0.75	closed
by	14	0.62	closed	as	14	0.72	closed
that	15	0.62	closed	with	15	0.71	closed
emission	16	0.59	open	be	16	0.71	closed
this	17	0.58	closed	on	17	0.69	closed
at	18	0.56	closed	his	18	0.62	closed
engine	19	0.56	open	at	19	0.60	closed
vehicle	20	0.51	open	by	20	0.57	closed
system	21	0.48	open	not	21	0.54	closed
car	22	0.48	open	had	22	0.54	closed
catalyst	23	0.46	open	this	23	0.52	closed
it	24	0.45	closed	but	24	0.49	closed
which	25	0.44	closed	from	25	0.46	closed

Table 3. A contrastive analysis of a special-language and a general-language corpus

Now, if we look at the 25 most frequent words in Table 3, it turns out that for the LOB corpus, the first 25 words are closed-class words and comprise over 30% of the total words of the corpora[6]. However, whilst the first 25 words in the special-language corpus also comprise just over 30% of the texts, there are at least six words that are open class, all nouns, comprising over 3% of the total corpus. All six of these open-class words are potentially key terms of the domain: *emission*, *engine*, *vehicle*, *system*, *car* and *catalyst*. These nouns are as frequent as the important closed-class words, like *by, not, had*, etc., in the general-language corpus. The first two open-class words in the LOB corpus do not appear until rank 53 (the reporting verb *said*) and rank 62 (the common noun *time*) respectively.

If we compare the relative frequency of the first six open-class words from the 25 most frequent words in the automotive engineering corpus with their relative frequency in the LOB Corpus, we find that the co-efficient of the relative frequency is some guide to the quantitative differences between special-language texts and general-language texts. The very high values of this co-efficient for some words indicates that, perhaps, these words are used almost exclusively, say, for automotive engineering. The high-frequency open class words identified in Table 3 have a large co-efficient of relative frequency ranging between 16 and infinity. Terms such as *emission* and *catalyst*, together with related terms like *autocatalyst, converter*, and *hydrocarbon(s)*, have zero frequency in the LOB Corpus, but a finite frequency in the automotive engineering corpus; hence, the co-efficient of weirdness for these terms, when computed by comparison against the LOB corpus, is *infinity* (Table 4a).

Word	Surrey Automotive Engineering corpus (369,751)		Lancaster Oslo-Bergen corpus (1,013,737)		Co-efficient of
	Absolute Freq.	Relative Freq. (%)	Absolute Freq.	Relative Freq. (%)	Weirdness
	(a)	(b)	(c)	(d)	(b/d)
autocatalyst	27	0.0073%	0	0.0000%	Infinity
car	1,790	0.4841%	272	0.0268%	18.04
catalyst	1,700	0.4598%	0	0.0000%	Infinity
control	1,517	0.4103%	199	0.0196%	20.90
emission	2,194	0.5934%	0	0.0000%	Infinity
engine	2,083	0.5634%	70	0.0069%	81.58
hydrocarbon	140	0.0379%	0	0.0000%	Infinity
hydrocarbons	290	0.0784%	0	0.0000%	Infinity
system	1,795	0.4855%	298	0.0294%	16.51
vehicle	1,884	0.5095%	20	0.0020%	258.27

Table 4a. The preponderance of open-class words in special-language literature
(Figures in columns 'b' and 'd' have been rounded up)

In contrast, for the most frequently occurring closed-class words, like *the, of, and, to, a* and *in* comprising just under 20% of the LOB Corpus <u>and</u> the automotive engineering corpus, the co-efficient of relative frequency is close to unity (Table 4b). For other closed-class words, like *we, what*, and *would*, for example, the co-efficient of relative frequency is far less than unity: it appears that scientists in particular and specialists in general tend to 'suppress' the use of certain closed-class category words (Table 4b). This suppression is as much an idiosyncrasy of the specialist texts as is the preponderance of nominals in such texts: a kind of weirdness, a departure from the norm, a departure from the general language of everyday usage.

Word	Surrey Automotive Engineering corpus (369,751)		Lancaster Oslo-Bergen corpus (1,013,737)		Co-efficient of Weirdness
	Absolute Freq.	Relative Freq.(%)	Absolute Freq.	Relative Freq.(%)	
	(a)	(b)	(c)	(d)	(b/d)
the	26,634	7.20%	68,351	6.74%	1.068
of	12,434	3.36%	35,745	3.53%	0.954
and	8,792	2.38%	27,873	2.75%	0.865
to	8,319	2.25%	26,781	2.64%	0.852
a	7,100	1.92%	22,647	2.23%	0.860
in	7,750	2.10%	21,248	2.10%	1.000
about	431	0.12%	1,898	0.19%	0.623
we	278	0.08%	3,128	0.31%	0.244
what	171	0.05%	1,925	0.19%	0.244
would	464	0.13%	2,799	0.28%	0.454

Table 4b. The 'suppression' of the closed-class words in special-language literature (Figures in columns 'b' and 'd' have been rounded up)

Following Malinowski's (1935) comments on the language of *magicians* in remote tribal communities, we refer to the co-efficient of the relative frequency of words in special-language text and in general-language texts as the *co-efficient of weirdness*. This weirdness may be said to give a distinctive texture to scientific writing and in some cases helps the scientists to report the unusual and the esoteric, whilst in others it makes such text rather opaque to a layperson.

2.2 A Typology of Scientific and Technical Writing

The most obvious source of special-language terminology of a domain is the archive of *learned* texts of the domain: learned papers and advanced text books are amongst the best and most frequent examples of this type of text. Here, one can find the terms in their earliest phase of their life-cycle, that is, when they have just been coined by a scientist and are being introduced to the specialist community for the very first time. Articulate scientists elaborate on their neologisms and are also frequently involved in elaborating neologisms created by others. Elaboration involves either extending or restricting the scope of a neologism.

Advances in science and technology are also reported in popular science magazines, hobby journals and in the news bulletins of learned societies[7]. Another important variant of the scientific writing genre is found in the language used in technical manuals, imperative in style and containing many verb-initial sentences in English. The popular science and the technical manual text are an important source of terminology: these texts may not contain as many neologisms as, say, the learned texts, but may allow access to more mature and more established terms.

Scientific and engineering artefacts are bought and sold, and the vendors of such artefacts rely on advertisements in the news media, in popular magazines, and, sometimes in learned journals. The advertisement text is yet another source of terminology: here we may find popularised and deprecated forms of terms: a *honey-combed three-way catalytic converter* in learned journals becomes *catalytic converter* or *autocatalyst* in popular magazines and in quality newspapers, and is reduced even further to *cat con* or *cat* in advertisements[8].

Public interest in the impact of science and technology means that (quality) newspapers carry editorial comments and news reports on science and technology topics. Apart from the terminology found in newsworthy stories - for instance, the discovery of a cure for a certain type of cancer, the collision of meteors with planets - much of the terminology in the newspaper genre of texts relies on mature terminology. News journalists, on the whole, tend to elaborate the terms they use: acronyms are expanded and display boxes in the middle of the text contain salient terms and their definitions.

One can identify at least six different types of texts produced by or with the help of a scientific or technological community: *learned journals* and advanced text books and *popular science texts*, texts designed to inform, and in the latter case, texts designed to entertain as well; *technical manuals* and *introductory text books*, texts designed with pedagogic or instructional purposes in mind; and *newspaper* and *advertisement* texts, texts that require imagination on the part of both the reader and writer, a kind of semi-fictional account of a scientific discovery or an artefact.

Specialist texts, like general language text, can be generally divided into two broad (sub-) genres: informative texts and imaginative texts. The designers of the Brown, the LOB and to an extent the other more modern corpora, distinguish between these types of text. The informative genre contains the non-narrative text, texts like essays, government documents, and the learned genre, though this genre was for all intents and purposes popular science texts. The imaginative text was essentially narrative text and comprised fiction, covering the spectrum from detective fiction to science fiction and from adventure fiction to romantic fiction.

Indeed, there are many more text types produced by the specialist community. For example, Sager, Dungworth and McDonald (1980) have discussed *100* different text types, including memos, patents, and so on. Newer text types appear regularly: the poster presentation in learned conferences, essentially mounted displays that require the presence of the author at certain fixed times; written texts containing voice annotations; electronic-mail communications between the members of a specialist domain.

2.3 Design of Special-language Corpora

Corpora designed for lexicographical purposes are designed according to author, title, date of publication, length of the text, nationality of the author, language variety, and so on. The literature on corpus-based lexicography includes discussions on how to select the texts so as to minimise the selectors' bias: a distinction is made between a randomly-selected corpus of texts and a corpus that contains deliberately selected texts (by *random selection* it is meant that texts are chosen from a catalogue of books in print at random). The LOB and Brown corpora are randomly selected corpora, whereas the Birmingham Collection of English Text was selected by a group of linguists, literature experts and lexicographers (Renouff 1987). The Longman Corpus of Contemporary English is a hybrid corpus in that one-half of the corpus is randomly selected whilst the other half was selected deliberately (Summers 1991). Corpus linguists vary in their choice of the length of texts: the LOB and Brown corpora contain 500 texts of approximately 2,000 words; the Longman corpus has an upper limit of 40,000 words and the Birmingham collection contains texts in their entirety.

Most general-language text corpora of English are *contemporary* in that the focus is on text published in the second half of the twentieth century[9]. Language variety, especially for monolingual corpora, is sometimes an important consideration. Corpora of English texts are clearly labelled in terms of the national origins of the various texts, like American English, British English, Australian English and Indian English.

Recall that it has been argued that a specialist text corpus would be a good source of neologisms and would be equally effective in showing which terms of the domain are preferred by the domain community and which ones are out of favour. Our focus is on obtaining pragmatic data related to the terms of a domain. This requires that we have a certain pragmatic balance in our corpus. In part, such a balance is achieved by having at least texts of the six different text types mentioned above comprising the informative and the imaginative texts of a specialist domain.

Pragmatic balance can also be achieved in part by making sure that texts used to build a specialist corpus are current: diachronic studies of language apart, there would be little point in looking for neologisms in older texts! Innovations in science and technology seldom have well-defined national or regional boundaries: pragmatic balance requires that the specialist corpus contain texts in two or more national varieties of a given language used by a discourse community. An up-to-date corpus of scientific and technical English texts should contain British, American and Australian English texts. Furthermore, as more and more scientists join the innovative fray and use English as a second language, for instance, Indian English, Euro-English, it is important to incorporate other English variants in a pragmatically-balanced specialist-corpus.

It must be noted that there is a whole range of continuously-growing text for general language, while the number of texts available for a specialist domain is bound to be smaller. In other words, the choice of a terminologist working with special-language text corpora is more limited than that of a lexicographer working with general-language text corpora.

The corpus-minded terminologist, unlike his or her lexicography counterpart, cannot make a decision on the size of the text he or she is going to use: LOB corpus designers restricted the size of text to 2,000 words primarily because of memory restrictions on computer systems; Longman Contemporary Corpus designers restrict the size of the text to 40,000 words. The terminologist cannot easily pass judgement on which text fragment to choose; perhaps there are more terms in the introduction, or perhaps they are in the middle of the text, or perhaps in the conclusion, or the author of a text may have even decided not to use certain terms. The weirdness of specialist texts, that is, the profusion of nominals and suppression of some closed-class words, coupled with the fact that one has more texts to choose from in general language means that the terminologist has little choice but to use full texts.

Lexicographers can pick and choose texts on the basis of the authors of the texts. These authors are well known in the sense that some would have been reviewed in the press, and, indeed, the lexicographer can select texts purely on his or her subjective judgement of the texts. The lexicographer is in a position to select texts for building lexica, because he or she can appreciate, analyse and understand general language texts without much help from others. However, such freedom of choice is not available to a terminologist who can neither appreciate nor analyse/understand specialist texts in the way a domain expert may do. Seldom does a terminologist have any formal knowledge of a specialist domain, and indeed, even if he or she knows something about a domain, it is quite probable that the next terminology assignment for a terminologist would be in a specialist area of which the terminologist knows very little. The terminologist either has to rely on a domain expert for selecting terminologically relevant texts or just has to take any text that becomes available.

2.4 Pragmatic Balance and the Design of Specialist Corpora

The Surrey automotive engineering corpus is one of the ten special-language corpora developed at the University of Surrey for building term banks and for studying special-language texts. Roughly the same number of words are available for German and for Spanish. These texts contain a mixture of British and American English texts, otherwise all others are British English texts. Table 5 contains the details of the English texts in the automotive engineering corpus.

Text Type	Total No. of Texts	Total No. of Tokens	Average	Maximum	Minimum
Popular Science	6	19,700	3,283	5,607	731
Journals	50	203,079	4,062	19,785	154
Manuals	7	36,027	5,147	8,116	2,027
Books	5	31,105	6,221	14,430	755
Advertisements (inc.Brochures)	38	42,749	1,125	2666	184
News Reportage and Features	24	37,091	1,545	5,884	206
Grand Total	130	369,751	2,844	19,785	154

Table 5: Details of the English section of the Surrey's Automotive Engineering Corpus

These texts were collected specifically for the purpose of building a multi-lingual terminology data bank, containing terms for emission control and anti-lock braking systems in two varieties of English (British and American), Spanish and German, for use in translation and in technical documentation. The objective of building such a specialised term bank was to initiate and evaluate the efficacy of corpus-based methods and tools in terminology management: this effort was sponsored by the European Commission's ESPRIT Programme (Ahmad et al 1992, 1993).

An analysis of the distribution of words in the different text types of the corpus shows that there was a degree of uniformity in their distribution so far as the co-efficient of weirdness is concerned. Table 6 shows that despite the differences in text types, authors of specialist texts, whether they are scientists, technical authors, specialist correspondents for newspapers and popular magazines, or advertising copy writers, show similar tendencies in using some categories of words more frequently than others when compared with general-language texts.

Co-efficient of Weirdness		News Reportage and Feature	Advertise-ment inc. Brochure	Book	Manual	Journal	Popular Science	Average
Lower Bound	Upper Bound							
<0.1		1%	1%	1%	1%	1%	0%	1%
>=0.1	<0.75	14%	14%	11%	12%	15%	12%	13%
>=0.75	<1.5	15%	14%	12%	9%	12%	11%	12%
>=1.5	<10	38%	39%	37%	29%	38%	37%	36%
>=10	<100	15%	16%	20%	19%	15%	21%	18%
>=100	<500	4%	4%	5%	6%	3%	4%	4%
>=500	<1000	4%	4%	6%	7%	4%	7%	5%
>=1000	<5000	1%	1%	1%	1%	0%	2%	1%
>=5000		0%	1%	1%	1%	0%	1%	1%
Infinity		9%	8%	7%	14%	10%	5%	9%
		100%	100%	100%	100%	100%	100%	100%

Table 6. A comparison of the co-efficient of weirdness in special-language texts across different types

Table 6 shows that all six types contain, on average, 9-10% words that do not exist in a contemporary corpus of English, like the Longman Corpus: the co-efficient of weirdness for such words is *infinity*. Again, over 10% of the words are used at least 10 times, or as much as 100 times, and in some cases 5,000 times, more in a specialist text than in a general-language text. Furthermore, Table 6 shows that over a third of words in specialist texts are used at least 1.5 times more, and in some cases as many as 10 times more, than in general-language texts. These words are likely to be closed-class words and a linked set of open-class words. There is only a small proportion of words, totalling about 12%, that have roughly the same frequency distribution in the automotive engineering corpus as in the Longman Corpus: the co-efficient of weirdness of such words, generally determiners and modal verbs, is *one*. But pronouns and a number of nouns of everyday use like *society, people,* and *child* are avoided almost completely in science and technology texts, and, surprisingly, in the advertisement, news reportage and features, and popular science genres. (Note that the genre *manual* has its own characteristic behaviour, though still within the norm of the corpus as a whole, and shows a preponderance of open-class nominals and suppression of closed-class items like pronouns, etc.)

2.5 A Note on the Choice of General-language Corpus for Computing *Weirdness*

The computation of the co-efficient of weirdness depends upon the availability of frequency information related to a relevant corpus of general language. By *relevant* we mean a general-language corpus that will help in the extraction of hitherto unidentified terms, particularly neologisms. Once used in science and technology, terms which have some impact on our everyday lives become absorbed quite quickly in general language. The LOB corpus does not have any instances of words like *emission*, *catalyst*, *catalytic converter* and *electronic*. However, all these words can be found in the Longman-Lancaster Corpus and the dictionaries that are associated with these corpora. These once-neologisms still occur with much lower frequency in contemporary general language corpora than, say, in a specialist text. Thus, a relevant general-language corpus should be as near contemporaneous as possible for identifying neologisms. The computation of the co-efficient of weirdness, through the use of a contemporaneous corpus, will help to avoid spending too much time investigating a potential term which may already have had some currency.

Note that the general-language corpus used for comparison presented in Table 6 was the more contemporary Longman-Lancaster Corpus. The bulk of the text in this 20 million word corpus was published during 1968-85; the smaller Lancaster-Oslo Bergen Corpus (1 million words), which was compiled in 1961, is more outdated, the bulk of the text having been published during the 1940s and 1950s.

In computing weirdness, we also looked at the question of genre balance in the general language corpus. Therefore, we focused on a corpus that has as wide a coverage of the written genre as possible and attempts were made to minimise selectors' bias: recall that half of the Corpus is randomly selected and the other half was the choice of a panel. Longman-Lancaster, mainly a British English Corpus, has coverage of American English also. And, despite the upper limit of 40,000 tokens on all texts, Longman-Lancaster contains excerpts from long narrative texts together with the kaleidoscopic newspaper texts. Above all, Longman-Lancaster is available to all academic institutions at a reasonable price.

3. Acquiring Terminology from a Text Archive

A text-based approach to terminology can be of help to a terminologist not only in semi-automatically identifying terms, through the computation of the co-efficient of weirdness, but also by making available other kinds of text-derived data. By viewing text fragments, containing keywords-in-context (KWIC), a terminologist can deduce a variety of syntactic, semantic and pragmatic details that can be found much more easily than by manual scanning methods, introspection or interrogation of domain experts.

Using such methods, we have been able to create term banks in at least ten different subject fields, ranging from drug addiction to automotive engineering, and from information technology, including artificial intelligence, to environmental protection. This work has been supported by 'System Quirk'[10] (Holmes-Higgin & Ahmad 1992), an intelligent terminology and lexical development system.

3.1 System Quirk: A Terminology and Lexicography Support System

System Quirk is essentially an integrated set of programs or software 'tools' for examining and extracting relevant material from evidence sources, such as an organised special-language text corpus, and for creating, deleting, modifying and maintaining a reference source such as terms in a term bank. There are tools for dealing with each phase of a term's life-cycle.

The literature in corpus linguistics, particularly in corpus-oriented lexicography, contains descriptions of software tools that are used for gathering data about lexicogrammatical properties of words. Leech has discussed the need for developing at least three different types of software tools that comprise a 'sophisticated computational environment' for retrieving data from a corpus and for processing linguistically the corpus itself. Leech's specification includes (i) general-purpose data retrieval tools, (ii) tools to facilitate corpus annotations at various levels, and (iii) tools to provide interchange of information between corpora and lexical and grammatical databases (1991:22-23).

System Quirk contains general-purpose data retrieval tools and tools for exchange of information between corpora and lexical (and terminology) databases. (System Quirk does not contain any corpus annotation tools, but it is capable of importing and exporting texts encoded in SGML format and terminology in a number of terminology interchange formats[11]). In addition to the text (and term) analysis tools and corpus and term bank organisation tools (see Table 7 for details), System Quirk contains the so-called visualisation tools. These tools can be used for elaborating a term, selectively browsing a text corpus or corpora, and tools for visualising the inter-relationships between terms. The visualisation tool has some facility for deducing new facts from old, through the use of knowledge representation formalisms, and a facility for identifying semantic relations based on linguistic cues. Table 7 below shows the functional characteristics of the tools:

Analysis Tools	
Text Analysis	Lexical/Term Analysis
Concordance, Collocation, Statistical Analysis. Term identification.	Relationships with other lexical items, Foreign Language Equivalents.
Organisational Tools	
Corpus Organisation	Term Bank Organisation
Classification and Representation of full text units. Organisation along pragmatic lines. SGML mark-up.	Creation, maintenance, and quality control of term banks. Accessing other term banks. TIF mark-up.
Visualisation Tools	
Selective Explication	Illustrative Explication
Access within and across corpus. Goal-oriented browsing. Selectional constraints on fragments.	Selection of illustrative text fragments - contextual examples. Use of semantic nets for illustrating inter-term relations. Publishing tools.

Table 7: Functional characteristics of the System Quirk toolbox

3.2 Text Analysis and Term Identification

The work-horse of System Quirk is the concordance and text analysis (sub-)program KonText. KonText is used in the first stage of terminological work following document selection, i.e., it is used to search the corpus, or sections of it, initially in order to capture term candidates.

Four basic operations can be performed on the texts selected: concordance (an alphabetical list of all the words in a text shown together with their context and reference to lines in the source text); collocation (a list of the co-occurrences of specified terms within sentence boundaries); wordlist (an alphabetical or frequency-sorted list of words); word index (as wordlist with references to lines in source texts). These operations can be refined and customised by a series of further options (A detailed discussion has been presented in Ahmad and Rogers forthcoming).

The KonText module can be used to compute the co-efficient of weirdness to identify terms. The computation is dependent on the four tasks performed by KonText. First, the relative frequency of each word form in the selected special-language texts is computed. Second, KonText provides the choice of a general-language corpus. Third, the relative frequency of the word forms in the selected special-language texts divided by the relative frequency of the same word forms in a general-language corpus specified by the user is computed (known as *ratio*). And, fourth, a facility to define the *ratio* level is given. The results for one such computation involving the execution of all the four tasks are shown in Figure 2.

Computing the *ratio* of word forms in special-language and general-language texts allows a provisional distinction to be made between general-language open-class words on the one hand, and special-language open-class words on the other hand, i.e. term candidates. For instance, in Figure 2 below, the word form *company* is shown occurring 18 times in the selected information technology text, while the word form *configuration* occurs only once. When the *ratios* are computed, however, we see that they are <10 and >10,000 respectively, indicating *configuration* as a term candidate, but not *company*. The particular *ratio* level at which term candidates can be optimally identified needs to be further explored in relation to a number of factors including the type of general-language corpus used as a comparison, and the type of domain covered by the special language.

▽				**Results**
command	6	7.84e-04	16.22	
commands	7	9.14e-04	INFINITY	** Note Ratio **
commentary	2	2.61e-04	12.62	
companies	8	0.001045	23.55	
company	18	0.002351	9.1	
compatible	1	1.31e-04	INFINITY	** Note Ratio **
compile	3	3.92e-04	INFINITY	** Note Ratio **
compiled	1	1.31e-04	10.19	
complete	2	2.61e-04	1.464	
completed	1	1.31e-04	1.815	
component	1	1.31e-04	5.519	
compulsory	1	1.31e-04	4.273	
computer	9	0.001176	56.77	
concept	1	1.31e-04	2.597	
concepts	3	3.92e-04	12.04	
concerned	10	0.001306	6.248	
conduct	1	1.31e-04	2.88	
configuration	1	1.31e-04	INFINITY	** Note Ratio **
configure	1	1.31e-04	INFINITY	** Note Ratio **
confirm	26	0.003396	287.0	
confirmation	3	3.92e-04	18.92	
confirmed	1	1.31e-04	5.095	
consistent	1	1.31e-04	5.298	
consult	7	9.14e-04	77.27	
consulted	1	1.31e-04	8.831	
consulting	3	3.92e-04	INFINITY	** Note Ratio **
consults	1	1.31e-04	INFINITY	** Note Ratio **
contain	1	1.31e-04	3.785	
contained	1	1.31e-04	3.08	

(OK) (Print) (To Clipboard) (Save to New File)

Fig. 2. Typical results from an information technology corpus showing all single word forms with a co-efficient of weirdness in excess of 10,000

4 Term Pragmatics and Terminology Organisation

During a translation session or a technical writing session, a typical translator or technical writer may need only a limited subset of data from the record format of a term in a term bank: a term and its foreign language equivalent, for instance. Furthermore, the translator or technical writer only needs to consult terms which he or she seldom or never uses: some terms may never be looked up, others could be consulted very frequently. The organisation of a term bank should, in principle, reflect this need of its end-users.

Our intention is to identify and implement a machine-assisted procedure that will use four pragmatic properties of a term, that is, language variety, style, frequency of the term in a text archive, and the age of the term, to partition a term bank into two parts: a mother term bank and its associated daughter term bank. The former containing terms with which technical writers or translators may be very familiar, and the daughter term bank containing terms with which the technical writer or translator may not be familiar.

Using these four pragmatic properties, an *ad hoc* score can be computed automatically, whereby each property contributes a partial familiarity score and all the partial scores are added up to give a total familiarity score for each term.   For instance, terms that occur very frequently in a given specialism, were coined in a widely-recognised geographical/regional variety, and have been in use over a considerable period of time in popular science texts (or newspaper texts) would not be looked up frequently by translators or terminologists. Such terms will have a high familiarity score. On the other hand, terms that are 'unfamiliar', in that they had been coined recently, reported in an esoteric learned journal by an author who is more familiar with a lesser used variety of, say, English, will have a low familiarity score.

The 'familiarity' scores can be used as a basis for dividing a term bank into the mother and daughter components, such that the access to daughter terms is quicker than, say, the mother terms. Later, in Section 4.2 we report on a software tool, Lexicon Distiller, a component of System Quirk, that can be used to divide a term bank into mother and daughter components.

4.1 Computing the Pragmatic Familiarity Score for a Term

We will show how the partial familiarity score for each of the four pragmatic factors associated with a given term can be computed automatically. An arbitrary scale ranging from +2 to -2 has been assigned to each of the properties. The partial score +2 indicates that for a given pragmatic property the term is familiar and a score of -2 means that on that particular pragmatic basis the term is unfamiliar.

For instance, a term would be assigned to the mother term bank if the total familiarity score is +8, that is, each of the four partial familiarity scores is +2, and to a daughter term bank if the familiarity score is -8. For intermediate scores, a policy can be laid out by the administrator of a given term bank and a threshold familiarity score can be assigned: terms above the threshold, any positive number between 0 and 8, will be assigned to the mother term bank and below that threshold can be assigned to the daughter term bank.

Language Variety   Terminology collections do acknowledge regional variations: *silencer* in British English is equivalent to *muffler* in the American English variety. This type of information is included in the record format for most typical term banks. The terminologist or technical writer will, perhaps, be more familiar with terms in the native language variety, or some varieties that are closer to the terminologist's or translator's variety. In Figure 3a we show how a partial familiarity score can be computed, if it is assumed by a term bank's administrator that the term bank users are British English speakers:

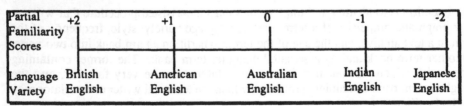

Fig. 3a. Partial Familiarity Score based on language variety

Regional variants are usually noted in the record formats of extant term banks.

Style Register Translators and technical writers usually deal with 'learned' texts, including learned papers and text books, and with technical manuals. Such texts are characterised by their formal style. The *formality* shows itself *inter alia* in the usage of standardised terms, in the avoidance of variants, and in the absence of popular equivalents of standardised terms. However, popular science material, advertisements and brochures, contain popularised terms: for example, *cat* for *catalytic converters*.

Figure 3b shows how partial familiarity scores can be computed for individual terms in a term bank. The assumption here is that the term bank user usually translates learned text or technical manuals.

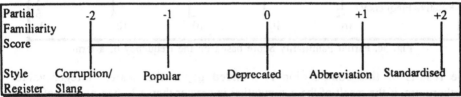

Fig. 3b. Partial Familiarity Score based on style

Most term bank record formats contain some *stylistic* data for a number of terms.

Frequency of occurrence Some terms are more frequent in the text of a specialist domain than others: in genetics and in neurology, the term *cell* will be amongst the most frequent, in that the term is usually a part of a compound nominal, like *Purkinjee cell*, *Pyramidal cell* or may appear as one of its morphological variants, e.g., *cells* (plural), *cellular* (derived adjective). The same is true of other *carrier* terms, like *nucleus* in nuclear physics; *force, stress, strain* in material sciences, and so on.

One can argue that if a term, single or complex or multiword, occurs more frequently than other terms in, say, a corpus of special-language texts, then the translator or technical writer will either know it already or will subconsciously memorise the elaboration of such a term. In contrast, the terms that occur with very low frequency in a special-language text archive, for example, terms used in the reporting of a new device or a novel concept, will be the terms with which the translator or technical writer will not be familiar.

Recall that the most frequently occurring words in a specialist corpus (and in a general-language corpus) are the closed-class words, and that these words have a relative frequency of between 1-5%. In special-language corpora, the closed-class words are followed by terms, usually nouns or noun compounds, which have a relative frequency of less than 1%. Following the closed-class words and the more frequent terms are terms that have lower frequency, ranging between 1 in 1000 (relative frequency of 0.001%) to one in 10 million words (relative frequency of 0.00000001%).

Now on the basis of relative frequency of words in a given corpus, a partial familiarity score can be computed. This computation involves taking the logarithm of the relative frequency and adding the number *four* (4) to the logarithm. Thus, any term occurring with a frequency of 1 in 100 (relative frequency of 0.01 or 10^{-2} in scientific notation), will have a partial familiarity score of +2 and a term which occurs with a frequency of less than or equal to 1 in 10000 (relative frequency of 0.0001 or 10^{-4}) will have a partial familiarity score of 0, and if the frequency of the word is less than or equal to 1 in 1 million (a relative frequency of 10^{-6} or less) then the partial familiarity score will be -2. Figure 3a shows how the partial familiarity score is related to the relative frequency of a term.

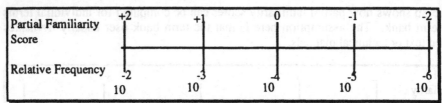

Fig. 3c. Partial Familiarity Score based on the frequency of a term

The results of this computation is rounded up to the nearest integer value. Furthermore, if the result of the computation is greater than +2, then a value of +2 is used. Similarly, if the result is less than -2, then a value of -2 is used.

It should be noted here that since most term banks are developed without reference to a text corpus it is not usual to note the frequency of a term in typical record formats used by existing term banks.

Life-cycle details Term banks are, or rather ought to be, updated at regular intervals and new terms added at a greater frequency than, say, to a conventional general-language dictionary. The progress of a scientific discipline is characterised not only by the introduction of new terms, but also by a gradual obsolescence of established terms. Translators and documentors will be more familiar with terms that are established and in use for 10 or more years. However, terms that have entered a specialism more recently, for instance in the last decade or so, have to be established even though their use may not be widespread. Well established terms can then be assigned a higher partial familiarity score, and less established terms can be assigned lower partial familiarity scores, and be stored in the daughter term bank. Figure 3d shows how partial familiarity scores can be computed by looking at the age of a term:

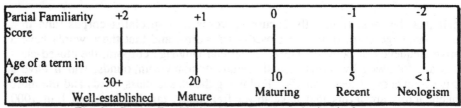

Fig. 3d. Partial Familiarity Score based on the 'age' of a term

Existing term banks do not directly record the 'age' of a term. However, a note is made of when the term was entered into a term bank.

4.2 Towards a 'Pragmatic' Basis for Organising Term Banks

As mentioned above, we will regard a term with a score of *-8* as very unfamiliar and a term with a score of *+8* as very familiar, with a gradable scale in-between. Consider the following automotive engineering terms, shown in Table 8, together with their *familiarity* scores that may be assigned for, say, a British English speaking translator or documentor: the figures in brackets show our *devised* score based on the polar scales mentioned above.

Term	Relative Frequency in Text	Language Variety	Style Register	Life-cycle History/ Age of the term	Familiarity Score
catalyst	0.46 *(+2)*	British English *(+2)*	Standardised *(+2)*	Well-established *(+2)*	*8*
catalytic converter	0.00108357 *(+1)*	British English *(+2)*	Standardised *(+2)*	Maturing *(+0)*	*5*
silencer	4.7719E-05 *(-1)*	British English *(+2)*	Standardised *(+2)*	Well-established *(+2)*	*5*
cat	0.00011831 *(0)*	British English *(+2)*	Popular *(-1)*	Maturing *(+0)*	*1*
muffler	0 *(-2)*	American English *(+1)*	Popular *(-1)*	Well-established *(+2)*	*0*

Table 8. Familiarity points score, shown in bold italics, for a number of terms from the automotive engineering (AE) domain. (Frequency data from Surrey's AE corpus)

Suppose now that we choose a familiarity threshold of +6; terms that have a score of less than *6* will be stored in the daughter term bank, and all other terms will be stored in the mother term bank. Thus, terms like *catalyst, catalytic converter* and *silencer* will be stored in the mother term bank, and terms like *cat* and *muffler* in the daughter term bank. The arguments relating to the life-cycle history of a term need to be looked into much more carefully in future research.

Lexicon Distiller, a recent addition to System Quirk[12], helps in exploiting the pragmatic properties of a term for assigning it to a mother or to a daughter term bank (Figure 4).

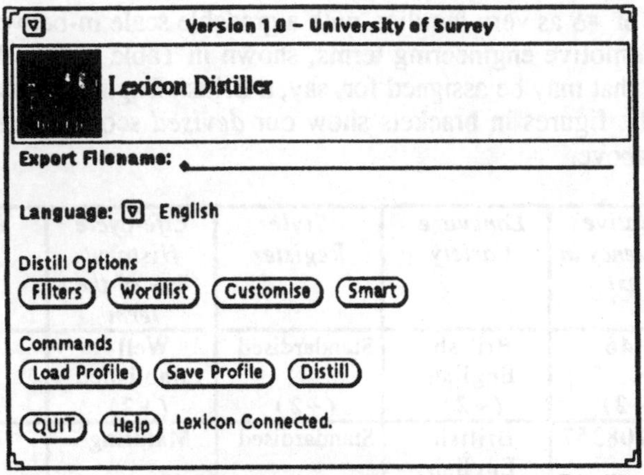

Fig. 4. The graphical user-interface for Lexicon Distiller

The Lexicon Distiller allows options for choosing a variety of *filters* for assessing a familiarity points score based on the pragmatic properties of a term such as its language variety, style register, frequency of usage, and its life-cycle history or age. The administrator of a term bank has the option of selecting, or *filtering*, a certain number of terms to a new term bank. Once the user of Lexicon Distiller has worked on creating part or whole of a daughter term bank, then the administrator can store them in a daughter term bank (see Figure 5).

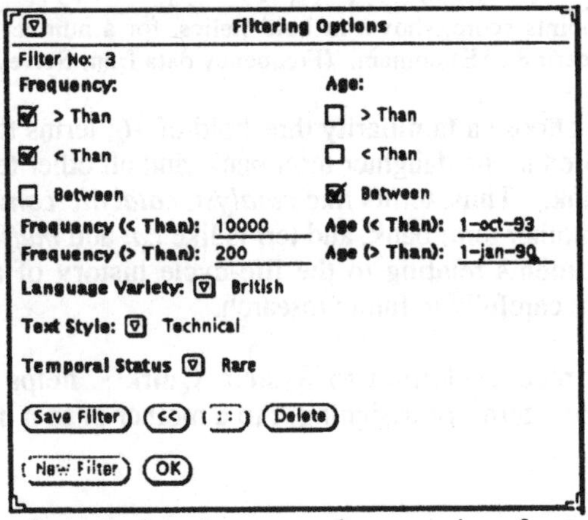

Fig. 5. Assigning the pragmatic properties of a term

5 Conclusions

The above discussion of the pragmatics of specialist terms, particularly its role in extracting terms from texts and efficiently organising the terms, shows the effectiveness of corpus-linguistic methods and techniques in terminology. We feel that such methods and techniques are in some sense more relevant to terminology than, say, to lexicography. Questions relating to the authenticity of terms can be settled by seeking the opinions of experts, and since these opinions are more frequently expressed in text, then special-language text is arguably a more important source, and perhaps sometimes the only source of evidence for the existence or non-existence of a term. The representativeness of texts, a vexed issue in lexicography and language studies, is a less ideologically-sensitive issue in terminology, since special-language texts do not usually involve subjective questions related to economic and social class-differences.

Terminology can benefit from being viewed and treated in the context of pragmatics, corpus linguistics and other paradigms in linguistics and in philosophy dedicated to the study of text for investigating problems related to knowledge of language and knowledge of matters scientific and technological.

The discussion in this paper was based on extracting and elaborating terms in English. Corpus-linguistic methods and techniques appear as equally effective for related languages like Dutch, and typologically different languages like Welsh (Ahmad and Davies, in press).

Acknowledgements

The author would like to thank Dr. M Rogers for her comments and criticisms on this paper, Paul Holmes-Higgin and Syed Sibte Raza Abidi who wrote the Lexicon Distiller program and Andrea Davies who helped in the debugging of the program and helped with the layout of this paper. Caroline McInnes was as usual patient with my handwriting and reminded us all of the various deadlines: her efforts deserve many thanks. Petra Steffens used her wit and editorial charm to persuade the author to produce this paper almost in time, for which I am very grateful.

References

Ahmad, Khurshid & Davies, Andrea E. (Forthcoming) '"Weirdness" in Special-language Text: Welsh Radioactive Chemicals Text as an Exemplar'. Internationales Institut für Terminologieforschung Journal.

Ahmad, Khurshid & Rogers, Margaret A. (Forthcoming) 'The analysis of text corpora for the creation of advanced terminology databases'. In (Eds.) Sue-Ellen Wright and Gerhard Budin The Handbook of Terminology Management. Amsterdam and Philadelphia: John Benjamins.

Ahmad, Khurshid & Rogers, Margaret A. (1992) Translation and Information Technology: The Translator's Workbench, in ReCALL, No. 6: 3-9.

Ahmad, Khurshid, Davies, Andrea, & Rogers, Margaret A. (1993) The Contrastive Analysis of Special-language and General-language text: Towards Automatic Term Identification. University of Surrey: Guildford. CS-93-12.

Aijmer, Karin and Altenberg, Bengt (Eds.) (1991) English Corpus Linguistics: Studies in Honour of Jan Svartvik. London and New York: Longman Publishers.

de Beaugrande, Robert & Dressler, Wolfgang (1981) Introduction to Text Linguistics. New York: Longman.

Crystal, David (1992). A Dictionary of Language and Linguistics. Oxford: Blackwell.

Geertz, Clifford (1988) Work and Lives - The Anthropologist as Author. Stanford (California, USA): Stanford University Press. (Also marketed in the UK under the imprint of Polity Press/Blackwell Publishers, Oxford).

Halliday, Michael A.K. & Martin, James R. (1993) Writing Science: Literary and Discursive Power. London and Washington D. C.: The Falmer Press.

Halliday, Michael A. K. (1978) Language as Social Semiotic: the social interpretation of language and meaning. London: Edward Arnold.

Harris, Zellig (1990) A Theory of Information and Knowledge. Oxford: Oxford Univ. Press.

Heisenberg, Werner (1963) Physics and Philosophy - The Revolution in Modern Science. London: George Allen and Unwin.

Heisenberg, Werner (1983) Encounters with Einstein (And Other Essays on People, Places and Particles). Princeton (New Jersey, USA): Princeton University Press.

Holmes-Higgin, Paul & Ahmad, Khurshid (1992) Knowledge Processing 8 Machine-Assisted Terminology Elicitation. Guildford: University of Surrey. CS Report No. CS-92-14.

ISO/R 1087 (1969) The Vocabulary of Terminology. Geneva: International Organization for Standardization.

Kittredge, Richard & Lehrberger, John (Eds.) (1982) Sublanguage: Studies of Language in Restricted Semantic Domains. Berlin: de Gruyter.

Landau, Sidney I. (1989) Dictionaries: The Art and Craft of Lexicography. Cambridge (UK): Cambridge University Press. (First published 1984).

Leech, Geoffrey (1991) 'The state of the art in corpus linguistics'. In (Eds.) Karin Aijmer and Bengt Altenberg (1991) pp 8-29.

Malinowski, Bronislow (1935) Coral Gardens and their Magic 2. London: Allen and Unwin.

Renouff, Antoinette (1987) 'Corpus Development'. In (Ed.) John McH. Sinclair (1987) pp 1-40.

Roda, Roberts P. (1992) 'Exploring the frontiers of documentary research in the translation process'. In (Ed.) Edith F. Losa. Frontiers: Proceedings of the 33rd Annual Conference of the American Translators Association. (November 4-8, 1992, San Diego, California). Medford (New Jersey, USA): Learned Information, Inc., pp 361-375.

Sager, Juan C., Dungworth, David and McDonald, Peter F. (1980) English Special Languages. Wiesbaden: Brandstetter Verlag.

Sinclair, John McH. (Ed.) (1987) Looking Up. London: Collins.

Sinclair, John M. (Ed.) (1991) Corpus. Concordance. Collocation. Oxford: Oxford University Press.

Summers, Della (1991) Longman/Lancaster English Language Corpus. Criteria and Design. Unpublished ms.

Svartvik, Jan (1966) On Voice in the English Verb. Mouton: The Hague.

Footnotes

[1] It has been estimated that up to 40% of the content of 'unabridged unilingual general dictionaries' is devoted to specialised terminology (Roberts 1992). However, general-language dictionaries usually include only the well-established terms, especially those terms that may appear in school text books.

[2] Computer scientists, including software engineers and the artificial intelligence community, are involved in the creation of *ad hoc* term collections: a data dictionary used in the specification and design of a software system contains substantial amounts of unstructured knowledge, and those involved in knowledge engineering get much closer to building term banks that comprise the building blocks of the so-called knowledge bases of expert systems. This is not to argue that the computer scientists should use currently available term banks as these data banks have been designed for translation or technical documentation. But the data available in such term banks can be of considerable use for building data dictionaries and for building fact bases of a knowledge base (Ahmad 1993).

[3] Scientific writing, a sub-genre of specialist writing, is on its way to becoming a well-established genre that has its own publications and, indeed, like general literature has its own prizes for distinguished writing.

[4] The literature concerning terminology is sharply divided into two major groups. For one group, concepts are the primary source of terminology, where conceptual hierarchies and part-whole relationships are the organising frameworks for building collections of terminology. For the other group, sense-related data is of paramount importance and the imposition of the hierarchies and part-whole relations perhaps mitigates against the creative use of language. This debate has its roots in the Platonist versus non-Platonist basis of knowledge and of language.

[5] See, for instance, observations on the language of physics by Werner Heisenberg (1963, 1983), and on the language of anthroplogy by Clifford Geertz (1988). These authors discuss philosophical issues connected to their discipline by looking at the vocabulary and the discourse structures of the texts of their respective disciplines.

[6]Very similar results are also found in more modern corpora such as the Lancaster/Longman Corpus (c. 1900-1985) and the Birmingham Collection of English Texts (c. 1965-1985).

[7] News bulletins, as opposed to learned journals, carry news *about* the members of the society and news about those who can or who have had influence on the society, etc.

[8]The real reduction is the use of the drawing of a cat's eye in advertisements for automobiles that are fitted with catalytic converters.

[9] The exceptions include the Helsinki Corpora of Historical English that for obvious reasons contain texts *produced* during different periods of this millennium.

[10] System Quirk is written in Quintus-Prolog, a logic programming language available on a SUN-SPARC station, running the UNIX operating system. Paul Holmes-Higgin, together with Stephen Hook, Stephen Griffin and Syed Sibte Raza Abidi, developed this program for the ESPRIT-sponsored Translator's Workbench Projects (1989-1992; 1992-94) and MULTILEX (1990-93).

[11]Corpus annotation is important for automatically analysing corpora with a view to determining the grammatical texture of tokens, texts and indeed text corpora. Grammatical tagging, a popular method of annotating texts, relies on the foreknowledge of the grammatical properties of all the tokens that may exist in a text. Our concern is identifying a neologism, and if a neologism has just been coined and reported in literature, then perhaps little would be known about its grammatical properties.

[12] Lexicon Distiller was written by Syed Sibte Raza Abidi and Paul Holmes-Higgin.

The Cambridge Language Survey

Paul Procter

Cambridge University Press, The Edinburgh Building, Shaftesbury Road,
Cambridge, CB2 2RU

Abstract. The Cambridge Language Survey is a research project whose activities centre around the use of an Integrated Language Database, whereby a computerised dictionary is used for intelligent cross-reference during corpus analysis – searching for example for all the inflections of a verb rather than just the base form. Types of grammatical coding and semantic categorisation appropriate to such a computerised dictionary are discussed, as are software tools for parsing, finding collocations, and performing sense-tagging. The weighted evaluation of semantic, grammatical, and collocational information to descriminate between word senses is described in some detail. Mention is made of several branches of research including the development of parallel corpora, semantic interpretation by sense-tagging, and the use of a Learner Corpus for the analysis of errors made by non-native-speakers. Sense-tagging is identified as an under-exploited approach to language analysis and one for which great opportunites for product development exist.

1 Introduction

Central to the activities of the Cambridge Language Survey is the concept of an Integrated Language Database (ILD). What this refers to is the intertwining of a dictionary system running under database software with corpora of particular languages, for example English. The corpora are of various types, including spoken and written material and the full range of literary genre. The Cambridge Language Survey intends to build monolingual ILDs for each of a range of European languages. As well as links between the dictionary and corpus in a language, there will be cross-links for translation equivalents between languages.

There are considerable advantages to working with an ILD. Among them is the facility to access the dictionary for specific linguistic information when making corpus searches. For example, when looking up a verb, the dictionary supplies information about the different inflected forms, the present participle perhaps or the past participle, and any corpus searching that is done can then be done across the range of these different inflected forms. This is very revealing for the lexicographer because it often demonstrates that one meaning is used with some inflected parts, but not with others. In the past where dictionary makers have tended to search the corpus separately from the dictionary, they have nearly always tended to look for the lemma, that is the base form, and to ignore other forms. In the case of a noun, this would mean searching for the singular whilst ignoring the plural form and would result in the loss of a lot of valuable information which should be recorded in dictionaries.

The Cambridge Language Survey is an ongoing project which takes a dynamic and opportunistic approach to collection of materials, that is, we do not set predetermined amounts of a particular kind of language that we would wish to collect, but collect a broad range as it becomes available. For example, newspaper material, novels, the language of film and television, pop music, etc. The corpus header on each sample clearly identifies the type of material involved, so that it is relatively easy, after the event, to adjust a selection from particular kinds of material so as to produce whatever is needed for a particular piece of research. The amounts of data involved are very large. Several hundred million words have been collected and are in the process of being indexed.

2   Linguistic Coding

The operation of an ILD clearly relies upon the availability on-line of a computerised dictionary, coding words according to their grammatical and syntactical functions. (Though activities are presently focussed upon English, it is our intention to produce a non-language-specific system of coding, which can be used to describe the vocabulary of various languages that we're interested in, and we hope, other languages in the future, including non Indo-European languages.)

The **Grammatical** coding held deals with such things as countability of nouns and complementation patterns, and includes syntactic restrictions upon the position of items – for example adjectives that may only appear in a predicative position. Other grammatical information includes whether or not a verb is able to passivise. The **Subject** codes used divide the world into a hierarchy of subject areas, an arrangement that allows us a great deal of flexibility in retrieving information. For example, one of the codes, *sports and games*, consists, at the top level, of a code G. On the second level down, TG, gives us team games. The level below this contains FBL, football, and below this the code AMFO, American football. These codes are used in the process of entry verification. By selecting a particular subject code we are able to compile a brief dictionary of terms relevant to a particular field. This list we then send for verification by an expert in that field. If we're lucky enough to find somebody who can cover the whole of *sports and games*, we would select the top level code. However, with something like sports, it's normally the case that experts specialise in one sport only and therefore we would pick at a lower level. In the case of life sciences and medicine, we might find someone who will cover a broad range at the top level, etc.

One of the most ambitious parts of the project is to greatly increase the role played by **semantic coding**. The idea is to describe the words in the language in terms of a dictionary of semantic features with associated values. For example, one of the features might be **colour** or **size**. A feature may have a fairly open-ended set of values associated with it – in the case of *colour*, all the possible colours that might be used in defining something. Or it may only have a set small number of values, such as with *size: large, medium*, or *small*.

This type of semantic coding system is based on multiple inheritance, a concept borrowed from Artificial Intelligence, which allows us to have not one single hierarchical tree but more than one. As an example of this, a type of gun, the bazooka may be described as a series of attibutes thus: it inherits from *gun* such things as *made from metal, constituents: barrel* and from higher up the tree, it inherits from *weapon*. From even higher up the tree it inherits from *object* such things as, *size: large, state: solid, movability: yes* (the fact that it can be moved). An example of multiple inheritance is that the feature, *made by humans*, is inherited not from this part of the tree but from a separate line. The reason for this is that this concept of *made by humans*, can be applied not just to objects but also to abstract things such as a Beethoven symphony.

One other thing I would like to mention in relation to semantic coding is our intention to carry out the analysis of verbs. This is much more complex than that of nouns, because as well as recording the semantic type of a particular verb, and the semantic restrictions on the subjects and objects, in the case of verbs which describe a transition, rather than a process, we also hold information about an initial, middle, or final state of those objects. For example, in the regular use of the verb *kill*, the object is in the initial state *alive*, before the action, and in the final state *dead*, after the action. This information can be held and used to interpret documents. It's one of our intentions to build additional software which will keep track of a state of affairs in a narrative so that it is possible to attach attributes to particular nouns, as to what condition or qualities they may have at any particular time.

3 Software Tools

The software tools we are using in the analysis of corpora fall into three main areas: parsing software, automatic collocations software, and software for sense tagging.

Parsing software is important for breaking down the structure of sentences so that it is possible to find the subjects and objects of verbs, even if they are quite complex. For example, if I say the sentence "John killed the beautiful lexicographic project", it's important to find the head noun *project* within the object, and differentiate it from the adjectives *beautiful* and *lexicographic*. Parsing software therefore allows us to get at the main elements of a sentence and when the dictionary is able to hold information about what sort of semantic restrictions there are on these objects and subjects, this can be used as one of the tools for automatic sense-tagging. In the sentence "John killed the project", *project* would be held in the dictionary and it would not carry a code *animate*, which one would normally associate with the objects of *kill*, such as *to kill a person* or *to kill a plant* and therefore this would give us a clue as to the meaning of *kill* in this case.

Another important area of software is in the finding of **collocations**. These are the words that are commonly associated with other words and we use mutual information statistics to find them. An example of this would be the word *frac-*

tion. We can look at all the sentences in our corpus containing the word *fraction* and we discover that the most significant statistical collocate is the word *tiny* as in a *tiny fraction*, and that *tiny* always occurs as the word directly before *fraction*. It is important to recognise that it's not just pure frequency that we are interested in here. It is the relevance or likelihood of a particular word occurring with another word. Therefore, a very infrequent word which always occurs with a particular word will be treated as important. In the phrase *learn by rote* the word *rote* is unusual and will nearly always occur with *learn* and therefore will score high, whereas a very frequent word such as *the* or *an*, which probably on a pure frequency basis is more common in association with nearly every word in the language, would not be given a very high score.

Tagging software will tag individual words with part of speech and allow lexicographers to search, for example, for nouns or a particular kind of noun, or to find complementation patterns such as whether a noun is followed by a particular kind of clause or a verb by a particular kind of infinitive. The significance of sense-tagging is that hitherto analysis of the words in a corpus has concentrated on word forms, thus confusing words with many meanings and words with few meanings occurring many times. The result has been not very useful. For an insight into what we should be doing in the future, we have to go back to the *General Service List* undertaken by [1], on data collected in the thirties, where a corpus of half a million words was hand-tagged with meanings. This data, even though now very old, has produced valuable results for publishers. For example, in the creation of graded vocabulary for readers and defining vocabularies for dictionaries. We think that it is time that in the world of the computer we are able to undertake this work on much larger bodies of data and to automate it to a high extent.

Our ultimate aim is to link each word in the CLS corpus to its corresponding CIDE (Cambridge International Dictionary of English) record. The first phase of this process will involve tagging a portion of the text and checking the results manually. It is also hoped that the information in the corpus itself can be used to enhance the accuracy of the tagging process.

To appreciate the process of sense-tagging it is useful to understand something of the organisation of the corpus itself. Associated with each word in the corpus is a code of 0 to 255. This range will be adequate to identify the meaning of even the most ambiguous word – at present, the CIDE entry with the greatest number of definitions is "go", having 135 possible meanings. Once each word has been fixed with an unequivocal sense, the corpus becomes far more amenable to computer analysis, and thus sense-tagging is a crucial step for any computerised text analysis, such as that involved in machine translation. However, the task of semantic tagging is far from trivial, and a great deal of research is needed.

In the area of machine translation, the traditional approach has been to start by tagging each word according to its part of speech. A word is identified as noun, verb, adjective and so forth, so that analysis can then proceed to the semantic level. The CLS, however, leaves the derivation of part of speech information until after the available semantic information has been sifted. Take, for example, the sentence *The general flew back to the front.* To analyse this text, each word is first matched against CIDE to generate a number of possible meanings. Comparison of the resulting subject codes will then point to the likely subject matter of the overall sentence. In our example, the words "general" and "front" will both have "military" among their possible subject codes. The program finds this match and assigns a weighting that points to a likely military context and hence also determines that "general" is being used as a noun rather than an adjective. In determining the meaning of words, other useful information is found in the collocations that I mentioned earlier. Significant collocations are often associated with particular meanings. One might find a use of *fire* with words like *gun*, or with words like *flame*. These will reveal the use of *fire* to mean *burn* or to mean *shoot*.

With the available semantic information exhausted, the program can proceed to form conclusions about the parts of speech in use. Part of speech, as well as sense information, is held for each individual word in the corpus. Thus, a word is typified by both sense and part of speech information. The CLS will have some 150 part of speech tags, as opposed to 50 in traditional programs. The larger set of tags is possible because the CLS program has more grammatical information to work with.

Most part of speech tagging uses a probability method. A "training corpus" of around a million words is tagged by hand and then used to generate a probability matrix containing the probabilities of any one part of speech tag (e.g., "determiner") being followed by another (e.g., "singular noun"). When reading the larger corpus, the computer is able to identify patterns which occurred in the training corpus and assign part of speech tags accordingly. This method has been used to tag the CLS corpus, but only with a 95% accuracy; i.e., one in every twenty words is tagged with an inappropriate part of speech. Another drawback is that training corpora are labour-intensive to produce and, while a number of training corpora are available, they are restricted to the traditional tags. In addition, a corpus of a million words, although it sounds like a lot of language, still does not provide all the grammatical combinations possible. The CLS is therefore developing a more rule-based approach.

In the past, rule-based systems have tended to fail because only a small proportion of the text held in a corpus conforms to the grammatical templates encoded. With the increased number of tags, CLS aims to permit more grammatical constructions and so produce a rule-based system that can deal with a wider range of grammatical possibilities. Human beings routinely decode complicated, confusing, even apparently nonsensical sentences. They can decipher the intended meaning because they can and do use context and other informational tools that the computer does not have. So while an utterance like "The cream tea at Table 4 wants the bill." may cause humans temporary confusion, they can soon build a context (restaurant, tea-room) with which to situate it. The CLS sense tagger program seeks to equip the computer with tools to help it successfully interpret the language it encounters.

The tagging system described is reasonably accurate even now, when the range of information that we are exploiting is still quite small. We are not making use, yet, of the selectional restriction information I mentioned about verb subjects and objects. The computer can still be confused by sentences like *The astronaut married the star*. Selectional restrictions would tell the computer that usually people rather than things marry, and therefore that *star* in this context means a *celebrity* rather than the celestial body suggested by the word *astronaut*.

There are several other ways that we can get a clue as to a word's intended meaning. Failing useful subject information at the sentence level we can look more widely to the paragraph or indeed to the corpus header itself, to find for example that an article came from the sports page of The Guardian. This might lead us to give some weight to the possibility that a meaning is a sports term, rather than some other meaning. Once we have accumulated sufficient information about the general frequency of particular meanings, we can also use this. If we find that one meaning predominates, then that would be another factor that would perhaps lead us, if no other information is available, to select one meaning rather than another. In doing the analysis, we do not ignore things like punctuation, which can provide useful information for the parser: for example capitalization, which will indicate proper nouns (in English) or nouns (in German).

One other type of software I should mention is **alignment tools**. If we have corpora of French and German, we can collect what are often called *parallel corpora*, where the same sorts of materials are being collected – perhaps sports articles from a newspaper – for both languages and where a study of the vocabulary of these in comparison with each other might provide useful information. But we are also interested in aligned corpora, where the one corpus is a direct translation or equivalent of the other. A famous example of this is the proceedings of the Canadian parliament, which appears in English and French simultaneously. Corpus software is to be developed which will automatically link sentences in these aligned corpora and allow very useful bilingual analysis to be undertaken.

4 The Learner Corpus

One feature that distinguishes the CLS from other language research projects is its use of learner-generated text. We are systematically collecting not just native speaker language but also non-native-speaker language, and are collaborating closely with the group of institutions which set exams in different countries. These are members of ALTE. In Germany they are represented by the Goethe Institut and in the UK by the University of Cambridge Local Examinations Syndicate (UCLES).

We are able to collect learner-generated language together with the examiners' marks. These marks are captured as codes and are used to provide a detailed analysis of the sorts of errors that learners make. Since there is a large amount of information associated with each learner (biographical information, age, gender, etc, as well of course as the native language of that learner), a great deal of useful information will result, not just for dictionary creation but for the creation of language teaching materials.

An important area of development for teaching materials will be to focus much more closely on what particular learners need. Maybe a learner from a particular language group will have difficulty with a particular grammatical structure or a particular vocabulary item, or set of vocabulary items. In the future, when we are working with large amounts of real data, rather than relying upon teachers' intuitions, we should be able to provide published materials which are much more useful and contain far less redundancy than in the past.

In addition to the corpus of learner English, we have accumulated what is probably the largest collection of "false friends" or "faux amis" available anywhere. These are words, such as the German *bekommen*, meaning *get* rather than *become*, which cause particular learner problems. In collecting them, we are able to cross-link with the evidence of the learner corpus to discover whether they are in actual fact a problem for the learner.

5 Conclusions: Products and Opportunities

Finally, I should like to say something about some of the purposes of all this activity, which as I mentioned earlier is very broad-based but which will lead to important product opportunities in the language industries as they are developing.

For publishing, we are clearly interested in products such as dictionaries, whether in printed paper form or electronic form, but we're now moving into a time where multimedia versions of these products allow us to incorporate audio material or video: to have clips from films, examples of pronunciation of words, etc., available in a very flexible interactive environment. The challenge to the publishing industry here is to create products which really exploit the opportunities of the new media, rather than simply transferring existing paper structures to electronic form.

Sense-tagging is one of the most significant things that can be undertaken in the development of lexicography. In the past, for frequent words, lexicographers have had to wade through tens of thousands, if not hundreds of thousands of instances of a word, and the more that this can be automated, the more useful the information can become and the more efficient can be the lexicographic process.

Another important area is that of machine translation or machine-assisted translation. Although people have been working in this field for twenty, perhaps twenty-five years, there has been a lack of really useful encoded data to help with the problem. Certainly we would regard sense-tagging software as a very useful foundation for any successful machine translation system, which is why we are working with a number of industrial companies who are interested in this area.

Looking a bit further ahead, we believe that software tools which allow natural language to be analysed and understood will start to help with such areas as sophisticated man-machine interaction. One might wish to instruct a machine to carry out an activity or ask for the central heating in a house to be turned up, or activate some household machines. As time goes on, it should be possible to instruct robots or computer systems to do things and to interrogate computer systems for information with natural language queries rather than through programming.

6   End Note

The Cambridge Language Survey is a multilingual research project involving partners from several European countries. There are four distinct types: **publishers** such as Cambridge University Press in the UK and Ernst Klett Verlag of Stuttgart in Germany; **industrial partners** such as Sharp Laboratories of Europe in Oxford and IBM Heidelberg; **academic partners** such as the University of Stuttgart and the Institute of Computational Linguistics in Pisa; and **members of ALTE**, the Association of Language Testers in Europe.

The funding for the project comes from several sources: a publishing development programme for the creation of dictionaries; various projects financed by the European Union; and a project partially funded by the Department of Trade and Industry in the UK. As well as being used in the creation of publishing products, the software resulting from our endeavours is intended to be of benefit to the scholarly community.

References

1. A General Service List of English Words, compiled and edited by Michael West. 1953. Longmans.

Memory-Based Lexical Acquisition and Processing

Walter Daelemans *

Institute for Language Technology and AI, Tilburg University
P.O.Box 90153, 5000 LE Tilburg, The Netherlands
Walter.Daelemans@kub.nl

Abstract. Current approaches to computational lexicology in language technology are knowledge-based (competence-oriented) and try to abstract away from specific formalisms, domains, and applications. This results in severe complexity, acquisition and reusability bottlenecks. As an alternative, we propose a particular performance-oriented approach to Natural Language Processing based on automatic memory-based learning of linguistic (lexical) tasks. The consequences of the approach for computational lexicology are discussed, and the application of the approach on a number of lexical acquisition and disambiguation tasks in phonology, morphology and syntax is described.

1 Introduction

In computational lexicology, three basic questions guide current research: (1) which knowledge should be in the lexicon, (2) how should this knowledge be represented (e.g., to cope with the problems of lexical gaps), and (3) how can this knowledge be acquired. Current lexical research in language technology is eminently *knowledge-based* in this respect. It is also generally acknowledged that there exists a natural order of dependencies between these three research questions: acquisition techniques depend on the type of knowledge representation used and the type of knowledge that should be acquired, and the type of knowledge representation used depends on what should be represented.

Also uncontroversial, but apparently no priority issue for many researchers, is the fact that the question which knowledge should be represented (which morphological, syntactic, and semantic *senses* of lexical items should be distinguished, Pustejovsky 1992) depends completely on the natural language processing *task* that is to be solved. Different tasks require different lexical information.

* I would like to thank my colleagues in the *Atila* project (Steven Gillis, Gert Durieux, and Antal van den Bosch) for their contributions to the approach described in this paper. The *Atila* (Antwerp-Tilburg Inductive Language Acquisition) project is a research corporation between the University of Antwerp and Tilburg University focusing on the application of Machine Learning techniques in linguistic engineering and in developmental psycholinguistics. Thanks also to the participants of the Heidelberg workshop on Machine Translation and the Lexicon for useful comments and suggestions.

Also, different theoretical formalisms, domains, and languages require different types of lexical information and therefore possibly also different types of lexical knowledge representation and different acquisition methods. It makes sense to work on "a lexicon for HPSG parsing of Dutch texts about airplane parts" or on "lexicons for translating computer manuals from English to Italian", but does it make equal sense to work on "the lexicon"? Because it is uncontroversial that lexicon contents is a function of task, domain, language, and theoretical formalism, the *reusability problem* has been defined as an additional research topic in computational lexicology, an area that should solve the problem of how to translate lexical knowledge from one theory, domain, or application to the other. Unfortunately, successful solutions are limited and few.

In this paper, we propose an alternative approach in which a performance-oriented (behaviour-based) perspective is taken instead of a competence-oriented (knowledge-based) one. We try to automatically *learn* the language processing task on the basis of examples. The effect of this is that the priorities between the three goals discussed earlier are changed: the representation of the acquired knowledge depends on the acquisition technique used, and the knowledge acquired depends on what the learning algorithm has induced as being relevant in solving the task. This shift in focus introduces a new type of reusability: reusability of *acquisition method* rather than reusability of acquired knowledge. It also has as a consequence that it is no longer a priori evident that there should be different components for lexical and non-lexical knowledge in the internal representation of an NLP system solving a task, except when the task learned is specifically lexical.

The structure of the paper will be as follows. In Section 2 we will explain the differences between the knowledge-based and the behaviour-based approach to Natural Language Processing (NLP). Section 3 introduces *lazy learning*, the symbolic machine learning paradigm which we have used in experiments in lexical acquisition. In Section 4, we show how virtually all linguistic tasks can be redefined as a classification task, which can in principle be solved by lazy learning algorithms. Section 5 gives an overview of research results in applying lazy learning to the acquisition of lexical knowledge, and Section 6 concludes with a discussion of advantages and limitations of the approach.

2 Knowledge-Based versus Behaviour-Based

One of the central intuitions in current knowledge-based NLP research is that in solving a linguistic task (like text-to-speech conversion, parsing, or translation), the more linguistic knowledge is explicitly modeled in terms of rules and knowledge bases, the better the performance.

As far as lexical knowledge is concerned, this knowledge is represented in a lexical knowledge base, introduced either by hand or semi-automatically using machine-readable dictionaries. The problem of reusability is dealt with by imposing standards on the representation of the knowledge, or by applying filters or translators to the lexical knowledge. Not only is there a huge and costly *lin-*

guistic engineering effort involved in the building of a knowledge-based lexicon in the first place, the effort is duplicated for every translation module between two different formats of the lexical knowledge. In practice, most NLP projects therefore start lexicon construction from scratch, and end up with unrealistically few lexical items.

In this paper, we will claim that regardless of the state of theory-formation about some linguistic task, simple data-driven learning techniques, containing very little a priori linguistic knowledge, can lead to performance systems solving the task with an accuracy higher than state-of-the art knowledge-based systems. We will defend the view that all linguistic tasks can be formulated as a *classification* task, and that simple memory-based learning techniques based on a *consistency heuristic* can learn these classifications tasks.

> **Consistency Heuristic.** "Whenever you want to guess a property of something, given nothing else to go on but a set of reference cases, find the most similar case, as measured by known properties, for which the property is known. Guess that the unknown property is the same as that known property." (Winston 1992)

In this approach, reusability resides in the *acquisition method*. The same, simple, machine learning method may be used to induce linguistic mappings whenever a suitable number of examples (a corpus) is available, and can be reused for any number of training sets representing different domains, sublanguages, languages, theoretical formalisms, and applications. In this approach, emphasis shifts from knowledge representation (competence) to induction of systems exposing useful behaviour (performance), and from knowledge engineering to the simpler process of data collection. Fig. 1 illustrates the difference between the two approaches.

3   Supervised Machine Learning of Linguistic Tasks

In supervised Machine Learning, a learner is presented with a number of examples describing a mapping to be learned, and the learner should extract the necessary regularities from the examples and apply them to new, previously unseen input. It is useful in Machine Learning to make a distinction between a *learning component* and a *performance component*. The performance component produces an output (e.g., a syntactic category) when presented with an input (e.g., a word and its context) using some kind of representation (decision trees, classification hierarchies, rules, exemplars, ...). The learning component implements a learning method. It is presented with a number of examples of the required input-output mapping, and as a result modifies the representation used by the performance system to achieve this mapping for new, previously unseen inputs. There are several ways in which *domain bias* (a priori knowledge about the task to be learned) can be used to optimize learning. In the experiments to be described we will not make use of this possibility.

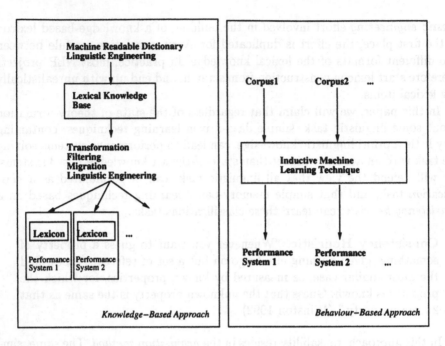

Fig. 1. Knowledge-Based versus Behaviour-Based approaches to lexical acquisition

There are several ways we can measure the success of a learning method. The most straightforward way is to measure *accuracy*. We randomly split a representative set of examples into a training set and a test set[2], train the system on the training set, and compute the success rate (accuracy) of the system on the test set, i.e., the number of times the output of the system was equal to the desired output. Other evaluation criteria include learning and performance speed, memory requirements, clarity of learned representations, etc.

3.1 Lazy Learning

Recently, there has been an increased interest in Machine Learning for *lazy learning* methods. In this type of similarity-based learning, classifiers keep in memory (a selection of) examples without creating abstractions in the form of rules or decision trees (hence *lazy* learning). Generalization to a new input pattern is achieved by retrieving the most similar memory item according to some distance metric, and extrapolating the category of this item to the new input pattern (applying the consistency heuristic). Instances of this form of *nearest neighbour method* include instance-based learning (Aha et al. 1991), exemplar-based learning (Salzberg 1990, Cost and Salzberg 1993), memory-based reasoning (Stanfill and Waltz 1986), and case-based reasoning (Kolodner 1993). Advantages of the

---

[2] To have reliable results, this process is repeated 10 times with different partitions of 90% training and 10% test items, and the average success rate of these ten experiments is computed (Weiss and Kulikowski 1991).

approach include an often surprisingly high classification accuracy, the capacity to learn polymorphous concepts, high speed of learning, and perspicuity of algorithm and classification (see e.g., Cost and Salzberg 1993). Learning speed is extremely fast (it consists basically of storing patterns), and performance speed, while relatively slow on serial machines, can be considerably reduced by using k-d trees on serial machines (Friedman et al. 1977), massively parallel machines (Stanfill and Waltz 1986), or Wafer-Scale Integration (Kitano 1993). In Natural Language Processing, lazy learning techniques are currently also being applied by various Japanese groups to parsing and machine translation under the names *exemplar-based translation* or *memory-based translation and parsing* (Kitano 1993).

Lazy learning has diverse intellectual dependencies: in AI techniques like memory-based reasoning and case-based reasoning, it is stressed that "intelligent performance is the result of the use of memories of earlier experiences rather than the application of explicit but inaccessible rules" (Stanfill and Waltz 1986). Outside the linguistic mainstream, people like Skousen, Derwing, and Bybee stress that "the analogical approach (as opposed to the rule-based approach) should receive more attention in the light of psycholinguistic results and new formalizations of the notion of analogy" (Skousen 1989; Derwing and Skousen 1989), In cognitive psychology (e.g., Smith and Medin 1981), exemplar-based categorization has a long history as an alternative for probabilistic and classical rule-based classification, and finally, in statistical pattern recognition, there is a long tradition of research on *nearest neighbour* classification methods which has been a source of inspiration for the development of lazy learning algorithms.

3.2 Variants of Lazy Learning

Examples are represented as a vector of feature values with an associated category label. Features define a pattern space, in which similar examples occupy regions that are associated with the same category (note that with symbolic, unordered feature values, this geometric interpretation doesn't make sense).

During *training*, a set of examples (the training set) is presented in an incremental fashion to the classifier, and added to memory. During *testing*, a set of previously unseen feature-value patterns (the test set) is presented to the system. For each test pattern, its distance to all examples in memory is computed, and the category of the least distant instance is used as the predicted category for the test pattern.

In lazy learning, performance crucially depends on the distance metric used. The most straightforward distance metric would be the one in equation (1), where X and Y are the patterns to be compared, and $\delta(x_i, y_i)$ is the distance between the values of the i-th feature in a pattern with n features.

$$\Delta(X, Y) = \sum_{i=1}^{n} \delta(x_i, y_i) \tag{1}$$

Distance between two values is measured using (2) for numeric features (using scaling to make the effect of numeric features with different lower and upper bounds comparable), and (3), an overlap metric, for symbolic features.

$$\delta(x_i, y_i) = \frac{|x_i - y_i|}{max_i - min_i} \qquad (2)$$

$$\delta(x_i, y_i) = 0 \text{ if } x_i = y_i, \text{ else } 1 \qquad (3)$$

3.3   Feature weighting

In the distance metric described above, all features describing an example are interpreted as being equally important in solving the classification problem, but this is not necessarily the case. Elsewhere (Daelemans and van den Bosch 1992a; Daelemans et al. 1993) we introduced the concept of information gain (also used in decision tree learning, Quinlan 1986) into lazy learning to weigh the importance of different features in a domain-independent way. Many other methods to weigh the relative importance of features have been designed, both in statistical pattern recognition and in machine learning (e.g., Aha 1990; Kira and Rendell 1992; etc.), but the one we used is extremely simple and produced excellent results.

The main idea of *information gain weighting* is to interpret the training set as an information source capable of generating a number of messages (the different category labels) with a certain probability. The information entropy of such an information source can be compared in turn for each feature to the average information entropy of the information source when the value of that feature is known. Those features that reduce entropy most are most informative.

Database information entropy is equal to the number of bits of information needed to know the category given a pattern. It is computed by (4), where p_i (the probability of category i) is estimated by its relative frequency in the training set.

$$H(D) = -\sum_{p_i} p_i log_2 p_i \qquad (4)$$

For each feature, it is now computed what the information gain is of knowing its value. To do this, we compute the average information entropy for this feature and subtract it from the information entropy of the database. To compute the average information entropy for a feature (5), we take the average information entropy of the database restricted to each possible value for the feature. The expression $D_{[f=v]}$ refers to those patterns in the database that have value v for feature f. V is the set of possible values for feature f. Finally, $|D|$ is the number of patterns in a (sub)database.

$$H(D_{[f]}) = \sum_{v_i \in V} H(D_{[f=v_i]}) \frac{|D_{[f=v_i]}|}{|D|} \qquad (5)$$

Information gain is then obtained by (6), and scaled to be used as a weight for the feature during distance computation.

$$G(f) = H(D) - H(D_{[f]}) \tag{6}$$

Finally, the distance metric in (1) is modified to take into account the information gain weight associated with each feature.

$$\Delta(X, Y) = \sum_{i=1}^{n} G(f_i)\delta(x_i, y_i) \tag{7}$$

Even in itself, information gain may be a useful measure to discover which features are important to solve a linguistic task. Fig. 2 shows the information gain pattern for the prediction of the diminutive suffix of nouns in Dutch. In this task, features are an encoding of the two last syllables of the noun the diminutive suffix of which has to be predicted (there are five forms of this suffix in Dutch). Each part (onset, nucleus, coda) of each of the two syllables (if present) is a separate feature. For each syllable, the presence or absence of stress is coded as well. The feature information gain pattern clearly shows that most relevant information for predicting the suffix is in the rime (nucleus and coda) of the last syllable, and that stress is not very informative for this task (which conforms to recent linguistic theory about diminutive formation in Dutch).

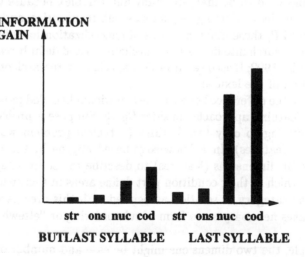

Fig. 2. An example of an information gain pattern. The height of the bars expresses, for each feature describing an input word, the amount of information gain it contributes to predicting the suffix. Features are stress (str), onset (ons), nucleus (nuc), and coda (cod) of the last two syllables of the noun.

3.4 Additional Extensions

Apart from the feature weighting solution, several other optimizations of the algorithm are possible. These concern, e.g., the use of symbolic features: when using the previous metric, all values of a feature are interpreted as equally distant to each other. This may lead to unsufficient discriminatory power between patterns. It also makes impossible the well-understood "Euclidean distance in pattern space" interpretation of the distance metric. Stanfill and Waltz (1986) proposed a *value difference metric* which takes into account the overall similarity of classification of all examples for each value of each feature. Recently, Cost and Salzberg (1993) modified this metric by making it symmetric.

In addition, the exemplars themselves can be weighted, based on typicality (how typical is a memory item for its category) or performance (how well is an exemplar doing in predicting the category of test patterns), storage can be minimized by keeping only a selection of examples, etc.

4 Lazy Learning of Linguistic Tasks

Linguistic tasks (including lexical tasks) are context-sensitive mappings from one representation to another (e.g., from text to speech, from spelling to parse tree, from parse tree to logical form, from source language to target language etc.). These mappings tend to be many-to-many and complex because they can often only be described by conflicting regularities, sub-regularities, and exceptions.

In current NLP, these different levels of generalization have been the prime motivation for research into inheritance mechanisms and default reasoning (Daelemans and Gazdar 1992; Briscoe et al 1993), especially in research on the structure and organisation of the lexicon.

To illustrate the difference between the traditional knowledge-based approach with the lazy learning approach, consider Fig. 3. Suppose a problem can be described by referring to only two features (a typical problem would need tens or hundreds of features). In a knowledge-based approach, the computational linguist looks for dimensions (features) to describe the solution space, and formulates rules which in their condition part define areas in this space and in their action part the category or solution associated with this area. Areas may overlap, which makes necessary some form of rule ordering or "elsewhere condition" principle.

For example, the two dimensions might be case and number of adjectives in some language, and the three categories might be different suffixes associated with different combinations of values for the case and number features.

In a lazy learning approach, on the other hand, knowledge acquisition is automatic. We start from a number of examples, which can be represented as points in feature space. This initial set of examples may contain noise, misclassifications, etc. Information-theoretic metrics like information gain basically modify this feature space automatically by assigning more or less weight to particular features (dimensions). In constructive induction, completely new feature

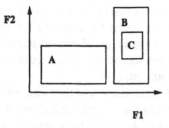

Linguistic Engineering Approach

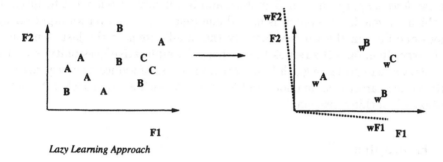

Lazy Learning Approach

Fig. 3. A graphical view of the difference between linguistic engineering (top, knowledge-based) and lazy learning (bottom, behaviour-based)

dimensions may be introduced for separating the different category areas better in feature space. Exemplar weighting and memory compression schemes modify feature space further by removing points (exemplars) and by increasing or decreasing the "attraction area" of exemplars, i.e., the size of the neighbourhood of an exemplar in which this exemplar is counted as the nearest neighbour. We are finally left with a reorganized feature space that optimally separates the different categories, and provides good generalization to unseen inputs. In this process, no linguistic engineering and no handcrafting were involved.

4.1 Linguistic Tasks as Classification

Lazy Learning is fundamentally a *classification* paradigm. Given a description in terms of feature-value pairs of an input, a category label is produced. This category should normally be taken from a finite inventory of possibilities, known beforehand[3]. It is our hypothesis that *all* useful linguistic tasks can be redefined this way. All linguistic problems can be described as context-sensitive mappings. These mappings can be of two kinds: *identification* and *segmentation* (identification of boundaries).

---

[3] This restriction can be circumvented by having multiple classifiers predict a different part of the output pattern, see Ling (1994) for this approach in learning decision trees.

- **Identification.** Given a set of possibilities (categories) and a relevant context in terms of attribute values, determine the correct possibility for this context. Instances of this include *part of speech tagging, grapheme-to-phoneme conversion, lexical selection in generation, morphological synthesis, word sense disambiguation, term translation, stress assignment*, etc.
- **Segmentation.** Given a target and a context, determine whether and which boundary is associated with this target. Examples include *syllabification, morphological analysis, syntactic analysis* (in combination with tagging), etc.

An approach often necessary to arrive at the context information needed is the *windowing* approach (as in Sejnowski and Rosenberg 1986 for text to speech), in which an imaginary window is moved one item at a time over an input string where one item in the window (usually the middle item or the last item) acts as a target item, and the rest as the context. An alternative possibility is to use *operators* as categories, e.g., shift and different types of reduce as categories in a shift-reduce parser (see Simmons and Yu 1992 for such an approach outside the context of Machine Learning).

5 Examples

The approach proposed in this paper is fairly recent, and experiments have focused on phonological and morphological tasks rather than on tasks like term disambiguation. However, we hope to have made clear that the approach is applicable to all classification problems in NLP. In this section we briefly describe some of the experiments and hope the reader will refer to the cited literature for a more detailed description.

5.1 Syllable Boundary Prediction

Here the task to be solved is to decide where syllable boundaries should be placed given a word form in its spelling or pronunciation representation (the target language was Dutch). In a knowledge-based solution, we would implement well-known phonological principles like the *maximal onset principle* and the *sonority hierarchy*, as well as a *morphological parser* to decide on the position of morphological boundaries, some of which overrule the phonological principles. This parser requires at least lexical knowledge about existing stems and affixes and the way they can be combined.

In the lazy learning approach (Daelemans and van den Bosch 1992a; 1992b), we used the windowing approach referred to earlier to formulate the task as a classification problem (more specifically, a segmentation problem). For each letter or phoneme, a pattern was created with a target letter or phoneme, a left context and a right context. The category was *yes* (if the target letter or phoneme should be preceded by a syllable boundary) or *no* if not. The lazy learning approach produced results which were more accurate than both a connectionist approach (backpropagation learning in a recurrent multi-layer perceptron) and a knowledge-based approach. The information gain metric also "discovered" an interesting asymmetry between predictive power of left and right context (right context turned out to be more informative).

5.2 Grapheme-to-Phoneme Conversion

Grapheme-to-phoneme conversion is a central module in text-to-speech systems. The task here is to produce a phonetic transcription given the spelling of a word. Again, in the knowledge-based approach, the lexical requirements for such a system are extensive. In a typical knowledge-based system solving the problem, morphological analysis (with lexicon), phonotactic knowledge, and syllable structure determination modules are designed and implemented.

In a lazy learning approach (Daelemans and van den Bosch 1993; van den Bosch and Daelemans 1993), again a windowing approach was used to formulate the task as a classification problem (identification this time: given a set of possible phonemes, determine which phoneme should be used to translate a target spelling symbol taking into account its context). Results were highly similar to the syllable boundary prediction task: the lazy learning approach resulted in systems which were more accurate than both a connectionist approach and a linguistically motivated approach. The results were replicated for English, French, and Dutch, using the same lazy learning algorithm, which shows its reusability.

5.3 Word Stress Assignment

Another task we applied the lazy learning algorithm to, was stress assignment in Dutch monomorphematic, polysyllabic words (Daelemans et al. 1993, 1994). A word was coded by assigning one feature to each part of the syllable structure of the last three syllables (if present) of the word (see the description of the diminutive formation task described earlier). There were three categories: final stress, penultimate stress, and antepenultimate stress (an identification problem).

Although this research was primarily intended to show that an empiricist learning method with little a priori knowledge performed better than a learning approach in the context of the "Principles and Parameters" framework as applied to metrical phonology, the results also showed that even in the presence of a large amount of noise (from the point of view of the learning algorithm), the algorithm succeeded in automatically extracting the major generalizations that govern stress assignment in Dutch, with no linguistic a priori knowledge except syllable structure.

5.4 Part of Speech Tagging

In this as yet unpublished research, a slightly more complex learning procedure was applied to the problem of part of speech tagging (an identification problem). First, a *lexicon* was derived from the training set. The training set consists of a number of texts in which each word is assigned the correct part of speech tag (its category). To derive a lexicon, we find for each word how many times it was associated with which categories. We can then make an inventory of *ambiguous categories*, e.g., a word like *man* would belong to the ambiguous category *noun-or-verb*. The next step consists of retagging the training corpus with these ambiguous categories. Advantages of this extra step are (i) that ambiguity is restricted to what actually occurs in the training corpus (making as much use as possible of sublanguage characteristics), and (ii) that we have a much more refined measure of similarity in lazy learning: whereas non-ambiguous categories can only be equal or not, ambiguous categories can be *more or less* equal. For the actual tagging problem, a moving window approach was again used, using patterns of ambiguous categories (a target and a left and right context). Results are only preliminary here, but suggest a performance comparable to hidden markov modeling approaches.

6 Conclusion

There are both theoretical and practical aspects to the work described in this paper. First, as far as linguistic engineering is concerned, a new approach to the reusability problem was proposed. Instead of concentrating on linguistic engineering of theory-neutral, poly-theoretic, multi-applicable lexical representations combined with semi-automatic migration of lexical knowledge between different formats, we propose an approach in which a single inductive learning method is reused on different corpora representing useful linguistic mappings, acquiring the necessary lexical information automatically and implicitly.

Secondly, the theoretical claim underlying this proposal is that language acquisition and use (and a fortiori lexical knowledge acquisition and use) are behaviour-based processes rather than knowledge-based processes. We sketched a *memory-based lexicon* with the following properties:

- The lexicon is not a static data structure but a set of lexical processes of identification and segmentation. These processes implement lexical performance.
- Each lexical process is represented by a set of exemplars (solved cases) in memory, which act as models to new input.
- New instances of a lexical process are solved through either memory lookup or similarity-based reasoning.
- There is no representational difference between regularities, subregularities, and exceptions.
- Rule-like behaviour is a side-effect of the operation of the similarity matching process and the contents of memory.
- The contents of memory (the lexical exemplars) can be approximated as a set of rules for convenience.

In a broader context, the results described here argue for an empiricist approach to language acquisition, and for exemplars rather than rules in linguistic knowledge representation (see Daelemans et al. 1994 and Gillis et al. 1993 for further discussion of these issues).

There are also some limitations to the method. The most important of these is the *sparse data problem*. In problems with a large search space (e.g., thousands of features relevant to the task), a large amount of training patterns is necessary in order to cover the search space sufficiently. In general, this is not a problem in NLP, where for most problems large corpora are available or can be collected. Also, information gain or other feature weighting techniques can be used to automatically reduce the dimensionality of the problem, sometimes effectively solving the sparse data problem.

Another problem concerns *long-distance dependencies*, especially in syntax. The methods described often make use of a moving window approach in which only a local part of an input representation is used. Whenever important factors determining a category decision are outside the scope of a pattern, the category assignment cannot be learned. A possible solution for this problem is the cascading of different lazy learning systems, one working on the output of the other. For example, a learning system for part of speech tagging could be combined with a learning system taking patterns of disambiguated tags as input, and producing constituent types as output. Taking patterns of constituent types as input, a third learning system should have no problem assigning "long-distance" dependencies: given the right representation, all dependencies are local.

References

Aha, D.: A study of Instance-Based Algorithms for Supervised Learning Tasks. University of California at Irvine technical report 90-42, 1990.

Aha, D., Kibler, D. and Albert, M.: Instance-Based Learning Algorithms. *Machine Learning* 6, (1991) 37–66.

Van den Bosch, A. and Daelemans, W.: 'Data-oriented methods for grapheme-to-phoneme conversion.' Proceedings of the Sixth conference of the European chapter of the ACL, ACL, (1993) 45–53.

Briscoe, T., de Paiva, V. and Copestake, A.: *Inheritance, Defaults and the Lexicon*. Cambridge: Cambridge University Press, 1993.

Cost, S. and Salzberg, S.: A weighted nearest neighbour algorithm for learning with symbolic features. *Machine Learning* 10, (1993) 57–78.

Daelemans, W. and Gazdar, G.: (guest eds.) Special Issue *Computational Linguistics* on Inheritance in Natural Language Processing, 18 (2) and 18 (3), 1992.

Daelemans, W. and van den Bosch, A.: Generalization Performance of Backpropagation Learning on a Syllabification Task. In: M.F.J. Drossaers and A. Nijholt (eds.) *Connectionism and Natural Language Processing*. Proceedings Third Twente Workshop on Language Technology, (1992) 27–38.

Daelemans, W. and van den Bosch, A.: 'A Neural Network for Hyphenation.' In: I. Aleksander and J. Taylor (eds.) *Artificial Neural Networks II: Proceedings of the International Conference on Artificial Neural Networks*. Elsevier Science Publishers, (1992) 1647–1650.

Daelemans, W. and van den Bosch, A.: 'TABTALK: Reusability in Data-oriented grapheme-to-phoneme conversion.' *Proceedings of Eurospeech*, Berlin, (1993) 1459–1466.

Daelemans, W., Gillis, S., Durieux, G., van den Bosch, A.: Learnability and Markedness in Data-Driven Acquisition of Stress. In: T. Mark Ellison and James M. Scobbie (eds) *Computational Phonology*. Edinburgh Working Papers in Cognitive Science 8, (1993) 157–178.

Daelemans, W., Gillis, S., and Durieux, G.: 'The Acquisition of Stress, a data-oriented approach.' *Computational Linguistics* 20 (3), (1994) forthcoming.

Derwing, B. L. and Skousen, R.: Real Time Morphology: Symbolic Rules or Analogical Networks. *Berkeley Linguistic Society* 15: (1989) 48–62.

Friedman, J., Bentley, J., and Finkel, R., an algorithm for finding best matches in logarithmic expected time. *ACM Transactions on Mathematical Software*, (1977) 3 (3).

Gillis, S., Daelemans, W., Durieux, G. and van den Bosch, A.: 'Learnability and Markedness: Dutch Stress Assignment.' In: *Proceedings of the Fifteenth Annual Conference of the Cognitive Science Society*, Boulder Colorado, USA, Hillsdale: Lawrence Erlbaum Associates, (1993) 452–457.

Kira, K. and Rendell, L.: A practical approach to feature selection. Proceedings International Conference on Machine Learning, 1992.

Kitano, H.: Challenges of massive parallelism. Proceedings IJCAI 1993, 813–834.

Kolodner, J.: Case-Based Reasoning. San-Mateo: Morgan-Kaufmann. 1993.

Ling, C.: Learning the past tense of English verbs: The symbolic Pattern Associator vs. Connectionist Models. *Journal of Artificial Intelligence Research* 1, (1994) 209–229.

Pustejovsky, J.: Dictionary/Lexicon. In: Stuart C. Shapiro (ed.), *Encyclopedia of artificial intelligence*, New York: Wiley, 1992, 341–365.

Quinlan, J. R.: Induction Of Decision Trees. *Machine Learning* 1, (1986) 81–106.

Salzberg, S.: A nearest hyperrectangle learning method. *Machine Learning* 6, (1990) 251–276.

Sejnowski, T. and Rosenberg, C.: NETtalk: a parallel network that learns to read aloud. *Complex Systems* 1, (1986) 145–168.

Simmons, R. and Yu, Y.: The acquisition and use of context-dependent grammars for English. *Computational Linguistics* 18 (3) (1992), 391–418.

Smith, E. and Medin, D.: *Categories and Concepts*. Cambridge, MA: Harvard University Press, 1981.

Skousen, R.: *Analogical Modeling of Language*. Dordrecht: Kluwer, 1989.

Stanfill, C. and Waltz, D.L.: Toward Memory-based Reasoning. *Communications of the ACM* (1986) 29: 1213–1228.

Weiss, S. and Kulikowski, C.: *Computer systems that learn*. San-Mateo: Morgan Kaufmann, 1991.

Winston, P.: Artificial Intelligence. Reading Mass.: Addison-Wesley, 1992.

Part II

Managing Lexical Data

Typed Feature Formalisms
as a Common Basis for Linguistic Specification[*]

Hans-Ulrich Krieger
krieger@dfki.uni-sb.de

German Research Center for Artificial Intelligence (DFKI)
Stuhlsatzenhausweg 3
D-66123 Saarbrücken, Germany

Abstract. Typed feature formalisms (TFF) play an increasingly important role in NLP and, in particular, in MT [27, 28, 10]. Many of these systems are inspired by Pollard and Sag's work on Head-Driven Phrase Structure Grammar (HPSG), which has shown that a great deal of syntax and semantics can be neatly encoded within TFF. However, syntax and semantics are not the only areas in which TFF can be beneficially employed. In this paper, I will show that TFF can also be used as a means to model finite automata (FA) and to perform certain types of logical inferencing. In particular, I will (i) describe how FA can be defined and processed within TFF and (ii) propose a conservative extension to HPSG, which allows for a restricted form of semantic processing within TFF, so that the construction of syntax and semantics can be intertwined with the simplification of the logical form of an utterance. The approach which I propose provides a uniform, HPSG-oriented framework for different levels of linguistic processing, including allomorphy and morphotactics, syntax, semantics, and logical form simplification.

1 Introduction

Pollard&Sag's seminal work on Head-Driven Phrase Structure Grammar has shown that a great deal of syntax and semantics can be neatly encoded within typed feature structures, thus leading for the first time to a highly lexicalized theory of language [20, 21]. Moreover, the formalisms underlying these structures can be given a precise set-theoretical semantics along the lines of Smolka and others.[2] However, there are certain areas within computational linguistics, for which, until recently, no satisfactory formulation in a uniform, constraint-based (or more specifically, HPSG-oriented) theory has been provided. Two of these representation problems will be addressed in this paper, viz., *finite automata* and *logical form simplification*.

---

[*] I would like to thank Elizabeth Hinkelman for reading a draft of this paper. I'm especially indebted to Petra Steffens for carefully reading the pre-final version and for making detailed suggestions.

[2] In the following, we will assume a basic familiarity with unification-based grammar theories [23, 25] and their logics [9, 7, 24].

2 Finite Automata as Typed Feature Structures

Finite automata (FA) and similar devices are heavily used in computational linguistics and natural language processing as a descriptive means of stating certain facts about natural language. They have been employed in the description of morphophonemics [11, 3] and in the formulation of word order constraints [26]; moreover, the use of FA allows for the integration of allomorphy and morphotactics [15, 12].

While it is unsurprising that the languages accepted by FA may also be encoded as typed feature descriptions, it is not clear how FA themselves can be specified as feature structures, how they can be processed, and, furthermore, what closure properties they have within TFF. These questions and, of course, their solutions will be addressed in this section.

2.1 Preliminaries

Assuming a familiarity with the basic inventory of automata theory and formal languages [6], we shall, in the following, formally refer to a *deterministic finite automaton* (DFA) by a 5-tuple $\langle Q, \Sigma, \delta, q_0, F \rangle$, where Q is a finite set of *states*, Σ a finite *input alphabet*, $\delta : Q \times \Sigma \mapsto Q$ is the *transition function*, $q_0 \in Q$ the *initial state*, and $F \subseteq Q$ the set of *final states*. A *nondeterministic finite automaton* (NFA) differs from a deterministic one in that the transition function δ maps to elements of the power set of Q, i.e., $\delta : Q \times \Sigma \mapsto 2^Q$ (Q, Σ, q_0, and F as before).

This is all we need to explain the encoding technique for FA within a typed feature logic. For reasons of simplicity, we start with the simplest form of FA, viz., *deterministic* finite automata *without* ϵ-moves, which consume *exactly one* input symbol at a time. Note that this is not a restriction w.r.t. the set of recognized words: given an arbitrary NFA, we can always construct a deterministic one which recognizes the same language (however, in the worst case with exponentially more states).

Fortunately, our approach is also capable of directly representing and processing non-deterministic FA with ϵ-moves, and allows for edges which are multiple-symbol consumers (see next section). It is worth noting that edges may not only be annotated with atomic symbols. They can also be labelled with complex ones, i.e., with possibly underspecified feature structures, where unification is a means for testing equality (for instance, in case of 2-level morphological descriptions; see [16] for an example of a paradigm-based inflectional morphology).

2.2 Encoding Finite Automata Within Typed Feature Formalisms

To specify an automaton as a typed feature structure, we introduce for every state $q \in Q$ a possibly recursive feature type with the same name as q. We will call such a type a *configuration*. Exactly the attributes EDGE, NEXT, and INPUT are appropriate for such a configuration, where EDGE encodes the *outgoing edges* of q, NEXT the *successor states* of q, and INPUT the symbols which remain on the *input list* when reaching q.[3] A configuration does thus not just model a state of the automaton, but an entire description of the FA at a given point in computation.[4] In order to formally define a configuration as a feature structure type, we first introduce the notion of a proto configuration that specifies the appropriate attributes and their values.

$$proto\text{-}configuration \equiv \begin{bmatrix} \text{EDGE } input\text{-}symbol \lor undef \\ \text{NEXT } configuration \lor undef \\ \text{INPUT } list(input\text{-}symbol) \end{bmatrix} \qquad (1)$$

We now define two natural subtypes of *proto-configuration*. The first one represents the *non-final states* $Q \setminus F$. Because we assume that exactly one input symbol is consumed every time an edge is traversed, we separate the input list into the first element and the rest list, structure-share the first element with EDGE (the consumed input symbol), and pass the rest of the list one level deeper to the next state.

$$non\text{-}final\text{-}configuration \equiv \begin{bmatrix} proto\text{-}configuration \\ \text{EDGE } \boxed{1} \\ \text{NEXT}|\text{INPUT } \boxed{2} \\ \text{INPUT } \langle \boxed{1} \, . \, \boxed{2} \rangle \end{bmatrix} \qquad (2)$$

The other subtype encodes the *final states* of F which possess no outgoing edges, therefore no successor states (and vice versa), or in our terminology: EDGE and NEXT are undefined (are of type *undef*). In addition, successfully reaching a final state with no outgoing edge implies that the input list is *empty*.

$$final\text{-}configuration \equiv \begin{bmatrix} proto\text{-}configuration \\ \text{EDGE } undef \\ \text{NEXT } undef \\ \text{INPUT } \langle \ \rangle \end{bmatrix} \qquad (3)$$

Of course, there will also be final states *with* outgoing edges, but such states are subtypes of the following *disjunctive* type specification:

$$configuration \equiv non\text{-}final\text{-}configuration \lor final\text{-}configuration \qquad (4)$$

To make things more concrete, let us look at an example, viz., the FA A_1 which recognizes the language $\mathcal{L}(A_1) = (a + b)^*c$.

---

[3] There might exist states in an FA with no outgoing edges and thus with no successor states. To cope with this fact, we introduce a special subtype of the most general type $\top$, called *undef*, which is *incompatible* with every other type (except with itself and $\top$).

[4] Note the similarity between a configuration and a closure in functional programming or a machine state in operational semantics—all notions exhaustively describe the corresponding computing device at a certain point in time.

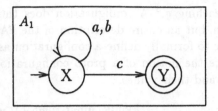

A_1 consists of the two states X and Y; therefore, we have to define two types X and Y, where Y (given in (5)) is only an instantiation of a final configuration. Note that we make use of *distributed disjunctions* [5] (depicted by the disjunction name $1) in the definition of X to express the covariation between edges and successor states: if a is processed, use type X (and vice versa), if b is processed, use again type X, but if c is chosen, choose type Y.

$$X \equiv \begin{bmatrix} \textit{non-final-configuration} \\ \text{EDGE } _{\$1}(a \vee b \vee c) \\ \text{NEXT } _{\$1}(X \vee X \vee Y) \end{bmatrix} \tag{5}$$

$$Y \equiv [\ \textit{final-configuration}\ ]$$

Whether a FA A *accepts* a given input string or not is thus equivalent to the question of *feature term consistency/satisfiability*: if we want to know whether w (a list of input symbols) will be recognized by A, we must *expand the type* which is associated with the initial state q_0 of A and specify w as its INPUT. Speaking in Carpenter's terms [4], we thus require that

$$q_0 \wedge [\text{INPUT } w]$$

be *totally well-typable*, i.e., that there is at least one model that satisfies the input description.[5]

The processing of FA within TFF is thus achieved by type expansion of possibly recursive feature types. However, type expansion not only tests for the satisfiability of a description but also makes the idiosyncratic and inherited constraints of a type explicit (see below). In our case, type expansion *always terminates*, either with a *unification failure* (the FA does not accept w) or with a fully expanded feature structure, representing a successful recognition.

Coming back to our example, let us ask whether abc belongs to the language $\mathcal{L}(A_1)$ accepted by A_1. By expanding type X with [INPUT $\langle a,b,c \rangle$], we can decide this question. This will lead to the following consistent feature structure, which represents the *complete recognition history* of abc, i.e., *all* its "solutions" in the FA (recall that because X is a subtype of *non-final-configuration* and *proto-configuration*, it will *inherit* all constraints of these types; similar for Y):

---

[5] Type expansion here is analogous to a top-down parsing method in syntactic analysis, viz., *recursive descent parsing*. Note that the satisfiability problem for recursive type descriptions is *in general* undecidable, although this is not the case for our encoding [14].

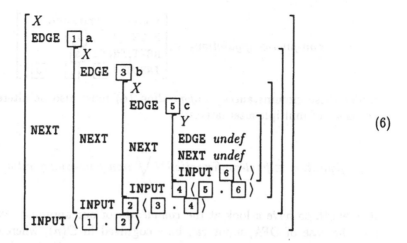

$$\tag{6}$$

We now change our focus from DFA to arbitrary NFA. The first question we have to ask is whether *nondeterminism* in general makes the whole encoding method invalid. In fact, nondeterminism does not introduce any problems at all. There is no difference in our framework between a DFA and a NFA, neither from a descriptive nor from an expressive standpoint, because outgoing edges labelled with the same symbol (the NFA criterion) can be easily captured by distributed disjunctions, as is done in the DFA example above (cf. the description of type X given by (5) in FA A_1).[6]

In addition, changing from Σ- to Σ^*-consuming edges leads only to minor modifications in the definition of *non-final-configuration* (2). Multiple-symbol consuming edges are modelled through lists of symbols instead of declaring single symbols appropriate for EDGE: an ϵ-transition (Σ^0) is encoded as the empty list (7), a single input symbol (Σ^1) through a list over this symbol (8), two input symbols (Σ^2) are represented using a list of two symbols (9), and so on. Therefore, we substitute the definition of *non-final-configuration* by giving a family of specialized definitions, where the number of definitions depends on the length of the longest word associated with an edge in the FA.

$$non\text{-}final\text{-}configuration_0 \equiv \begin{bmatrix} proto\text{-}configuration \\ \text{EDGE } \langle\,\rangle \\ \text{NEXT|INPUT } \boxed{1} \\ \text{INPUT } \boxed{1} \end{bmatrix} \tag{7}$$

$$non\text{-}final\text{-}configuration_1 \equiv \begin{bmatrix} proto\text{-}configuration \\ \text{EDGE } \langle\,\boxed{1}\,\rangle \\ \text{NEXT|INPUT } \boxed{2} \\ \text{INPUT } \langle\,\boxed{1}\,.\,\boxed{2}\,\rangle \end{bmatrix} \tag{8}$$

---

[6] From a *processing* standpoint, of course, a DFA differs from a NFA in our approach. We will come back to this later.

$$\textit{non-final-configuration}_2 \equiv \begin{bmatrix} \textit{proto-configuration} \\ \texttt{EDGE} \; \langle \; \boxed{1} \, , \; \boxed{2} \; \rangle \\ \texttt{NEXT|INPUT} \; \boxed{3} \\ \texttt{INPUT} \; \langle \; \boxed{1} \, , \; \boxed{2} \; \cdot \; \boxed{3} \; \rangle \end{bmatrix} \qquad (9)$$

Under these circumstances, *configuration* (4) must also be altered, since it now consists of multiple alternatives:

$$\textit{configuration} \equiv \textit{final-configuration} \vee \bigvee_{i=0}^{n} \textit{non-final-configuration}_i \qquad (10)$$

It is worth to have a look at the *complexity* of our approach. We all know that in the case of DFA, input can be recognized in $O(n)$, whereas the time complexity for a NFA is $O(2^n)$ in the worst case, where n is given by the length of the input string. Because we employ disjunctions to describe the covariation between edges and successor states, one might assume that the complexity of our treatment is already exponential for the DFA case as a result of the fact that the satisfiability problem for disjunctive formulae is $\mathcal{NP}$-complete [9], thus a unification algorithm will have a non-polynomial complexity, assuming that $\mathcal{P} \neq \mathcal{NP}$. Recall that we are using unification as a means for testing equality.

However, when modelling DFA in our approach, the disjunctions under EDGE and NEXT will *collapse* into one element as a consequence of the fact that in a DFA *at most one* arc can be traversed at a time (the one whose label matches the input). We therefore have to expand only *one* type under NEXT and unification only operates on conjunctive descriptions. But if this is the case, our treatment has nearly the same complexity as in theory: there exist well-known *quasi-linear* unification algorithms for conjunctive formulae, for instance Aït-Kaci's unification algorithm employed in LOGIN [1], which is an extension of Huet's method for fixed-arity, first-order terms. By encoding general NFA in our framework, we obtain the same theoretical result as is the case for a direct encoding, viz., exponential time complexity.

2.3 Intersection, Union, and Complementation of FA

As a nice by-product of our encoding technique, we can show that *unification*, *disjunction*, and *classical negation* in the underlying feature logic directly correspond to the *intersection*, *union*, and *complementation* of FA. The correspondences can be easily shown when assuming a sorted set-theoretical semantics for feature descriptions [24].

Take, for instance, the intersection of two arbitrary FA, A_1 and A_2. Intersecting A_1 and A_2 means construction of an FA A which recognizes the intersection of $\mathcal{L}(A_1)$ and $\mathcal{L}(A_2)$. But exactly this is achieved through unification: constructing A is equivalent to unifying the types associated with the start states of A_1 and A_2, q_0 and q_0'; the denotation of $q_0 \wedge q_0'$ is then given by the intersection of the objects denoted by q_0 and q_0'. The same argumentation holds for union and complementation of FA.

To see how this is accomplished, consider A_1 (as before) and A_2, which recognizes the language $\mathcal{L}(A_2) = a(b+c)^*$.

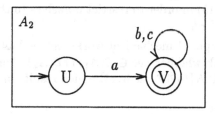

To model A_1 and A_2, we refer to the types X and Y of (5) and to U and V, which are defined in (11).

$$U \equiv \begin{bmatrix} \textit{non-final-configuration} \\ \text{EDGE } a \\ \text{NEXT } V \end{bmatrix}$$

$$V \equiv \begin{bmatrix} \textit{configuration} \\ \text{EDGE } \$_1(b \vee c \vee \textit{undef}) \\ \text{NEXT } \$_1(V \vee V \vee \textit{undef}) \end{bmatrix} \tag{11}$$

The intersection of A_1 and A_2 then corresponds to the unification of X and U, which leads to the following structure (assuming that our logic is based on an open-world semantics [17]):

$$\begin{bmatrix} X \\ \text{EDGE } \$_1(a \vee b \vee c) \\ \text{NEXT } \$_1(X \vee X \vee Y) \end{bmatrix} \wedge \begin{bmatrix} U \\ \text{EDGE } a \\ \text{NEXT } V \end{bmatrix} = \begin{bmatrix} X \wedge U \\ \text{EDGE } a \\ \text{NEXT } X \wedge V \end{bmatrix} \tag{12}$$

Testing whether a given string w belongs to $\mathcal{L}(A_1) \cap \mathcal{L}(A_2)$ is equivalent to testing for the satisfiability of $q_0 \wedge q_0' \wedge [\text{INPUT } w]$. Again, type expansion decides the consistency of the given input description; see (13). Note that the unification of q_0 and q_0' has the same effect as running A_1 and A_2 in "parallel" which is equivalent to the intersection of A_1 and A_2, exactly what we want to achieve. Again, a similar argumentation holds for the union and complementation of FA; see (14) and (15).

$$w \in \mathcal{L}(A_1) \cap \mathcal{L}(A_2) \iff q_0 \wedge q_0' \wedge [\text{INPUT } w] \neq \bot, \tag{13}$$

$$w \in \mathcal{L}(A_1) \cup \mathcal{L}(A_2) \iff (q_0 \vee q_0') \wedge [\text{INPUT } w] \neq \bot \tag{14}$$

$$w \in \overline{\mathcal{L}(A_1)} \iff \neg q_0 \wedge \textit{configuration} \wedge [\text{INPUT } w] \neq \bot \tag{15}$$

Because we are working in the domain of FA (although they are encoded via feature structures), complementing an FA means to complement the language it accepts with respect to Σ^* and not to complement the set of objects denoted by q_0 with respect to the domain of feature descriptions, i.e., the whole universe (which represents a much larger set). We, therefore, have to intersect/unify $\neg q_0$ with *configuration* in (15) in order to restrict ourselves to the domain of feature structures which *model* FA.

To see how the proposed mechanism works, let us look at the FA A_1 and A_2 again and let us ask whether $abc \in \mathcal{L}(A_1) \cap \mathcal{L}(A_2)$? Deciding this question means to expand $X \wedge U \wedge [\text{INPUT } \langle a, b, c \rangle]$ which results in (16).

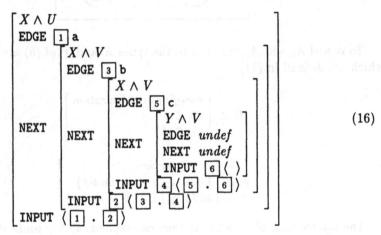

$$\tag{16}$$

It has to be noted that the intersection of FA via unification does not work in general for FA with ϵ-moves. This problem is inherent and well-known but is no restriction w.r.t. expressivity (see [14] for more details and related aspects).

2.4 Concatenation and Kleene Closure

Let us now focus on the *concatenation* and *Kleene closure* of regular expressions/FA. It turns out that the feature logic on which our approach is based together with a weak form of *functional uncertainty* [8] allows for a characterization of these operations [14]. Let $A_1 = \langle Q_1, \Sigma_1, \delta_1, q_0, F_1 \rangle$ and $A_2 = \langle Q_2, \Sigma_2, \delta_2, q_0', F_2 \rangle$ be two arbitrary FA. The concatenation of A_1 and A_2 is given by

$$A_1 \cdot A_2 \equiv q_0 \wedge [(\text{NEXT})^* \ q_0' \wedge \bigvee_i f_i] \tag{17}$$

where the f_i must be subtypes of *non-final-configuration*, although on the FA level, they belong to the set of final states. While $A_1 \cdot A_2$ would usually be constructed by introducing an ϵ-move between A_1 and A_2 [6, p. 31], we account for concatenation by connecting every final state $f_i \in F_1$ with the start state q_0' of A_2; thus, we have to write $(\vee_i f_i) \wedge q_0'$. Connection here does *not* mean introducing an ϵ-move but to *unify* every f_i with q_0', which requires us to turn the final states of A_1 into non-final ones to allow for successful unifications; this is why f_i must be a subtype of *non-final-configuration*.

At this point, functional uncertainty comes into play because we do not know for a concrete input $w = w_1 \cdot w_2$ how many iterations of NEXT are necessary in A_1 to successfully recognize w_1, so that w_2 can be further processed by A_2. Note that the functional uncertainty constraint in (17) can be restated by using the following recursive type definition—thus there is no need for a richer logic:

$$[(\text{NEXT})^* \ \sigma] \quad \rightsquigarrow \quad \Phi \equiv \sigma \vee [\text{NEXT} \ \Phi] \tag{18}$$

The iteration or Kleene closure of A_1 is constructed in a similar way: the final states $f_i \in F_1$ are *unified* with the start state q_0 (to be more precise, with the types associated with these states). The construction of A_1^* then looks as follows:

$$A_1^* \equiv A^0 \vee A^+ \tag{19}$$

where A^0 is an instantiation of *final-configuration* (the empty string case) and $A^+ \equiv q_0 \wedge [(\text{NEXT})^* \ \vee_i f_i]$. However, f_i must be a subtype of the disjunctive type *configuration* (4) because the f_i serve as final states as well as non-final states in this construction, which is in accordance with the definition of *configuration*.

Although concatenation and Kleene closure are directly encodable in our logic, we recommend against using the above technique for reasons of efficiency. In this regard, it is better to construct the composite automaton first by hand—which is fairly straightforward—and then apply the encoding mechanism for non-complex FA.

3 Logical Form Simplification Within HPSG

Typed feature formalisms in general, and HPSG in particular, serve as a basis for many NLP/MT systems [27, 28, 10]. Even though most of these systems represent the semantic content of an utterance as a feature structure, they do *not* use a parser (or generator) or a uniform deduction component to simplify logical form or to draw domain-specific inferences within the calculus of HPSG in order to derive legal, simpler expressions represented as a feature structure again (cf. [2] to get an impression of simplifying/resolving (quasi) logical form within the core language engine of SRI).

Instead, all systems either translate the semantic representation directly into an application language (e.g., a database language), which means that semantic inferences are not seen as essential in the front-end, or transform feature structures into a term of a semantic representation logic (for instance the language $\mathcal{NLL}$ [18]), on which a deduction component operates to yield another, denotation-preserving expression. Given such an intermediate language, the method of processing the semantics of a sentence is as follows:

1. incrementally construct a feature structure f representing the semantics of a given sentence,
2. transform the content of f into a term t of the intermediate language,
3. apply simplification schemata iteratively to t, yielding a simpler term t',
4. translate t' into an application language expression e,
5. interpret e with the inference machinery of the application language.

We will argue in this paper that semantic inferences can be carried out locally as part of the parsing (generation) process so that step (2.) and (3.) are in fact *not* needed and that f can be directly translated into e. Doing away with an intermediate level of semantic representation has many advantages:

- PROCESSING: semantic inferences can be carried out locally during the parsing process (if needed); since inconsistencies can thus be detected at an early stage of analysis, processing efforts can be reduced
- ARCHITECTURE: semantic inferences are integrated into the parser—which leads to a simpler architecture of the whole NLP system
- EFFICIENCY: there is no need to transform a feature structure into an expression of the intermediate language—which saves time and space
- UNIFORMITY: it is theoretically appealing to provide a coherent framework in which all levels of linguistic description are represented and in which artificial interface problems are thus avoided

Because HPSG in general allows for higher order expressivity through unrestricted relations and recursive types, the notion of *logical equivalence* of descriptions is undecidable, and moreover, not even recursively enumerable. Hence the subject of this paper will not be a restricted decision procedure for testing the equivalence of two descriptions, but, rather, a limited method of logical form simplification. This is achieved by enriching the feature logic underlying HPSG—however, without sticking to external relational constraints.

3.1 Encoding Logical Form Simplification

In the following, we refer to Pollard and Sag's first volume of HPSG [20]. Even though the examples given throughout this section are simplified in that the structure of SEM is *flat*, i.e., only consists of top level attributes like OP (operator), SC (scope), CONN (connective), etc., the idea developed here can be easily adapted to more complex forms of HPSG and other constraint-based grammar formalisms which have similar notions of what English (or any natural language) is [20, p. 147]:

$$English = P_1 \wedge \cdots \wedge P_{n+m} \wedge (L_1 \vee \cdots \vee L_p \vee R_1 \vee \cdots \vee R_q) \qquad (20)$$

In the introductory section, we said that during parsing the primary reason for using feature structures is the need for storing information obtained so far (e.g., semantic content). A parser, however, will, for instance, *not* simplify nested

occurrences of an operator like a *semantic not* ¬.[7] There's a notable exception
to what we said about the lack of semantic inferences in HPSG: most of the
effects of *β-reduction*, used by many semanticists growing out of the Montagovian
tradition, can be easily captured by *unification* (see for instance [19]).

In this section, we intend to present the necessary inventory for *logical form
simplification* within HPSG. What we need is

1. an immediate dominance (rule) schema R_{proj} formulated as (Project) in (22)
   to record semantic inferences, and
2. for each simplification schema exactly one *extralinguistic/metalogical principle* P_{meta_i} $(1 \leq i \leq k)$ realized as (a special form of) an implication.

Therefore, we must redefine (20) by adding the rule schema and the principles. This results in the following definition of *English*:

$$P_1 \wedge \cdots \wedge P_{n+m} \wedge P_{\text{meta}_1} \cdots \wedge P_{\text{meta}_k} \wedge (L_1 \vee \cdots \vee L_p \vee R_1 \vee \cdots \vee R_q \vee R_{\text{proj}}) \quad (21)$$

The rule schema R_{proj} serves to represent both sides of an inference step
by projecting the simplified semantics to the top level SEM and storing the non-
simplified representation under DTRS; see (22). Note the similarity between R_{proj}
and an R_i: R_i serves as an instruction to build up phrase structure. However, the
number of branches in such a derivation tree is in general greater than one—this
is in contrast to the single daughter of R_{proj}. The idea now is to postulate a similar structure which allows us to construct a *proof tree*. Topologically speaking,
such a proof tree corresponds to a linear chain. Because we are interested in the
value of the SEM attribute, we structure-share PHON and SYN on the top level with
the same attributes of the single daughter under the path DTRS|NON-SIMPL-DTR.
This is necessary for a parser to continue (syntactic parsing) properly.

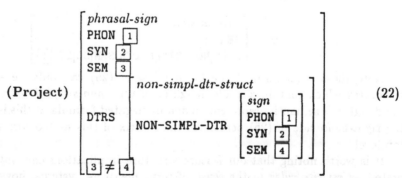

$$\textbf{(Project)} \quad \begin{bmatrix} \textit{phrasal-sign} \\ \text{PHON} \;\; \boxed{1} \\ \text{SYN} \;\; \boxed{2} \\ \text{SEM} \;\; \boxed{3} \\ \text{DTRS} \;\; \begin{bmatrix} \textit{non-simpl-dtr-struct} \\ \text{NON-SIMPL-DTR} \begin{bmatrix} \textit{sign} \\ \text{PHON} \;\; \boxed{1} \\ \text{SYN} \;\; \boxed{2} \\ \text{SEM} \;\; \boxed{4} \end{bmatrix} \end{bmatrix} \\ \boxed{3} \neq \boxed{4} \end{bmatrix} \quad (22)$$

Note that it is always possible to instantiate such a structure, if needed,
during the construction of syntax and semantics in order to simplify the value
of SEM (cf. the examples in Section 3.2). After a successful simplification step,
we may then continue with syntactic analysis and possibly perform some more
simplification steps again later.

---

[7] For example, an expression like [SEM|CONT [OP ¬, SC [OP ¬, SC ψ]]] should be simpli-
fied in many cases to [SEM|CONT ψ].

To avoid *interferences* between linguistic principles and extralinguistic ones, we assume DTRS to be of type *non-simpl-dtr-struct*; see (22). Thus, we exclude the application of principles like the Head Feature Principle, the Semantics Principle, or the Subcategorization Principle. Because those principles are of the form

$$[\text{DTRS } [\textit{headed-structure}]] \implies [\cdots] \tag{23}$$

they cannot be applied to structures which are licensed by the projection rule schema (22). The same argument also holds for the opposite case: structures admitted by the four rule schemata of HPSG-I, cannot be constrained by our extralinguistic principles, because the antecedents of such principles assume a single daughter of type *non-simpl-dtr-struct*, which would cause the principles to fail.

We now present two well-known simplification schemata and show how to represent them in terms of feature structure implications—actually, we only represent *one* direction of the biconditional (otherwise we would have to state two implications). We start with the simplification schema for *double negation*, i.e.,

$$\frac{\neg\neg\psi}{\psi} \tag{24}$$

or as an implication

$$(\text{2Neg}) \quad \begin{bmatrix} \textit{phrasal-sign} \\ \text{DTRS} \begin{bmatrix} \textit{non-simpl-dtr-struct} \\ \text{NON-SIMPL-DTR|SEM} \begin{bmatrix} \textit{op-sc-struct} \\ \text{OP } \neg \\ \text{SC|OP } \neg \end{bmatrix} \end{bmatrix} \end{bmatrix}$$
$$\implies \begin{bmatrix} \textit{phrasal-sign} \\ \text{SEM } \boxed{1} \\ \text{DTRS|NON-SIMPL-DTR|SEM|SC|SC } \boxed{1} \end{bmatrix} \tag{25}$$

Note the special form of the left-hand side: (25) can only be applied to structures which contain a single daughter of type *non-simpl-dtr-struct*, where the daughter's semantics represents a doubly negated formula. If this is the case, the right-hand side of (25) percolates the matrix of this nested formula to the top level.

It is worth noting that our feature structure implications can *not* be interpreted as *rewrite rules* in the sense of term rewriting systems; however, they *encode* a rewrite rule through phrase structure trees. Real rewriting, instead, would violate the main assumption of the unification-based grammar paradigm, viz., *monotonicity*.

Our next example concerns one of *De Morgan's rules*, i.e.,

$$\frac{\neg(\phi \wedge \psi)}{\neg\phi \vee \neg\psi} \tag{26}$$

which corresponds to the following implication:

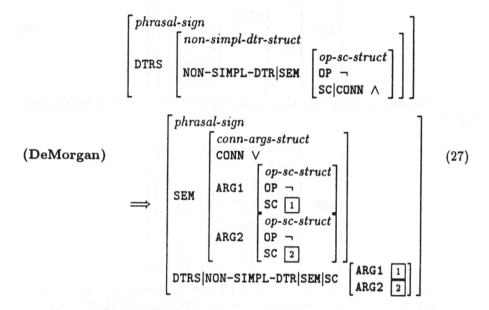

$$\text{(DeMorgan)} \qquad (27)$$

3.2 An Improved Version

The proposal presented so far has one significant disadvantage: extralinguistic principles can only be applied to top level forms which are licensed by the projection rule but can *not* be taken into consideration in the case of embedded structures, unless deeper reaching principles have been provided. While from a practical point of view, this may not be considered a severe drawback, it is unacceptable from the viewpoint of expressiveness.

Let us illustrate this claim with an example. Consider, for instance, the following derivation tree.

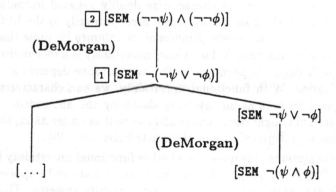

This example shows that everything works fine until De Morgan's rule is applied a second time. Given the structure of $\boxed{1}$,

$$
\left[\text{SEM} \begin{bmatrix} \textit{op-sc-struct} \\ \text{OP } \neg \\ \text{SC} \begin{bmatrix} \text{CONN } \vee \\ \text{ARG1} \begin{bmatrix} \text{OP } \neg \\ \text{SC } \psi \end{bmatrix} \\ \text{ARG2} \begin{bmatrix} \text{OP } \neg \\ \text{SC } \phi \end{bmatrix} \end{bmatrix} \end{bmatrix} \right] \tag{28}
$$

we can successfully apply (27), thus producing the following simplified semantics for $\boxed{2}$:

$$
\left[\text{SEM} \begin{bmatrix} \textit{conn-args-struct} \\ \text{CONN } \wedge \\ \text{ARG1} \begin{bmatrix} \text{OP } \neg \\ \text{SC} \begin{bmatrix} \text{OP } \neg \\ \text{SC } \psi \end{bmatrix} \end{bmatrix} \\ \text{ARG2} \begin{bmatrix} \text{OP } \neg \\ \text{SC} \begin{bmatrix} \text{OP } \neg \\ \text{SC } \phi \end{bmatrix} \end{bmatrix} \end{bmatrix} \right] \tag{29}
$$

The problem now is that the schema for double negation stated in (25) cannot be applied to (29) because the structure under DTRS|NON-SIMPL-DTR|SEM would be of type *conn-args-struct* after the application of (Project) but not of type *op-sc-struct*. Although the arguments of the connective ∧ fulfill the antecedent of (25), the metalogical principle cannot fire. Note that this problem is not restricted to top level parts of the semantics of the immediate daughter but can arise at an arbitrary depth.

To overcome this shortcoming, we need the ability to *iterate* certain attributes/paths in the antecedent of an implication. The relevant attributes in example (29) are the arguments of the connective, ARG1 and ARG2. Here however, the iteration is only of depth 1. If the feature logic allows us to specify *regular path expressions*, we are able to restate the antecedent of the principle for double negation in such a way that we can characterize doubly negated formulae at deeper levels; see (30). There exists a mechanism used primarily in the LFG community which fulfills exactly our needs: *functional uncertainty* [8] (note that Section 2.4 also makes use of this device). Functional uncertainty is a mechanism for dealing elegantly with linguistic phenomena like long distance dependencies or constituent coordination. With functional uncertainty, we can characterize a nested doubly negated formula at an arbitrary depth by the antecedent of (30). Because such a formula might occur under ARG1 as well as under ARG2, the Kleene star * is applied to a disjunction + of these attributes; see (30).

Advocates of rewrite systems may question whether functional uncertainty is really called for here. They might propose simplification rules that can be applied anywhere within a feature structure as is known from rewrite systems. This, however, would assume a different semantics for feature structure implications— in order to *encode* the universal applicability of rewrite rules in term rewriting systems, functional uncertainty seems to be the only viable solution. The seeming disadvantage of specifying exactly the path where a matching structure must be located turns out to be a benefit: in our case, the specified path *guides the search* of an inference engine that, for a given principle, tests for the applicability of its antecedent. In the case of general rewrite systems, this search is not guided, i.e., the rewrite system is "blind" or must rely on heuristics.

Unfortunately, functional uncertainty is *not* sufficient to cope with structures embedded at deeper levels. This is because we must extract certain substructures under DTRS, which, however, should *not* be percolated entirely. Moreover, these structures might be specified by a *regular path*, since we do *not* know how deep they are located. Take, for instance, our example of double negation. What we would like to state is that the (top level) value of SEM is identical to the value under DTRS|NON-SIMPL-DTR|SEM with one important *exception*: the value under DTRS|NON-SIMPL-DTR|SEM|(ARG1+ARG2)* (the doubly negated formula) has to be *substituted* with DTRS|NON-SIMPL-DTR|SEM|(ARG1+ARG2)*|SC|SC (the matrix of the formula). This requires a special form of *monotonic substitution*. Since our notion of substitution is similar to the one used in the λ-calculus, we write $X_{\{Y \backslash Z\}}$ meaning:

Substitute in a copy of X every Y' with Z, where Y' is subsumed by Y.

The notion of a copy is defined as follows: X is a *copy* of X' iff $X \Rightarrow X'$ and $X' \Rightarrow X$, such that $X \neq X'$.

Functional uncertainty together with monotonic substitution now allows us to state an improved version of the principle for double negation, which subsumes (25).

$$
\begin{bmatrix}
phrasal\text{-}sign \\
DTRS \begin{bmatrix} non\text{-}simpl\text{-}dtr\text{-}struct \\ \text{NON-SIMPL-DTR|SEM } \boxed{1} \begin{bmatrix} conn\text{-}args\text{-}struct \\ (\text{ARG1+ARG2})^* \ \boxed{2} \begin{bmatrix} op\text{-}sc\text{-}struct \\ \text{OP } \neg \\ \text{SC } \begin{bmatrix} \text{OP } \neg \\ \text{SC } \boxed{3} \end{bmatrix} \end{bmatrix} \end{bmatrix} \end{bmatrix}
\end{bmatrix}
$$

$$
\implies \begin{bmatrix} phrasal\text{-}sign \\ \text{SEM } \boxed{1} {}_{\{\boxed{2} \backslash \boxed{3}\}} \end{bmatrix}
$$

$$(30)$$

Coming back to our example, we are now able to simplify the value of SEM after the application of De Morgan's rule by using the improved principle for double negation. Note that (30) is applied to *both* arguments of the connective $\wedge$ in $\boxed{1}$. The derivation tree then looks as follows:

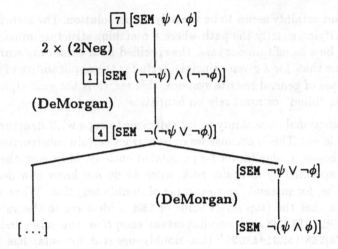

$$\boxed{7}\ [\text{SEM}\ \psi \wedge \phi]$$

$2 \times (2\text{Neg})$

$$\boxed{1}\ [\text{SEM}\ (\neg\neg\psi) \wedge (\neg\neg\phi)]$$

(DeMorgan)

$$\boxed{4}\ [\text{SEM}\ \neg(\neg\psi \vee \neg\phi)]$$

$$[\text{SEM}\ \neg\psi \vee \neg\phi]$$

(DeMorgan)

$$[\ldots] \qquad [\text{SEM}\ \neg(\psi \wedge \phi)]$$

where

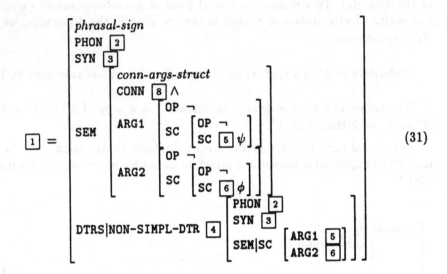

$$\boxed{1} = \begin{bmatrix} \textit{phrasal-sign} \\ \text{PHON}\ \boxed{2} \\ \text{SYN}\ \boxed{3} \\ \text{SEM}\ \begin{bmatrix} \textit{conn-args-struct} \\ \text{CONN}\ \boxed{8}\ \wedge \\ \text{ARG1}\ \begin{bmatrix} \text{OP}\ \neg \\ \text{SC}\ \begin{bmatrix} \text{OP}\ \neg \\ \text{SC}\ \boxed{5}\ \psi \end{bmatrix} \end{bmatrix} \\ \text{ARG2}\ \begin{bmatrix} \text{OP}\ \neg \\ \text{SC}\ \begin{bmatrix} \text{OP}\ \neg \\ \text{SC}\ \boxed{6}\ \phi \end{bmatrix} \end{bmatrix} \end{bmatrix} \\ \text{DTRS|NON-SIMPL-DTR}\ \boxed{4}\ \begin{bmatrix} \text{PHON}\ \boxed{2} \\ \text{SYN}\ \boxed{3} \\ \text{SEM|SC}\ \begin{bmatrix} \text{ARG1}\ \boxed{5} \\ \text{ARG2}\ \boxed{6} \end{bmatrix} \end{bmatrix} \end{bmatrix} \quad (31)$$

and

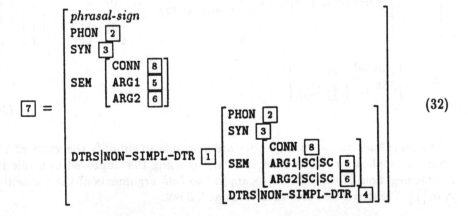

$$\boxed{7} = \begin{bmatrix} \textit{phrasal-sign} \\ \text{PHON}\ \boxed{2} \\ \text{SYN}\ \boxed{3} \\ \text{SEM}\ \begin{bmatrix} \text{CONN}\ \boxed{8} \\ \text{ARG1}\ \boxed{5} \\ \text{ARG2}\ \boxed{6} \end{bmatrix} \\ \text{DTRS|NON-SIMPL-DTR}\ \boxed{1}\ \begin{bmatrix} \text{PHON}\ \boxed{2} \\ \text{SYN}\ \boxed{3} \\ \text{SEM}\ \begin{bmatrix} \text{CONN}\ \boxed{8} \\ \text{ARG1|SC|SC}\ \boxed{5} \\ \text{ARG2|SC|SC}\ \boxed{6} \end{bmatrix} \\ \text{DTRS|NON-SIMPL-DTR}\ \boxed{4} \end{bmatrix} \end{bmatrix} \quad (32)$$

If the principle of double negation should also be able to handle other cases of embedded constructions (quantifier within the scope of ¬, etc.), we must specify this as is the case for rewrite schemata in term rewriting systems. This can be achieved either by adding new principles for each case or, more generally, by making the improved version of (2Neg) sensitive to these special situations (cf. [13] for more details).

Our last extension concerns the introduction of *set values*. A truly robust, HPSG-inspired approach to logical form simplification must be able to unify the following two structures:

$$\begin{bmatrix} conn\text{-}args\text{-}struct \\ \text{CONN} \ \wedge \\ \text{ARG1} \ \phi \\ \text{ARG2} \ \psi \end{bmatrix} \qquad \begin{bmatrix} conn\text{-}args\text{-}struct \\ \text{CONN} \ \wedge \\ \text{ARG1} \ \psi \\ \text{ARG2} \ \phi \end{bmatrix} \qquad (33)$$

Although $\phi \wedge \psi$ and $\psi \wedge \phi$ are equal in a model-theoretic sense (that is, the extensions are equal, i.e., denote the same set of objects), standard unification would fail. We, therefore, suggest to replace the keyword approach ARG*n* by a set-valued treatment as shown in (34). Moreover, this has the advantage of allowing more than two arguments for connectives like $\wedge$ or $\vee$ (see [19] for a similar proposal). In addition, there is no longer a need for specifying commutativity via a principle/schema; instead, commutativity is now handled internally through set unification.

$$\begin{bmatrix} conn\text{-}args\text{-}struct \\ \text{CONN} \ \wedge \\ \text{ARGS} \ \{\phi, \psi, \ldots\} \end{bmatrix} \qquad (34)$$

However, the question still remains which form of set values and set unification is really needed in our case (see for instance [22]). And perhaps, more important, what is the price we have to pay when using set-values. However, an examination of these aspects would exceed the scope of this paper.

4 Summary and Conclusions

In this paper, I have shown how FA can be neatly integrated and processed within TFF. The encoding method assumes that the logic makes recursive type definitions available. Some examples of German inflectional morphology [16] have been implemented in the typed feature formalism *TDL* [17].

The second area addressed in this paper concerns a proposal for logical form simplification within TFF/HPSG. The approach makes strong assumptions about the expressivity of the feature calculus (set values, functional uncertainty/recursive types and monotonic substitution).

Both approaches extend the domain of "ordinary" constraint-based grammars beyond the construction of syntax and semantics, thus avoiding artificial interface problems between different components in that everything is represented within the same formalism. This integration need *not* lead to a heavy decrease of efficiency as explained in Section 2 and 3, so that the advantages of these proposals prevail against non-integrated, multi-component oriented systems.

References

1. Hassan Aït-Kaci and Roger Nasr. LOGIN: A logic programming language with built-in inheritance. *Journal of Logic Programming*, 3:185–215, 1986.
2. Hiyan Alshawi, editor. *The Core Language Engine*. ACL-MIT Press Series in Natural Language Processing. MIT Press, 1992.
3. Steven Bird. Finite-state phonology in HPSG. In *Proceedings of the 14th International Conference on Computational Linguistics, COLING-92*, pages 74–80, 1992.
4. Bob Carpenter. *The Logic of Typed Feature Structures*. Tracts in Theoretical Computer Science. Cambridge University Press, Cambridge, 1992.
5. Jochen Dörre and Andreas Eisele. Determining consistency of feature terms with distributed disjunctions. In Dieter Metzing, editor, *Proceedings of 13th German Workshop on Artificial Intelligence, GWAI-89*, pages 270–279, Berlin, 1989. Springer.
6. John E. Hopcroft and Jeffrey D. Ullman. *Introduction to Automata Theory, Languages, and Computation*. Addison-Wesley, Reading, MA, 1979.
7. Mark Johnson. *Attribute Value Logic and the Theory of Grammar*. CSLI Lecture Notes, Number 16. Center for the Study of Language and Information, Stanford, 1988.
8. Ronald M. Kaplan and John T. Maxwell III. An algorithm for functional uncertainty. In *Proceedings of the 12th International Conference on Computational Linguistics, COLING-88*, pages 297–302, 1988.
9. Robert T. Kasper and William C. Rounds. A logical semantics for feature structures. In *Proceedings of the 24th Annual Meeting of the Association for Computational Linguistics*, pages 257–266, 1986.
10. Martin Kay, Jean Mark Gawron, and Peter Norvig. *Verbmobil: A Translation System for Face-to-Face Dialog*. CSLI Lecture Notes, Number 33. Center for the Study of Language and Information, Stanford, 1994.
11. Kimmo Koskenniemi. Two-level model for morphological analysis. In *Proceedings of the 8th International Joint Conference on Artificial Intelligence*, pages 683–685, 1983.
12. Hans-Ulrich Krieger. Derivation without lexical rules. In C.J. Rupp, M.A. Rosner, and R.L. Johnson, editors, *Constraints, Language and Computation*. Academic Press, 1994. A version of this paper is available as DFKI Research Report RR-93-27. Also published in IDSIA Working Paper No. 5, Lugano, November 1991.
13. Hans-Ulrich Krieger. Logical form simplification within HPSG. Technical report, Deutsches Forschungszentrum für Künstliche Intelligenz, Saarbrücken, Germany, 1994. Forthcoming.
14. Hans-Ulrich Krieger. Representing and processing finite automata within typed feature formalisms. Technical report, Deutsches Forschungszentrum für Künstliche Intelligenz, Saarbrücken, Germany, 1994. Forthcoming.

15. Hans-Ulrich Krieger and John Nerbonne. Feature-based inheritance networks for computational lexicons. In Ted Briscoe, Valeria de Paiva, and Ann Copestake, editors, *Inheritance, Defaults, and the Lexicon*, pages 90–136. Cambridge University Press, New York, 1993. A version of this paper is available as DFKI Research Report RR-91-31. Also published in Proceedings of the ACQUILEX Workshop on Default Inheritance in the Lexicon, Technical Report No. 238, University of Cambridge, Computer Laboratory, October 1991.

16. Hans-Ulrich Krieger, John Nerbonne, and Hannes Pirker. Feature-based allomorphy. In *Proceedings of the 31st Annual Meeting of the Association for Computational Linguistics*, 1993. A version of this paper is available as DFKI Research Report RR-93-28.

17. Hans-Ulrich Krieger and Ulrich Schäfer. *TDL*—a type description language for constraint-based grammars. In *Proceedings of the 15th International Conference on Computational Linguistics, COLING-94, Kyoto, Japan*, pages 893–899, 1994.

18. Joachim Laubsch and John Nerbonne. An overview of *NLL*. Technical report, Hewlett-Packard, 1991.

19. John Nerbonne. A feature-based syntax/semantics interface. In Alexis Manaster-Ramer and Wlodek Zadrozny, editors, *Mathematics of Language, Vol. 2*. Annals of Artificial Intelligence and Mathematics, 1992. Also available as DFKI Research Report RR-92-42.

20. Carl Pollard and Ivan A. Sag. *Information-Based Syntax and Semantics. Vol. I: Fundamentals*. CSLI Lecture Notes, Number 13. Center for the Study of Language and Information, Stanford, 1987.

21. Carl Pollard and Ivan A. Sag. *Head-Driven Phrase Structure Grammar*. Studies in Contemporary Linguistics. University of Chicago Press, Chicago, 1994.

22. William C. Rounds. Set values for unification-based grammar formalisms and logic programming. Technical Report CSLI-88-129, Center for the Study of Language and Information, 1988.

23. Stuart M. Shieber. *An Introduction to Unification-Based Approaches to Grammar*. CSLI Lecture Notes, Number 4. Center for the Study of Language and Information, Stanford, 1986.

24. Gert Smolka. A feature logic with subsorts. LILOG Report 33, WT LILOG–IBM Germany, Stuttgart, May 1988. Also in J. Wedekind and C. Rohrer (eds.), Unification in Grammar, MIT Press, 1991.

25. Hans Uszkoreit. From feature bundles to abstract data types: New directions in the representation and processing of linguistic knowledge. In A. Blaser, editor, *Natural Language at the Computer—Contributions to Syntax and Semantics for Text Processing and Man-Machine Translation*, pages 31–64. Springer, Berlin, 1988.

26. Hans Uszkoreit. Linear precedence in head domains. Paper presented at the *HPSG in German* workshop, 1992.

27. Hans Uszkoreit, Rolf Backofen, Stephan Busemann, Abdel Kader Diagne, Elizabeth A. Hinkelman, Walter Kasper, Bernd Kiefer, Hans-Ulrich Krieger, Klaus Netter, Günter Neumann, Stephan Oepen, and Stephen P. Spackman. DISCO—an HPSG-based NLP system and its application for appointment scheduling. In *Proceedings of COLING-94, Kyoto, Japan*, 1994.

28. Rémi Zajac. A transfer model using a typed feature structure rewriting system with inheritance. In *Proceedings of the 27th Annual Meeting of the Association for Computational Linguistics*, pages 1–6, 1989.

European Efforts Towards Standardizing Language Resources

Nicoletta Calzolari

Istituto di Linguistica Computazionale
Via della Faggiola, 32
56100 Pisa, Italy

Abstract. This paper aims at providing a broad overview of the situation in Europe during the past few years, regarding efforts and concerted actions towards the standardization of large language resources, with particular emphasis on what is taking place in the fields of Computational Lexicons and Text Corpora. Attention will be focused on the plans, work in progress, and a few preliminary results of the LRE project EAGLES (Expert Advisory Group on Language Engineering Standards).

1   Introduction and Historical Background

This paper aims at providing a broad picture of the situation in Europe, concerning efforts and concerted actions towards the standardization of language resources, with particular emphasis - given the topic of this book - to what is taking place specifically in the fields of Computational Lexicons and Text Corpora. Attention will be focused on the plans, work in progress, and preliminary results of the LRE project EAGLES (Expert Advisory Group on Language Engineering Standards),[1] in particular with respect to two of its five Working Groups. In order to fully comprehend the motivation behind the setting up of this project, a short description of the general *Zeitgeist* in our field over the past few years is necessary.

The major event which set in motion, in a very focused and innovative way, efforts towards standardization of language resources was the Grosseto Workshop on "Automating the Lexicon: Research and Practice in a

---

[1]EAGLES is an LRE project (Linguistic Research and Engineering), funded by the CEC's DGXIII. EAGLES consists of five Working Groups hosted by designated R&D centres (Instituto Cervantes - Spain, GSI-ERLI - France, DFKI - Germany, CST - Denmark, Vocalis Ltd. - U.K.) and coordinated by the Consorzio Pisa Ricerche, Italy. EAGLES material produced within the Working Groups has been used in preparing this paper. For further information please contact the EAGLES secretariat at eagles@icnucevm.cnuce.cnr.it.

Multilingual Environment" organized by Zampolli, Walker and myself in 1986 and sponsored by the EC (see Walker, Zampolli, Calzolari, 1994).

There, for the first time, the topic of the *Computational Lexicon* was tackled from a broad perspective, giving to this field the prominent position that it deserves in Computational Linguistics, in Natural Language Processing, and in - what is today called - Language Engineering or Language Industry. This new perspective was made possible by our careful efforts in bringing together prominent experts from very different areas, ranging from theoretical linguistics to machine translation, computational linguistics, natural language processing, information retrieval, lexicography, publishing, psycholinguistics, and so on. It was the first time that representatives of these fields had been offered a forum for exchanging their ideas and experiences with regard to lexical issues. Insights on lexical matters were freely voiced, whereupon a reciprocally fruitful interchange took place. This interchange was characterized by a commonly observable effort to integrate each other's insights into one's own discipline and to take account of the deficiencies, needs, and requirements that came to light.

The lexicon was rightfully defined as the major bottleneck for Natural Language Processing (NLP), and a clear statement emerged as a summary from a set of more detailed recommendations (see Walker et al, 1994; Zampolli 1987), according to which a priority was assigned to the design and development of "large, reusable, multifunctional, precompetitive, multilingual linguistic resources".

The concept of *reusability* of resources (see Calzolari, 1990) made its appearance, in both the sense of i) exploiting and reusing information implicitly present in pre-existing resources (even though designed for other purposes), and ii) constructing computational lexicons in such a way that various users, systems, and applications can extract - given appropriate interfaces - the relevant lexical information. The word *reusability* has become, since then, a key word in the field, applied in many different contexts, stressing the need for integration of results, and offering the possibility of building on each other's achievements.

The above recommendation can be viewed as providing the key words of the program and the set of coordinated actions which were both launched and promoted by the EC in the subsequent years. We mention here only those projects which, from our point of view, are closely connected to the type of recommendations stemming from the Grosseto Workshop, to give an idea of how the trend, begun there, has become more and more concrete and well-established.

The first two projects, directly connected to the two meanings of *reusability*, to be set up were the ESPRIT BRA ACQUILEX (see Calzolari,

Briscoe, 1993) and the ET-7 (see Heid, McNaught, 1991) projects, associated respectively to the first and second sense of *reusability* given above.

Other large European projects having as their objective or as background motivation the design or development of large, reusable resources are ESPRIT MULTILEX, EUREKA GENELEX, MLAP NERC, as well as a number of ET-10 and of LRE projects.

ET-7 in particular deserves mention. Its goal was to assess the feasibility of designing large scale, reusable lexical and terminological resources. A broad range of different possible sources of lexical material, and in particular of different applications requiring a lexical component, was carefully evaluated, focusing attention on different theoretical frameworks, different needs with respect to granularity of information, depth and coverage of description, and so on, providing an account, as far as it is possible to completely do so, of a variety of diverging needs.

An important observation, which led to a methodological recommendation for future actions towards developing shareable specifications for linguistic resources, was - stated in very simplistic terms - that different theories describe essentially the same facts, but make different generalizations and use different descriptive devices. The methodological claim derived from this was, on the one hand, to go back to the most fine-grained, observable differences/phenomena, i.e., to reach an extreme particularization of linguistic observations, and, on the other hand, to reach a complete explicitness of descriptive devices and to provide explicit and reproducible criteria for each observable difference taken into account. This shared layer of granular observations can constitute - appropriately recorded - a common data pool which accounts for minimal facts, tested according to decision trees, and possibly represented in typed feature based language. The global *reuse scenario* defined within ET-7 foresaw a data pool model composed of three major areas: acquisition, representation, and application. Within this layered architecture, the representation of lexical information is located on a level, which is interfaced on one side - through specific acquisition tools - to the potential sources of information, and on the other side - through a compiler/interpreter level which takes care of *recombining* specific descriptive devices and of filtering out relevant information - to specific Application Lexicons which need to provide application specific lexical descriptions.

It is clear that the role of ET-7 was fundamental in opening up a pathway to a programmatic implementation of the designed model.

Other converging motivations giving impetus to the flowering of so many projects on large linguistic resources arose from the existing situation in the lexical area in the early '90s. As is well known, for many years previous to the '80s, the role of the lexicon in NLP systems was given far less consideration than, for instance, the system's underlying processes.

With the shift from merely toy applications to professional real-world systems, the situation began to change. State-of-the-art applications rely on large-scale, real size lexicons able to incorporate more and more linguistic information. At the same time, NLP developers and researchers have realized that reiterate construction of system-dependent lexicons is costly and ineffective. Reusability of lexical resources has, therefore, become one of the leading paradigms in the R&D community.

Reusability, however, presupposes agreement on a *neutral* shared lexicon model and a language to represent such a model. Developing common specifications for lexical phenomena and for lexical representation is therefore crucial in order to i) pave the way towards the construction of commonly usable basic lexicons, ii) enable merging of lexical material developed in different sites and coming from different sources, and iii) create the conditions for developing common and publicly available dictionary tools based on the common model.

2   Setting up of EAGLES

The situation sketched above created the appropriate conditions for the launching, firstly, of a project definition study in 1992 (EEG, i.e., European Expert Group) and then, in February 1993, of a project aiming specifically at defining standards or preparing the ground for future standard provision. EAGLES (Expert Advisory Group on Language Engineering Standards) was launched in the framework of the CEC's DGXIII Linguistic Research and Engineering (LRE) program.

The areas of concern to EAGLES are text corpora, computational lexicons, grammar formalisms, evaluation and assessment, and spoken language. In each of the five EAGLES Working Groups (WG), leading experts of both the research and the industrial communities are represented, combining their efforts towards the development of a common basic European infrastructure and of agreed linguistic specifications.

2.1   General Mode of Operation of EAGLES

The basic idea behind EAGLES work is for the group to act as a catalyst in order to pool concrete results coming from current major European projects. The major efforts concentrate on the following types of activities, which, in this sequence, show how, on very general lines, the work is organized in all the five WGs. A schematic account of the general methodology of work is outlined below:

- surveying and assessing available proposals of shared specifications in order to evaluate the potential for harmonization, convergences, and emerging standards;

- assessing and discovering areas where there is a consensus about existing linguistic resources;

- detecting those areas ripe for short-term standardization vs. areas still in need of basic research and development;

- proposing common specifications for the core set of basic phenomena on which a consensus can be found;

- setting up guidelines for representation of core sets of basic features;

- performing feasibility studies for less mature areas;

- suggesting actions to be taken for a stepwise procedure leading to the creation of multilingual reusable resources.

In the following section, more details will be given concerning the Lexicon WG.

2.2   Towards Standards in the Lexical Area

The EAGLES Lexicon WG is obviously not starting from scratch. There are numerous projects on which it can build; some of them have been mentioned in Section 1.

2.2.1   The Survey Phase

The survey phase in the lexical area includes, for each level of linguistic description, an assessment of the following aspects:

- existing lexical categories and features according to the most prominent linguistic schools;

- linguistic phenomena to be described (taken from linguistic descriptions, existing lexicons, corpus analysis, etc.) according to the ET-7 methodology of reaching the layer of minimal granular distinctions;

- existing practices in NLP lexicons;

- formalisms for representation of lexical information;

- requirements of NLP applications.

The assessment phase must lead to an evaluation of

- the feasibility of building on and reusing previous work;

- areas not covered so far or in need of further work;

- the adequacy of what exists vis-a-vis linguistic schools.

2.2.2 The Proposal Phase

All the above parameters, and their interaction, are taken into account in the process of designing a common proposal for a core set of descriptive features which satisfy the requirements identified in the survey phase. In particular:

- For each of the proposed features, tests and reproducible criteria for linguistic classification have to be devised.

- An evaluation must be made of the benefits of defining a minimal level of linguistic encoding for a computational lexicon that can be considered reusable and that is conformant to EAGLES specifications. Such a level could then be employed in the evaluation of future lexicon building projects.

For some areas, such as Semantics, it is not realistic to commit to the development of concrete proposals for standards in the short term. Here a feasibility study may be appropriate, proposing - after an evaluation of the existing results in the area - a series of steps to be taken in order to try to arrive at an adequate consensus at least on specific topics.

For each level of linguistic description, the following aspects are examined:

- types of objects/units to be dealt with and to be distinguished (e.g., simple words, compounds, word senses, etc.),

- minimal observable distinctions,

- relevant categories, features, and values (examples, consistency criteria, and assignment tests must be provided),

- denotational devices and formalisms for representation,

- links to other linguistic levels.

Moreover, the applicability of the results to all European languages, or to a subset thereof, has to be pointed out.

3 Some Preliminary Results: the Morphosyntactic Area

This section will focus on - only as an exemplification - some preliminary results in one of the areas tackled by EAGLES in its first year of life. Work on Morphosyntax, both within the Lexicon and the Corpus WGs, has led to a preliminary proposal which will be presented in the First EAGLES Interim Report (Calzolari and McNaught, eds., forthcoming), and which is based on the contributions by Monachini and Calzolari (1994) and Leech (1993 and 1994).

The morphosyntactic area was more mature than the others, and therefore a lot of material was available for the Survey and Assessment phase. In particular, we must mention the extensive study already conducted within the NERC project by Monachini and Östling (1992a, 1992b), where the most common tagging practices were compared and evaluated and a consensual nucleus of morphosyntactic features among the different tagsets was clearly highlighted. Within EAGLES, the NERC survey was enlarged to cover the major European lexical projects (such as MULTILEX and GENELEX) as well as the TEI (Text Encoding Initiative) proposal for Morphosyntax Encoding.

The first EAGLES proposal, based on a careful analysis of existing practice consists, for each category/POS, of an enumeration of all the potentially relevant features (attributes and possible values) for a number of different European languages. The chosen overall organization is a multilayered structure, instead of a flat one, which gives more flexibility to the proposal and allows the user to choose the appropriate level of encoding (which may vary, e.g., according to different applications). There is only one *obligatory feature*, i.e. the POS itself. All the other features are arranged on different levels according to their status of *recommended*, *optional*, or *language-specific* features. The recommended features are a basic set of core features, which are not only commonly accepted and shared by existing tagsets and lexicons, but for which - most importantly - tools also exist that allow the easy encoding at this level. This was an important aspect to be evaluated when designing the hierarchy of features.

The proposed EAGLES features are being applied to a large number of European languages. Under these concrete applications, they are tested on real corpora and lexica. For each language, a complete overview of the language-specific way in which the common proposal is constrained is given, in terms of the selection of the applicable attribute-value pairs among the possible ones.

It is at this level of language specific instantiation of the EAGLES proposal that aspects of hierarchical organization of the features have to be handled: monotonicity can be looked for, relevant constraints have to be specified, and the range of pertinent values for an attribute has to be made explicit.

An important aspect to be stressed is the close interrelationship between the work in the two WGs on Lexicons and Corpora. The outcome of EAGLES work in these two areas (morphosyntactic lexical encoding and tagsets), as a result of the close cooperation between the two groups, is not only absolutely compatible, but the EAGLES tagset (see Leech 1994) - seen as one of the possible applications of a Computational Lexicon - is immediately derivable from the EAGLES lexical features. The interdependence between lexicon development and corpus analysis is an essential issue to be taken into due consideration in any future action aiming at creating lexicons and/or tagsets.

4 Interaction between EAGLES and other Projects

The EAGLES morphosyntactic proposal is already being applied - and consequently tested and evaluated - in a number of national and European projects, such as LRE DELIS and MULTEXT. This interaction - in both directions - between EAGLES, which is an infrastructural or horizontal type of action, and a large number of topic specific research and development projects and applications, is an essential component of the EAGLES overall work style.

Standards must emerge from state-of-the-art developments, and as such they are not to be imposed. Consolidation of a standard proposal must be viewed, by necessity, as a slow process and, by definition, as a non-innovative action, involving i) a detailed analysis of an existing situation, ii) a phase of putting forward proposals, iii) a careful evaluation by the scientific community of the recommendations with regard to concrete applications, and iv) feedback and readjustment of the proposal until a rather stable platform is reached, on which a real consensus - acquiring its meaning by real usage - is arrived at.

What can be defined as *new* in this long process is the highlighting of the consensual areas and the gradual consciousness of the stability acquired within the communities involved. A first benefit is the possibility for those entering the field of focusing their attention on not yet solved problems without losing time on rediscovering and reimplementing what many others have already acquired. This is the only way our discipline can really move forward, but this entire process is not without dangers or posssible objections.

Cautiousness and watchfulness, together with involvement of all the relevant actors in the field, are, therefore, important and intentional methodological tenets must be adhered to, particularly in this first phase of the EAGLES enterprise where the basic building blocks of a long and steady work are being formed.

References

[1] N. Calzolari: "Lexical databases and textual corpora: perspectives of integration for a Lexical Knowledge-Base". In: U. Zernik (ed.): Lexical Acquisition: Exploiting On-line Resources to Build a Lexicon. Laurence Erlbaum, 1990, pp. 191-208.

[2] N. Calzolari, T. Briscoe: "ACQUILEX-I and -II: Acquisition of Lexical Knowledge from Machine-Readable Dictionaries and Text Corpora". In: A. Zampolli, N. Varile (eds.): Proceedings of the COLING-92 International Project Day, forthcoming, and Acquilex Working Paper, Pisa, 1993.

[3] N. Calzolari, J. McNaught (eds.): "EAGLES Second Progress Report". Internal report, November 1993.

[4] N. Calzolari, J. McNaught (eds.): "EAGLES Interim Report". Internal report, forthcoming.

[5] N. Calzolari, A. Zampolli: "Lexical Databases and Textual Corpora: a Trend of Convergence between Computational Linguistics and Literary and Linguistic Computing". In S. Hockey, N. Ide, (eds.): Research in Humanities Computing. Oxford: Oxford University Press 1991, pp. 273-307.

[6] GENELEX Consortium: "Couche syntaxique. Les unites syntaxique simple". Tome 1, Version 3.0, ASSTRIL, Gsi-Erli, IBM France, SEMA GROUP, September 1993.

[7] U. Heid, J. Mcnaught (eds.): "Eurotra-7 Study: Feasibility and Project Definition Study on the Reusability of Lexical and Terminological Resources in Computerised Applications". Eurotra-7 Final Report, Stuttgart, 1991.

[8] G. Leech: "Draft partial report on task 3: Assessment of of recommendations for linguistic annotation. Subtask 3.1 Assessment of recommendations for Morphosyntax level". Draft technical report, Lancaster, December 1993. EAG-CSG-T3.5.

[9] G. Leech, A. Wilson: "Tagset guidelines". Draft technical report. Lancaster, December 1993. EAG-CSG-T3.3.

[10] G. Leech, A. Wilson: "A morphosyntactic tagset for English, making use of the guidelines of the Pisa document". EAGLES Technical Report, Lancaster, 1994.

[11] Lexicon Working Group: "WG Computational Lexicon Workplan". Internal Report, Pisa, 1993. EAG-LWG-WP.

[12] M. Monachini, N. Calzolari: "Synopsis and Comparison of Morphosyntactic Phenomena Encoded in Lexicons and Corpora and Applications to European Languages". Draft Technical Report, ILC Pisa, January, 1994. EAG-LSG-T4.6/CSG-T3.2.

[13] M. Monachini, A. Östling: "Morphosyntactic corpus annotation - a comparison of different schemes". Technical report, ILC Pisa, September 1992. NERC-WP8-60.

[14] M. Monachini, A. Östling: "Towards a minimal standard for morphosyntactic corpus annotation". Technical report, ILC Pisa, September 1992. NERC-WP8-61.

[15] MULTILEX Consortium: "Standards for multifunctional lexicon". CAP GEMINI, Philips, University of Surrey, University of Bochum, University of Münster, April 1993.

[16] TEI AI 1W2: "List of common morphological feature for inclusion in TEI starter set of grammatical-annotation tags". June 1991.

[17] D. Walker, A. Zampolli, N. Calzolari (eds.): "Automating the Lexicon: Research and Practice in a Multilingual Environment". Proceedings of a Workshop held in Grosseto, Oxford: Oxford University Press 1994.

[18] A. Zampolli: "Perspectives for an Italian Multifunctional Lexical Database". In: A. Zampolli, A. Cappelli, A. Cipriani, C. Peters (eds.): Studies in Honour of Roberto Busa S. J. Linguistica Computazionale. VI, 1987, pp. 301-41.

Machine Translation and Terminology Database -
Uneasy Bedfellows ?

Machine Translation Group
- compiled by Katharina Koch[*] -
SAP AG
Neurottstr. 16
69190 Walldorf, Germany

Abstract. The software company SAP translates its documentation into more than 12 languages. To support the translation department, SAPterm is used as a traditional terminology database for all languages, and the machine translation system METAL for German-to-English translation. The maintenance of the two terminology databases in parallel, SAPterm and the METAL lexicons, requires a comparison of the entries in order to ensure terminological consistency. However, due to the differences in the structure of the entries in SAPterm and METAL, an automatic comparison has not yet been implemented. The search for a solution has led to the consideration of using another existing SAP tool, called Proposal Pool.

1 Introduction

SAP is a German software company that operates internationally, producing standard software for processing business data in application areas ranging from Financial Accounting and Materials Management to Human Resources. The company was founded in 1972 and currently employs some 3,500 people world-wide.

At present, SAP offers two product lines: the R/2 System and the R/3 System. The R/2 System is a strategic product for use in the technical environment of mainframe computers, whereas the R/3 System supports a three-level client-server concept in which database servers, application servers, and presentation servers work in LAN/WAN connections.

[*] My thanks go to Jennifer Brundage, Daniel Grasmick and Dirk Lüke whose cooperation in writing this article was invaluable.

The main application areas common to R/2 and R/3 include Asset Management, Financial Accounting, Financial Controlling, Materials Management, Plant Maintenance, Production Planning, Quality Assurance, Human Resources, and Sales & Distribution. The R/3 System additionally includes a number of industry solutions and further applications, such as the Project System.

The documentation on the SAP application modules is mostly written in German and translated into more than 12 languages. The translation volume is not the same for all languages. While all documentation - that is, online documentation, manuals, training materials, etc. - is translated into English, only the online documentation and the training materials are translated into other languages, such as French; and for a few languages, e.g., Danish, only the user interface is translated. SAP documentation in German comprises about 1 million lines of online documentation for R/2, 2 million lines for R/3 and altogether more than 1 GB of paper documentation.

SAP's translation department is organized in service groups: the translation service with individual groups for each language and the machine translation group (MT group).

The translation service comprises about 90 translators. There are 40 translators for German-to-English translations alone. The other 50 translate from German into French, Spanish, Italian, Portuguese, Russian, Dutch, Danish, Swedish, Norwegian, Japanese, etc. Translators of languages for which the translation volume is particularly high specialize in one application area. For the other languages, one translator is often responsible for several applications. To support their terminological work, all translators maintain and use SAPterm as a terminology database (TDB).

The MT group is made up of 5 full-time translators, who use the MT system METAL in order to provide the specialized translators with roughly post-edited machine translations and the SAP subsidiaries with preliminary versions of SAP manuals in English. At present, METAL is used productively for the language pair German-English; the English-German version is being tested. The METAL system is centrally maintained and controlled by the MT group, working closely together with the specialized translators as regards the definition of English equivalents of the German source terminology.

With two terminology databases, SAPterm and the METAL lexicons, the problem of terminological inconsistency arises. In the following, terminology maintenance at SAP with SAPterm on the one hand and METAL on the other hand is described. The emphasis of these sections is on the description of the structure of entries in SAPterm and METAL. Then, the difficulties in comparing SAPterm entries with METAL entries and thus in keeping the terminology databases consistent are shown. Afterwards, the SAP Proposal Pool, a translation memory used for the translation of the user interface of the SAP R/3 System, is presented. Finally, a program is introduced which allows an automatic comparison of the entries in the Proposal Pool with METAL entries.

2 Terminology Maintenance Using SAPterm

Since SAP not only produces but also translates its documentation in-house, there is a great need for a tool to guarantee terminological accuracy, consistency, and therefore quality. SAPterm is such a tool. It is not only a traditional terminology database, but also an integrated part of the SAP R/3 System and can be used for a number of purposes:

- Documentation developers, as SAP calls its technical writers, use SAPterm as a spell checker for online documentation and as a terminology checker to ensure that only authorized terms are used.
- Translators use SAPterm as a TDB for maintaining and looking up application-specific terminology.
- The SAP Enterprise Model, an information model representing the entities of a company and the relationships between these entities, is also part of SAPterm. It is stored under a separate path.
- Finally, SAPterm with its modular storing concept enables glossary definitions to be retrieved and displayed in F1 help throughout the SAP R/3 System.

SAPterm supports all languages used at SAP. It is implemented on the same relational database as the SAP R/3 System and the information it contains can be accessed by all SAP employees world-wide. It has been in use now for two years and currently contains some 15,000 German-English entries. It is based on a master language concept, the master language being German: target language entries are always made with reference to the German source entry. However, it is possible to display SAPterm entries in any possible language combination. It is also possible to print out multilingual dictionaries. In addition, there is an interface for the import and export of entries.

The structure of a SAPterm entry consists of two parts: linguistic information and administrative information.

The linguistic information part contains the following fields:

- head word
- semantic description of the head word
- abbreviations
- authorized short forms
- synonyms (these are unauthorized and can be identified by the terminology checker)

- relation between terms
- contexts
- reference specifications
- application-specific glossary definitions
- comments

The only field that is mandatory is the head word; all other fields are optional. Depending on the authorization of the individual user, all fields can be searched for. The specialized translators with display and maintenance authorization cannot search for the field *contexts, reference specifications, application-specific glossary definition* and *comments*. In order to be able to search for these fields, more extensive authorizations are required.

The administrative part of the SAPterm entry contains information that is automatically specified by the system, such as a quality indicator, which is relevant for the internal administration of the entries, the name of the person who created and who last changed the entry, and the dates of these actions.

The maintenance of SAPterm entries is not the task of the translators alone. German terminology and the information on it is entered into the database by the documentation developers. The translators then enter the translation and information for these terms with reference to a specific language and application.

3 Terminology Maintenance Using METAL

The steadily increasing volume of documentation at SAP made it necessary to look for alternatives to cope with the translation bottleneck. It was expected that the volume of documentation would increase by 30% when the new product R/3 was launched in 1992. In May 1990, the decision was therefore taken to introduce the MT system METAL. After a test and preparation phase, during which the suitability of SAP texts for machine translation was examined, the METAL lexicon built up and tools developed to establish a link between the SAP R/3 System and METAL, the system for German-to-English translation became productive in October 1991. Nearly all types of text at SAP can be translated using METAL, such as online documentation (screen texts, hypertext, F1 help texts), manuals, training material, etc.

Today, the METAL lexicon contains 45,000 SAP-specific German-English entries in addition to the 40,000 entries that were delivered with the system.

Unlike SAPterm, the METAL system is not implemented on a relational database, but a database system specially developed for multilingual applications. Its entries can only be accessed by members of the MT group and are therefore not a central source of information at SAP.

3.1 The METAL Lexicon

The METAL lexicon is subdivided into three individual lexicons: the German monolingual lexicon, the English monolingual lexicon and the German-English bilingual lexicon, called "transfer lexicon".

METAL Monolingual Entries

Monolingual METAL entries contain grammatical, syntactical, and semantic information on a term, which is much more extensive than the information included in SAPterm entries. This "extra" information is required to allow METAL to analyze the source text and to generate the target text correctly.

The grammatical, syntactical, and semantic information required by the system depends on the grammatical category of the entry. Examples of grammatical information required by METAL and not included in SAPterm are the specification of a verb frame defining all the possible arguments of the verb in question, and the singular and plural forms of a noun. Syntactical information includes, e.g., the definition of article usage. The article usage of English nouns can be controlled by specifying whether the definite article is required when the noun is used as a subject or after a preposition. Another example of syntactical information concerns English adverbs and specifies whether the adverb is to be placed before or after the verb. Semantic information only has to be provided for nouns: the user chooses one or more possible semantic types from a list of 15 different possibilities, such as *abstract, concrete, human, animal, process.*

METAL Transfer Entries

The METAL transfer entries establish the link between the monolingual entries of two languages and determine the desired target language entry for the source language entry for a particular application area. Thus, the transfer entries are essentially canonical word pairs. However, an entry is not made with a specific context as is the case for traditional TDBs. If the user wants to restrict the translation to a particular context, context information can be specified by means of so-called tests and transformations within the entry. With this function, the translation of *zur Verfügung stehen* can be defined as *to be available*, for example.

4 Problems in Comparing METAL and SAPterm Entries

As can be concluded from the above description, it is very difficult to compare the entries in SAPterm and METAL *automatically*. Up to now, it has in fact only been possible to *manually* compare the entries in the form of lists. Even then, the METAL entries containing tests and transformations cannot be used in the comparison, because this information is not included when creating simple lists of entries. The main difficulties in comparing the two TDBs result from different entry structures and the different maintenance and management procedures.

4.1 Difference in the Structure of Entries

The structure of METAL entries and SAPterm entries differs considerably. The minimum information that SAPterm requires is the head word. METAL, however, requires much more information, and this always has to be specified in full. In addition, the way terms are coded in METAL sometimes differs from the way terms are entered in SAPterm. Some examples of these differences are given below.

Adjectives and Nouns

Nouns modified by an adjective can be coded in METAL either as a noun entry with a test on the adjective or as one string. Since the information on context tests in METAL cannot be printed out, the MT group at SAP decided to code entries of this type in one string, as this is usually done in traditional TDBs as well. However, METAL requires, for example, the form *prozentuale Wert*, whereas SAPterm uses the form *Wert, prozentualer*.

Verbs With Separable Prefixes

In METAL, verbs with separable prefixes are entered in the infinitive form with a blank between the prefix and the verb stem to indicate to the system that the prefix is separable, for example, *ein geben*. SAPterm entries, on the other hand, specify the infinitive form of the verb without a blank, for example, *eingeben*.

Past or Present Participles Used as Adjectives

German present or past participles used as adjectives with a "real" adjective as an equivalent in the target language require a separate entry in SAPterm. Here is an example of such an entry: *bestimmt => specific*. In METAL, the entry is made on the basis of the verb entry (the German verb *bestimmen* in the example), which contains all the inflected forms of the verb, with a test on the use of the verb as past or present participle. In cases where the equivalent of the German participle is also a participle, no entry at all is needed. METAL automatically generates the requested translation.

Tests and Transformations

Translations that only apply in certain contexts are dealt with differently in METAL and SAPterm. In SAPterm, the term is entered with the context, whereas METAL integrates the context information into the entry using tests and transformations. The entry *ablaufen, dunkel => run in the background, to* is an example of a SAPterm entry. The same entry in METAL would be *ab laufen => run* associated with a test and a transformation telling the system to add *in the background* if the verb *ablaufen* is modified by the adverb *dunkel*.

4.2 Differences in Maintaining and Managing Entries

SAPterm is used above all as a source of information for translators and users of the SAP R/3 System. METAL, on the other hand, is used only for machine translation. The METAL lexicons need to be maintained to ensure that a given document can be translated correctly. As the two databases are not maintained for the same purposes, different maintenance strategies have been adopted. As a result, SAPterm and the METAL lexicons differ considerably in the number of entries. Examples of these maintenance strategies are given below:

- While SAPterm only contains entries that the translators believe are important and specific to their application area, the METAL lexicon *must* include all the terms a document contains. Otherwise, the system will not produce a correct translation. Thus, the MT group codes all terms not included in the METAL lexicons on the basis of lists of unknown words that the system creates after having analyzed the source text. This is one of the reasons why METAL contains a much larger number of entries than SAPterm.

- Another reason is that METAL includes more compounds than SAPterm. If a compound is not coded, it is nevertheless translated, providing its simplicia are known to the system. METAL thus generates the translation from the translation of the individual components stored in the lexicon. If this generated translation is correct, coding of the compound is not required. However, it is advisable to do so to avoid the generated translation of the compound from becoming incorrect if the translation of one simplex changes.

- Due to the hierarchical organization of the subject areas in METAL and the search sequence of the system, the METAL lexicon will always contain more entries than SAPterm. For example, if both METAL and SAPterm contain a very specific entry for a particular subapplication, the METAL system requires an additional, more general entry on a higher level of the subject area hierarchy.

This wide discrepancy between the number of entries makes a comparison even more difficult. Too many METAL entries do not have a corresponding entry in SAPterm.

The technical management of SAPterm entries is another factor hindering the terminological consistency of the two TDBs. Entries deleted from SAPterm do not receive a delete flag, but are physically deleted from the database. This means that the METAL group can only find out about entries which have been deleted in SAPterm, if they are informed by the translators. The same applies to changes made to SAPterm entries. If an entry is changed in SAPterm, it is not automatically changed in METAL. However, it is possible to extract all SAPterm entries that have been changed after a certain date. Since this check for changed entries is not run on a daily basis, it may take some time for changes to be carried out in METAL.

5 SAP Proposal Pool

An automatic comparison tool between SAPterm and the METAL lexicons has not yet been implemented. In the search for a possible solution, the option of using another existing SAP tool was considered: the so-called SAP proposal pool. It is a string-for-string translation memory that is fully integrated into the SAP R/3 online translation tools. A string can consist of a character, a word, or a full sentence. The proposal pool is used not only for German-to-English translation, but for all language pairs.

At the moment, the proposal pool is used solely for translating the user interface - that is, screen fields, menus, error messages, table and module titles. In translating these text elements, the tool is extremely efficient, because these texts are characterized by a high degree of repetition. For example, the SAP R/3 System contained more than 1 million screen entries for Release 2.1, but only 400,000 were stored in the proposal pool, which meant that the remaining 600,000 were identical with an existing entry.

5.1 Working With the SAP Proposal Pool

The proposal pool is subdivided into several subpools, one for each SAP application module (e.g., Financial Accounting (FI), Materials Management (MM), etc.). Before translators can start translating the user interface texts, they have to run a program which extracts the text parts for a specific application area. The result of this extraction is stored in the so-called work list. For each group of entries in this work list, the translators then access the proposal subpool of the corresponding application area (e.g., Financial Accounting). Strings for which a translation is available in the proposal pool are automatically replaced by their target language equivalent. If no translation has been defaulted, the translators can choose entries from a related area (e.g., Cost Accounting).

The strings remaining without a default translation have to be translated manually. When saving these translations, the proposal pool is automatically updated. This way, the subpools are constantly being added to, and working with the proposal pool becomes more and more efficient. Each time entries are stored, they are checked against existing entries in the proposal pool. If an entry is made that differs from an existing translation in the pool, the system will ask the translator to react in one of three ways. The translator may either

- change the entry and accept the pool entry, or
- change the pool entry, or
- define his entry as an exception for a specific screen.

5.2 Advantages of the SAP Proposal Pool

Using the SAP proposal pool has several advantages. It ensures terminological consistency across the user interface, especially when many translators are working in the same application area. It saves the translators tedious typing effort and therefore reduces the risk of typing errors. Translation with the proposal pool is at least twice as fast as conventional human translation, because it reduces the time required for typing and looking up terminology. Statistics have shown that about two thirds of the translated interface texts came from the pool. As access is very quick, working with the proposal pool is also a lot faster than the machine translation process since no time is needed for extracting, transferring, converting, and correcting files. The proposal pool can also be used for making changes throughout the system.

Obviously, these advantages mean a gain in productivity and an increase in quality.

5.3 The SAP Proposal Pool and the Benefits for METAL

Strings in the proposal pool are "real life" entries, i.e., they are closer to the system development than a TDB since they are actually used in the system.

To be able to use the information contained in the proposal pool and to allow the METAL system to benefit from it, SAP has developed a tool which makes it possible to compare proposal pool entries with METAL entries. This tool works as follows:

It extracts entries for a selected SAP application area from the proposal pool and creates two sequential files. One file contains the German entries and their English equivalents (as stored in the pool) and the second file contains only the German entries. The latter is sent to the METAL system for translation. Afterwards, the tool compares the translated file with the original file from the proposal pool and creates a third file with a list of entries that are different. On the basis of this list, new lexical entries are added to the METAL system or existing entries are changed.

6 Conclusion

The preceding sections have shown that SAP uses three different tools for terminology maintenance and translation: SAPterm, METAL, and the SAP proposal pool. Since these are different databases without any interconnection, they must be maintained in parallel. This can, of course, result in terminological inconsistencies. The ultimate solution to this problem would be to implement all these tools on a common database. For this purpose, the different tools would have to be adapted with respect to hardware and software requirements.

Currently, no commercial product is available on the market offering such an integrated solution. As long as producers of translation tools do not provide such a package, it is left up to the users to find a possibility of combining the individual products and techniques, e.g., terminology database, machine translation, and translation memory.

At SAP, the rapidly increasing number of entries in SAPterm and METAL means that it has become almost impossible to perform a comparison manually. As an intermediate solution, SAP is therefore planning to develop and implement a semi-automatic comparison tool for SAPterm and METAL. Comparison with such a tool necessitates the structural adaptation of existing METAL and SAPterm entries so as to create a common comparison and exchange format. As a project of this nature requires extensive knowledge of the internal structure of METAL entries, the implementation of this tool will have to be carried out by SAP in cooperation with the developer of the METAL system.

A Generic Lexical Model

Daniel BACHUT, Isabelle DUQUENNOY, Lee HUMPHREYS,
Tita KYRIAKOPOULOU, Anne MONCEAUX, Fiammetta NAMER[1],
Jean-Michel OMBROUCK[2], Claire PERREY, Anne PONCET-MONTANGE,
Maria-Claudia PUERTA, Caroline RAFFY, Brigitte ROUDAUD, Simon SABBAGH[3]

EUROLANG - SONOVISION ITEP-TECHNOLOGIES
BP 35 94701 Maisons Alfort Cedex
FRANCE

Abstract. Linguistic engineering presupposes lexical resources. For translation, it is highly desirable that a Machine Translation engine and human translators should have access to the same dictionary information. The present paper describes a multilingual dictionary model, which integrates information for use by both humans and a variety of NLP systems. The model is used as a reference in the design of commercial translation products.

1 Introduction

Consider some of the functionalities that might be offered by a translator or multilingual terminologists' workbench:

- multilingual spell checking with intelligent replacement proposals

- multilingual grammar checking (e.g., subject-verb agreement)

- controlled language conformance checking

- on-line access to a source language dictionary

- on-line access to a target language dictionary

- on-line access to a source-target bilingual dictionary

- construction, updating, and on-line access to multilingual terminology

- checking for consistent usage of terms in a text

- tools for identifying possible terms in texts/corpora

- automatic insertion of term/non-term translations in texts

- full machine translation of text

All these functions make use of lexical resources. Clearly these resources should be shared rather than separately supplied for each function. If lexical resources are not

---

1. Département de Linguistique, Université de Nancy, France
2. CNET, Lannion, France
3. Current address: GSI-ERLI, Paris, France

shared, the same information may be repeated in several function-specific lexicons (redundancy); there will also be arbitrary and unnecessary conflicts of lexical information.

The present paper describes a multilingual lexical data model which is designed to allow humans and NLP applications to share one and the same lexical resource. We have attempted to ensure that

- information used by humans and MT systems can be adequately represented

- lexical information is not strongly tied to any particular theory

- lexical information for different European languages can be consistently represented

- lexical information is fully-factorised, i.e., information such as morphology can be shared by sets of entries

- both general vocabulary and technical terms can be represented

The model was specifically designed for industrial language technology applications.

Initial work by the authors at EUROLANG was inspired by a number of key aspects of the MULTILEX model [1] - in particular, the factorisation of phonological and morphological information. However, at the time the work started, many parts of the MULTILEX model were incomplete; moreover, the model did not provide everything needed for MT support. For these reasons, the authors were obliged to create a new model with many new features, whilst conserving major aspects of the MULTILEX model.

The initial model produced over a 6 month period by the authors is known as the Reference Model. In a subsequent phase, a simplified version - the Operational Model - was developed with a view to simplifying the eventual engineering task.

In the present paper we present an overview of ideas present in both models. For reasons of space, detailed presentation of the linguistic feature sets has been avoided.

2 Sense vs Form

Dictionaries for humans are normally sense-based; that is, headwords carry indices indicating homographs and polysemes (sub-senses). Each homograph and sub-sense carries a definition.

It is highly desirable to maintain this structure in electronic dictionaries since (amongst other things) this allows full semantic cross-referencing.

Unfortunately, many commercial MT systems with which we are familiar have monolingual lexicons based on headword forms without sense distinctions. For example, the METAL [2] entry for the French verb *aborder* contains no sub-sense structure; subsenses are only implicitly identified in the transfer lexicon by tests on context where translation into a particular language absolutely requires that a particular usage must be identified. When *aborder* takes a person as its object, it translates into English as *approach*; when it takes an abstract object, it translates as *tackle* as in *tackle a problem*.

A standard monolingual French paper dictionary such as "Le Robert" clearly distinguishes these two contexts as sub-senses; in the METAL monolingual French dictionary this remains at best implicit.

The lack of explicit sense distinctions in MT monolingual dictionaries is justified on grounds of efficiency; introducing distinctions results in many more arcs in the parse chart. These extra arcs present ambiguities which may be difficult to remove in analysis and which may not correspond to a change in word form in translation.

Since the model we developed is sense-based, we have been obliged to spend considerable effort to ensure that this representation can be rapidly converted (perhaps in real-time) into its morphology-based equivalent for an MT system using the lexicon as a client application. This conversion in general involves collapsing the information contained in several Lexical Entries (see below) into a subsuming MT entry. For reasons of space, such conversion/compilation questions are not treated here.

3   Modelling Principles

We concentrate on a presentation of the principal Entities and Relations in the model and the linguistic/lexicographic justifications for the choices we have made. We have not attempted to describe the relational database implementation of the model and its user interfaces.

Although some basic linguistic constraints are enforced by the Entity-Relation structure of the model, additional constraints within and between entity instances can be specified. For example, inside the SYNTAX entity one could specify that only abstract (non-concrete) nouns can have complements.

Whilst the Entity-Relation set could be extended to directly model such constraints, the use of external constraints has a practical interest: the linguist/lexicographer can continue to add constraints to the implemented lexical database without thereby forcing system re-engineering.

4   The Lexical Entry

The principal organising element of our dictionary is the Lexical Entry (LE). Ideally, it is semantically unambiguous; however, in taking into account the fact that creating lexical resources for several languages is extremely time-consuming, we have allowed for the possibility that the LE can be used also to model sense-ambiguous entries recovered by automatic methods from existing MT-based lexical resources. Indeed, we have envisaged the situation where the same lexicon may provisionally contain both sense-distinguished and sense-ambiguous LEs; the latter would be progressively split by semi-automatic methods into sense-distinguished LEs as lexicographic resources become available.

An individual LE instance is composed of instances of the following units or modules:

- grapho-phono-morphological (GPMU)

- syntax

- semantics
- pragmatics
- process (control information for NLP systems - not discussed in this paper)

Monolingually, relational information is expressed by cross-references between elements. These cross-references can be between

- LEs
- SEMANTICS

Cross-references between LEs can be used to record word-level links such as free-variant forms. Cross-references between SEMANTICS can be used to record semantic or conceptual relations, such as hyperonymy. Each cross-reference can carry various pieces of information (a name, reflexivity/transitivity/symmetry properties, and so on).

Multilingually, relational information is grouped in the transfer module. A source LE is associated with one or several target LEs. These transfer links are multi-bilingual and one-way (irreversible).

The LE object in Fig. 1 must be seen as a central node giving access to the various types of lexical or even terminological information. For example, the relations between GPMU and syntax necessarily occur via the LE. There is no direct link between GPMU and syntax.

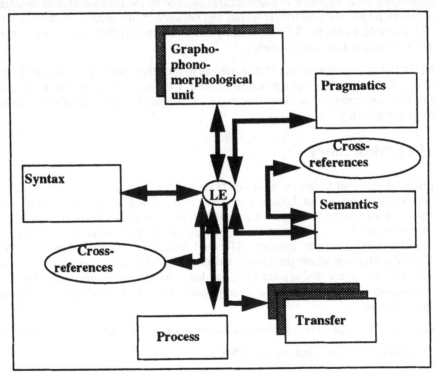

Figure 1 : Outline of LE Architecture

For presentation purposes, the architecture as shown in this figure is slightly simplified. The LE is identified by

- a character string (lemma)
- an identification number (usually interpreted as a **sense** number)
- the language in which the LE occurs
- an attribute with the type of the LE (i.e., "term" or "general word")
- an attribute specifying the grammatical category

The relationship of the LE to other entities is shown in Section 10 DATA MODEL.

4.1 The Individuation of LEs

LEs are individuated by classical lexicographic criteria:

Grammatical Category and Subcategory

> **Different LEs for homographic nouns and adjectives**
>
> *abricot, N (= the fruit "apricot")*
> *abricot, Adj inv (= the colour "apricot")*
>
> **Different LEs for homographic adverbs**
>
> *naturally, Adv-Clausal (Naturally, as a beginner, Jack was useless).*
>
> *naturally, Adv-Phrase (Even the benzene in Perrier occurs naturally).*

Morphology

Words which have different *canonical forms* have different LEs regardless of semantic considerations:

> *pregnant, Adj*
>
> *expectant (3), Adj (= pregnant)*

Gender and number constitute a criterion for separating LEs to the extent that they constitute a criterion for separating GPMUs (see Morphology Model):

> *DE der Leiter, die Leiter (= leader)*
> *DE die Leiter, die Leitern (= scale)*
>
> *FR bois, Nms (= wood)*
> *FR bois, Nmp (= woodwind instruments)*
>
> *FR oeil, yeux (= eye, eyes)*
> *FR oeil, oeils (des oeils-de-boeuf) (= bull's eye window(s))*

Frame Differences

Frequently - *but not necessarily* - variations in syntactic behaviour signal a variation in sense and hence the need for several rather than 1 LE.

Using syntactic criteria to separate meanings applies in particular to predicative words, which determine the simple sentence structure and argument types. For example, the French verb *louer* may be inserted into each of the following three syntactic frames :

louer (1) :

> *C0hum louer C1hum de C2*
>
> *Max loue Marie de sa réussite*
>
> *(= Max praises Marie for her success)*

louer (2) :

> *C0hum louer C1*
>
> *Max a loué une place d'opéra*
>
> *(= Max booked a seat at the opera)*

louer (3) :

> *C0hum louer C1 à C2hum*
>
> *Max loue un garage à Marie*
>
> *(= Max rents a garage to Marie)*

The situation is in fact more complex than this. The French verb *louer (3)* itself covers two distinguishable meanings, which are reflected by the translation into German:

louer (3) :

> *Max vermietet eine Garage an Marie (= Max rents a garage to Marie)*

louer (4) :

> *Max mietet eine Garage von Marie (= Max rents a garage from Marie)*

The morphological verb *louer*, therefore, corresponds to at least 4 lexical units. It is important to realise here that

- one syntactic frame may cover two distinct senses (reflecting different roles of the participants in the *louer* example). Only three of the senses are distinguishable on syntactic criteria.

- where two LEs are postulated on semantic grounds, the two distinct senses must be discoverable independently of translational criteria. LEs are established on monolingual grounds.

By contrast, variation in a syntactic frame does not necessarily signal a change in sense. Recall the familiar dative shift example:

> *John gave the book to Mary*
>
> *John gave Mary the book*

The only difference between these two is in focus. Hence we have only one LE; the frame alternation is recorded either by a feature or (equivalently) by assigning two surface frames.

Semantic Features

Different meanings which are reflected by different features:

> *FR une souris [N - animate] (= a mouse (computing))*
> *FR une souris [N +animate] (= a mouse (animal))*
>
> *a pound (N unit of measurement)*
> *a pound (N monetary unit)*

Sex

Where different forms signal differences in the sex of the referent, there are separate LEs:

> *emperor* (i.e., man who rules an empire)
>
> *empress* (1) (i.e., wife of emperor)
>
> *empress* (2) (i.e., woman who rules an empire)

Note that the two different senses of *empress* correspond to two different LEs. The relationship between *emperor* and *empress* is given by cross references.

5 Semantics

The SEMANTICS entity contains the *definition* of one or more words.

The model allows SEMANTICS to be *monolingual* or *multilingual*[1]. Monolingual SEMANTICS only point to LEs in one single language; multilingual SEMANTICS point to LEs in more than one language.

In this section we consider the individuation criteria for instances of the SEMANTICS entity.

5.1 Synonyms

An instance of SEMANTICS may be shared by several different LEs since morphologically independent words can share exactly the same definition. In each of the following, the two members of the synonym pair share the same SEMANTICS instance:

- standard synonyms
  measuring tape <---> tape measure

- register synonyms
  marsh gas <--> methane
  chemise <--> liquette

- dialect synonyms
  bonnet (UK) <--> hood (US)

---

1. e.g.,for terminological work

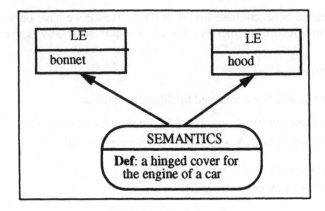

Figure 2 : Example of SEMANTICS linking two synonymous LEs

5.2 Terminology and the Concept of Concept

Terminology is usually based around the guiding proposition that terms are associated with concepts, and that concepts belong to a given domain of activity. Concepts carry definitions. Semantically co-referential terms share the same concept.

The terminologists' notion of concept can be directly modelled in by the SEMANTICS entity. Semantic or conceptual relations other than strict synonymy can be represented by the cross-reference components of the model which link SEMANTICS instances to create a conceptual network.

5.3 Grammatical Words

Grammatical words cannot easily be attributed a semantic definition. If a definition cannot be supplied for a grammatical word, the SEMANTICS will be empty. Nonetheless, the LEs for grammatical words share the same structure as those for content words.

Keeping grammatical words as LEs is empirically justified since in at least some cases they have a fixed translation (and/or syntax):

> *Pron : FR mien(ne)(s) -> EN mine*
> *Det : FR la plupart de -> EN most of*

6 GPMUs

GPMUs and CGPMUs (= Complex GPMUs) record information on morphology and pronunciation.

The inflection code gives access to the information necessary to construct the appropriate surface forms of the specified word. For example, the code N21 corresponds to a class of feminine nouns whose plural is formed by adding *s* to the end of the word, eg.

> *FR clef Nfs (= key) --> clefs Nfp (= keys)*

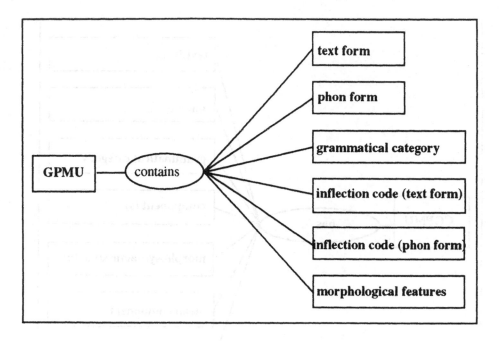

Figure 3 : Outline structure of GPMU

Since the same morphological and phonological unit can be associated with different senses and syntaxes, GPMUs can be shared between LEs. Thus, given that FR *apprendre*(1) with the sense "teach" and *apprendre*(2) with the sense "learn" share the same morphology, we have:

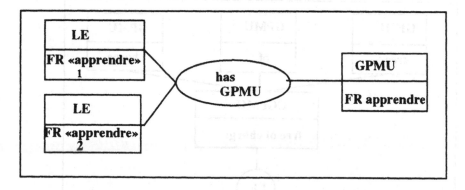

Figure 4 : Sharing of a GPMU instance by two LE instances: FR *apprendre*

A CGPMU is a variety of GPMU used to encode multiword units (compounds, idioms, fixed expressions, etc). CGPMUs point to their component GPMUs. That is, there are pointers from component morphemes in a CGPMU to the GPMUs that encode those morphemes. These component links allow inflection to be "inherited" by the complex expression from its component parts.

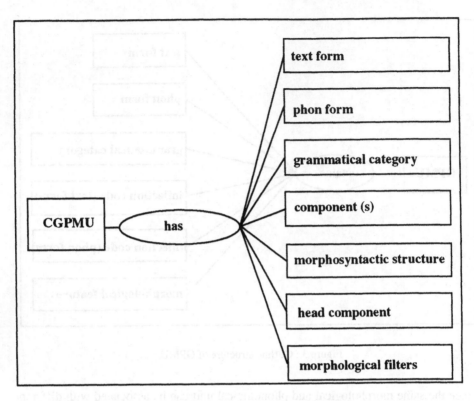

Figure 5 : Outline structure of a Complex GPMU

Thus the EN multiword *free of charge* is represented:

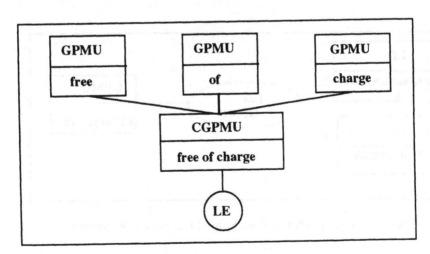

Figure 6 : Example of a Complex GPMU

The morphosyntactic structure attribute for this example would be the sequence *Adj Prep Noun*. Such a value can be used for default calculation of flexional properties.

Some CGPMUs contain morphemes which have no individual independent realisation. Such composants are usually semantically empty:

> *au fur et à mesure (= e.g., gradually, as one goes along)*

> *aujourd'hui (= today)*

> *prendre la poudre d' escampette (= to take to one's heels)*

These units are encoded with GPMUs which are only ever realised indirectly as components of a CGPMU. For this reason the relation GPMU -->LE is 0,N rather than 1,N.

Most CGPMU instances do not have a flexional code themselves; components inherit their flexional properties from their source GPMUs. Certain constraints on flexion that occur inside the CGPMU are handled by morphological filter features. Such features can be used to specify, for example, that the noun *fluide* in *FR mécanique des fluides* is always in the plural form.

6.1 Canonical Form and Variants

There are cases where the lexicographer wants to recognise that two forms having the same definition, although not morphologically identical, are sufficiently similar to be regarded as variant forms. Each variant form is recorded as a separate LE. The set of variants are cross-referenced by LE to LE links of type VARIANT. LEs in a variant group necessarily share the same SYNTAX and SEMANTICS. However, they differ in GPMU (obligatorily) and PRAGMATICS (optionally).

For single word forms, we have at least the following types of variants:

- **Free Spelling Variant**

  Variants which have the same pronunciation but slightly different spelling.

  bistrot <---> bistro

- **Conditioned Spelling Variant**

  Spelling variants which are pragmatically constrained or conditioned.

  colour <---> color (-> American versus British spelling)

  dog <---> doggie (-> baby-talk name for dog)

  bookmaker <---> bookie (-> informal name for bookmaker)

- **Reduction (Abbreviation, etc.)**

  receiver ---> RCVR

The underlying criterion for recognising a variant of a single word form is that both forms having the same definition share essentially the same stem.

For *multiword* forms, we have at least the following types of variants:

- **Permutation**

  à temps plein <---> à plein temps (= full time)

- **Head Shift**

  bowler hat ---> bowler

- **Reduction to Head**

  motor car ---> car

- **Structural Variants**

  festival de musique <---> festival musical (= music festival)

- **Grammatical Word Deletion**

  mémoire à fichier ---> mémoire fichier (= file memory)

- **Separator Variants**

  vidéo-cassette <---> vidéo cassette

The underlying criterion for recognising a variant of a multiword form is that both forms having the same definition share content words. Our model provides for various possible treatments.

7 Pragmatics

Extralinguistic information is information about usage constraints for LEs. It is coded in the PRAGMATICS entity.

We separate extralinguistic information into two parts:

- General Pragmatic Information

  Information which describes geographical, temporal and register limitations on words. This information applies to all words in the lexical database.

- Term Usage Information

  Information which describes usage constraints on words as determined by various organisations (user organisation, legal organisation, standards organisations). Words which are supplied with this information are terms.

Term usage information can be regarded as an *extension* of general pragmatic information.

Logically, extralinguistic constraints could be applied to every morphological, phonetic, and syntactic feature inside an LE; we can regard pragmatic information as an extra "dimension" in linguistic coding. Thus, in the following example, there are two sense-equivalent surface frames for the English verb *write*:

> *Mary wrote to John* (NP PP[to] - British English)

> *Mary wrote John* (NP NP - American English)

Here the choice of syntactic frame inside a single LE for *write* is constrained by dialect considerations.

Practically, allowing for all such possible cases in the model structure makes for considerable complication at the level of implementation and interface. The use of a single entity to record such extralinguistic information in the Operational Model is therefore a compromise[1]. To record the dialect-conditioned frame variation of *write* in a way accessible to an NLP system would require two LEs.

8 Syntax

For reasons of space, we give the barest outline of the SYNTAX entity.

An instance of a SYNTAX entry may be shared by several LEs.

For non-predicative words (e.g., concrete nouns), the feature set actually specified is limited; for predicative words, such as verbs, the syntax is based around the syntactic functions (subject, object, indirect object, prepositional object, subject complement, object complement). Each of these frame elements is characterised by a set of features indicating the category of the complement. Other features describe more global properties, such as the type of the auxiliary verb (for Romance languages), whether the verb is intrinsically reflexive, and the form of the support verb(s) in the case of predicative nouns.

Our Reference model provides a very rich sub-entity and feature set for syntactic description. In the Operational Model, only a subset of these features are used. This keeps the coding entries within reasonable time and cost bounds.

9 Transfer

Instances of the TRANSFER entity are used to specify possible translations for a word[2]. It consists of

- a reference to a source and target entry - a link
- a set of transfer features on the link

Even taking into account that transfer links are specified between sense-disambiguated LEs, a given LE (word) may have several possible translations (1,n). Equally, a given targt word may translate more than one source word (n,1). There will be a transfer link for each such pairing.

In the Reference Model we defined highly generic transfer features and transfer relations. In the Operational Model we limit ourselves to a set of features sufficient for the METAL MT system: subject area (TAG), local environment test features (TEST), preference (PREF) and mapping features (XFM). The preference value is used in some METAL transfer lexica for ordering rule applications. Mapping features are used when - for example - there is a category change between source and target. Comments, examples, administration information, and subject area tags are also relevant for human users.

---

1. The Reference model defines a complex "two level" pragmatic component allowing constraints to be specified on the syntax entity if required.

2. Strictly speaking, the transfer entity is a specialisation of the cross-reference entity. For this reason, it does not appear explicitly in Figure 8.

Some of the features on the link are redundant; for example, a difference in number between the source and the target word, which will be reflected in both test and transformation features, can be inferred directly by looking at the syntax and morphology of the source and target LEs. However, for the time being we have chosen to retain this redundancy to avoid expensive run-time calculation of test and transformation features.

Two source LEs which are synonyms (e.g., FR *clef (= key)* and *clé (= key))* will nonetheless each have a transfer link to their shared EN translation *key*.

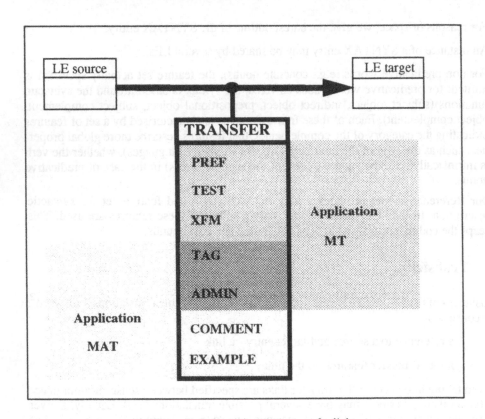

Figure 7 : Information on the transfer link

10 Data Model

The overall data model is summarised below. Each link is annoted with two sets of ratios which indicate the relation cardinality. For example, looking at the link between the LE entity and the SYNTAX entity, the ratio 1,1 means that each LE instance has one and only one SYNTAX instance (1,1) whilst each SYNTAX instance links to at least one and perhaps several LE instances (1,n).

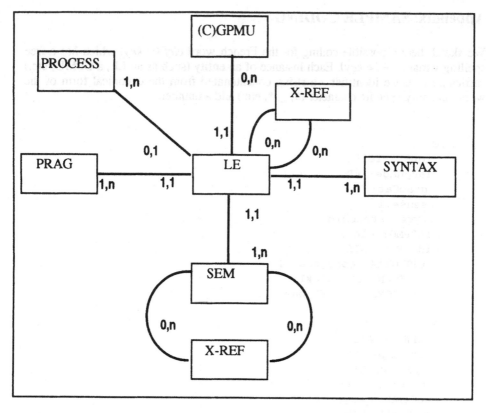

Figure 8 : Operational Model - Outline Entity-Relation Model[1]

11 Conclusion

We have briefly presented a dictionary model designed to allow a coherent treatment of lexical information for both humans and NLP systems. Some aspects of the model are realised in a EUROLANG product - *Le Lexicaliste*. The model is also proving particularly helpful in the design of lexical components for other EUROLANG translation-oriented products as well as future possible versions of SIETEC's METAL MT system. Current discussions with various clients serve to confirm our view that full integration of lexical resources is critical to the success of language technology products.

12 References

1. G. Heyer: The MULTILEX project - Génie Linguistique 91 - Versailles (1991)

2. T. Schneider: The METAL System - MT Summit II, Washington (1991)

---

1. We have not named the relations in this figure, nor have we shown GPMU internal structure and links with CGPMU.

Appendix: SAMPLE CODING

We sketch here a possible coding for the French word *clef* (= *key*) which has a free spelling variant *clé* (= *key*). Each instance of an entity (such as an LE, a GPMU, etc.) carries an instance identifier - a string concatenated from the canonical form of the word, an entity-specific character (#, _, *, etc.) and a number.

```
LE
    idLE: clef*1
    language: FR
    gramCat: N
    sense:1
    type: standard
    idGPMU: clé_1
    idCGPMU: NIL
    idSYNTAX: conc_noun_1
    idSEMANTICS: clé#1
    idPRAGMATICS: FR_basic_1

LE
    idLE: clé*1
    language: FR
    gramCat: N
    type: variant
    idGPMU: clé_2
    idCGPMU: NIL
    idSYNTAX: conc_noun_1
    idSEMANTICS: clé#1
    idPRAGMATICS: FR_basic_1

LE
    idLE: key*1
    language: ENG
    gramCat: N
    sense:1
    type: standard
    idGPMU: key_1
    idCGPMU: NIL
    idSYNTAX: conc_noun_1
    idSEMANTICS: clé#1
    idPRAGMATICS: EN_basic_1

GPMU
    idGPMU: clé_1
    writtenform: clef
    P-initial:CONSONANTAL
```

```
      gramCat: N
       substType: COMMON
      idMFG: n21
      -- morphological features
      -- other features

GPMU
      idGPMU: clé_2
      writtenform: clé
       P-initial:CONSONANTAL
      gramCat: N
      substType: COMMUN
      idMFG: n21
      -- morphological features
      -- other features
MFG
      idMFG: n21
      refMFG: clé
      rule
        stem: clé
        FF
           form: clé
           gender: fem
           nbr: sing
        FF
           form: clés
           gender: fem
           nbr: plur

SYNTAX
      idSYNTAX: conc_noun_1
      determinant: standard
      possessive: F
      -- other syntax features

SEMANTICS
      idSEMANTICS: clé#1
      definition:
      definition status:
      subject area:

PRAGMATICS
      idPRAGMATICS: FRbasic_1
      geography: ANY_FRENCH
      register: STANDARD

PRAGMATICS
      idPRAGMATICS: ENbasic_1
      geography: ANY_ENGLISH
```

```
    register: STANDARD

XREF
    idSOURCE: clé*1
    idTARGET: clé*2
    type: HAS-VARIANT
    inverse-type: HAS-VARIANT
    sub-type: FREE
    inverse-sub-type: FREE
    linked-entities: LEs
    XREF-PROPS
        reflexive: NO
        symmetric: YES
        transitive: YES

TRANSFER
    idSOURCE: clé*1
    idTARGET: key*1
TRANSFER
    idSOURCE: clé*2
    idTARGET: key*1
```

TransLexis:
An Integrated Environment for Lexicon and Terminology Management

Brigitte Bläser
IBM Germany Information Systems GmbH
Scientific Center
Vangerowstr. 18
D-69115 Heidelberg

Abstract. The IBM lexicon and terminology management system TransLexis provides an integrated solution for developing and maintaining lexical and terminological data for use by humans and computer programs. In this paper, the conceptual schema of TransLexis, its user interface, and its import and export facilities will be described. TransLexis takes up several ideas emerging from the reuse discussion. In particular, it strives for a largely theory-neutral representation of multilingual lexical and terminological data, it includes export facilities to derive lexicons for different applications, and it includes programs to import lexical and terminological data from existing sources.

1. Introduction

Quite a number of tools assisting translators, terminologists, and other professionals working in a multilingual environment are commercially available today. Recently announced systems, for example the Eurolang Optimizer, the IBM Translation Manager/2, and the Trados Translator's Workbench [13, 14, 17], offer an integrated working environment for translators including facilities for text processing, dictionary and terminology management, a translation memory, and in some cases even the possibility to interface a machine translation (MT) system.

In addition to these machine assisted translation systems (MAT systems), several fully automatic translation systems (MT systems) are available as well, e.g., LMT, LOGOS, and METAL [8, 9, 15]. Usually, these systems include their own facilities for the management of lexical data. Thus, where both MAT and MT systems are employed, often two distinct dictionaries have to be maintained in parallel. This doubles maintenance work and increases the danger of inconsistent and contradictory lexical data (see also the article by K. Koch in this volume).

Dictionaries for human translators and for automatic translation systems contain different kinds of information organized in different ways. While human translators need, for instance, natural language definitions, contexts, and usage notes, most MT systems require detailed morphological and syntactic information as well as semantic information represented in a formal knowledge represention language. Furthermore, the basic lexical units may not be identical. Basic lexical units of dictionaries for human users are usually so-called lemmas or citation forms of lexical items. In MT systems, on the other hand, the basic units can also be word stems or morphemes. This imposes special requirements on the design of a dictionary for use by both humans and MT systems (see also [1]).

Faced with the need to maintain lexicons which were developed for different NLP applications, to develop a lexicon for an MT system, and to provide terminologists and human translators with a tool for managing lexical and terminological data, IBM decided to design and implement a system for developing and maintaining a multifunctional lexicon. The system which resulted from these efforts is called TransLexis. TransLexis was developed in the context of the international IBM project Logic-Programming Based Machine Translation (LMT) [8, 9], where a central lexicon tool was required that not only supports the different language pairs under work in the project but also allows the acquisition of existant lexical data from different sources [5]. In addition, throughout the design and development of TransLexis, pilot users have contributed their expertise in terminology, have articulated their requirements, and have played an active role in testing and revising preliminary versions of the system.

In Section 2 of this paper, the structure of TransLexis will be described; in Section 3, the conceptual schema of the underlying database will be explained; Section 4 deals with the major elements of the user interface, and Section 5 outlines the import and export facilities of the system.

2. The Structure of the TransLexis System

TransLexis has four components:
- a database management system,
- an application programming interface (API),
- a graphical user interface for creating, displaying, and updating lexical and terminological information,
- components for exporting and importing lexical and terminological data in different formats.

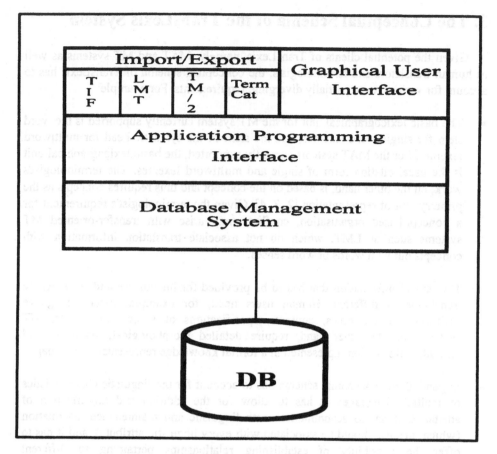

Figure 1: Structure of the TransLexis system

TransLexis runs under the operating system IBM OS/2. It can be employed in single-user as well as multi-user environments. Its design adheres to the principles of client/server architectures. For managing the database, the standard relational database system IBM DB2/2 has been employed. The user interface and the import and export components access the data via functions of the API. The API provides numerous functions for creating and updating lexical and terminological entries, for searching entries according to different filtering criteria, for navigating through the database, and for administering different users and user groups (e.g., by means of user profiles and by distinguishing different access rights). With the API functions, new application programs that access the lexical and terminological data in a different way can easily be developed. The import and export facilities currently allow the interchange of data between TransLexis and the MAT systems IBM Translation Manager/2 and Keck MemCat [16] as well as with the MT system LMT. In addition, a preliminary version of the Terminology Interchange Format (TIF) is supported [11, 12]. The user interface has been implemented using the functions of the IBM OS/2 Presentation Manager. It offers all the possibilities of direct manipulative interaction (e.g., dragging and dropping, notebook browsing, etc.).

3. The Conceptual Schema of the TransLexis System

Given the potential clients of TransLexis, namely, MAT and MT systems as well as human translators and terminologists, the conceptual schema of TransLexis has to account for various, even partially diverging, requirements. For example:

- The basic lexicographical unit for the MT system currently supported is the word stem for single word lexemes, and the stem of the syntactic head for multiword lexemes. For the MAT systems currently supported, the basic lexicographical unit is the usual citation form of single and multiword lexemes. The terminologist's work, on the other hand, is based on the concept and thus requires concepts as the primary unit of representation [2, 3, 4]. Given the terminologist's requirement for a concept-based organisation, conflicts may arise with transfer-oriented MT systems such as LMT, which do not associate translation information with concepts but with words or word senses.

- The lexical information that has to be provided for human use and for machine translation is different. Human users need, for example, natural language definitions, usage notes, contexts, specifications of subject areas, etc. MT systems, on the other hand, require detailed morphological, syntactic, and semantic information represented in a formal knowledge representation language.

- In general, the conceptual schema has to account for the linguistic characteristics of multiple languages, it has to allow for the addition and modification of attributes, it has to accommodate both linguistic and maintenance information (which, ideally, should be associated with every linguistic attribute), and it has to offer the possibility of establishing relationships pertaining to different dimensions of lexical description, such as semantic relations on the concept level (e.g., hyponymy and synonymy), translation relations on the sense level, and string relations on the word level (e.g., abbreviations and orthographic variants).

The conceptual schema of TransLexis has been designed to accommodate all of these requirements. Figure 2 shows the entities of the TransLexis conceptual schema and their interrelations (an earlier version of the schema which did not account for terminological information has been described in [5])[1].

---

[1]The boxes in Figure 2 represent types of entities, the diamonds represent types of relations between the entities. The labels associated with the arcs indicate whether the relation in question is a one-to-one (1,1), one-to-many (1,n), many-to-one (n,1), or many-to-many (n,m) relation. For the sake of simplicity, attributes of the entities and relations have been omitted.

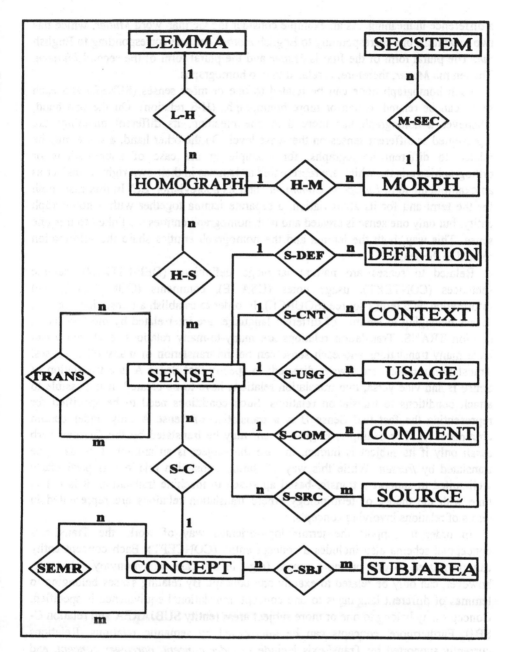

Figure 2: Conceptual schema of the TransLexis database

Citation forms are represented by the LEMMA entity. Each lemma is related to one or more homograph entities (HOMOGRAPH) through the lemma-homograph relation (L-H). A new homograph entity is generated whenever the citation form belongs to more than one part of speech (e.g., *program* as a noun and *to program* as a verb) or if the citation form has different morphological properties which also indicate a difference in meaning. As an example consider the German word *Mutter,* which has two meanings, one corresponding to English *mother* and one corresponding to English *nut.* The plural form of the first is *Mütter* and the plural form of the second *Muttern.* The lemma *Mutter,* therefore, is related to two homographs.

Each homograph node can be related to one or more senses (SENSE) and each sense can be related to one or more homographs (H-S relation). On the one hand, whenever a homograph has more than one meaning, its different meanings are represented as different senses on the sense level. On the other hand, a sense may be related to different homographs, for example in the case of abbreviations or orthographic variants, which are represented as lemmas in their own right. Consider as an example the term *European Community* and its abbreviation *EC.* In this case, both for the term and for its abbreviation, a separate lemma together with a homograph entity, but only one sense is created and both homograph entities are linked to this one sense. This way, both the lemma and the homograph entities share the information related to the sense.

Related to senses are natural language definitions (DEFINITION), sample sentences (CONTEXT), usage notes (USAGE), comments (COMMENT), and information on a term's source (SOURCE). In order to establish a translation relation, senses belonging to lemmas of different languages are interrelated by the translation relation TRANS. Translation relations are many-to-many relations: each sense can have many translations and each sense can be the translation of many other senses. Translation relations are always directed: to specify that Sense A is a translation of Sense B and vice versa, two translation relations have to be created. It is possible to attach conditions to translation relations. Such conditions need to be specified for representing the fact that Sense B is a translation of Sense A only under certain circumstances. For example, English *to eat* may be translated by the German verb *essen* only if its subject is human, in case the subject is an animal, it needs to be translated by *fressen.* While this way of stating translation relations is particularly well-suited to support a transfer-based approach to machine translation, it is not in tune with the theory of terminology where translation relations are represented in terms of relations involving concepts.

In order to support the terminology-oriented way of work, the TransLexis conceptual schema also includes a concept entity (CONCEPT). Each concept entity can be related to one or more senses (e.g., in the case of synonymy). A sense, however, can only be related to exactly one concept. By relating senses belonging to lemmas of different languages to one concept, translational equivalence is specified. Concepts may belong to one or more subject areas (entity SUBJAREA and relation C-SBJ). Furthermore, concepts can be interrelated by semantic relations. Relations currently supported by TransLexis include *broader concept, narrower concept,* and *related concept.*

165

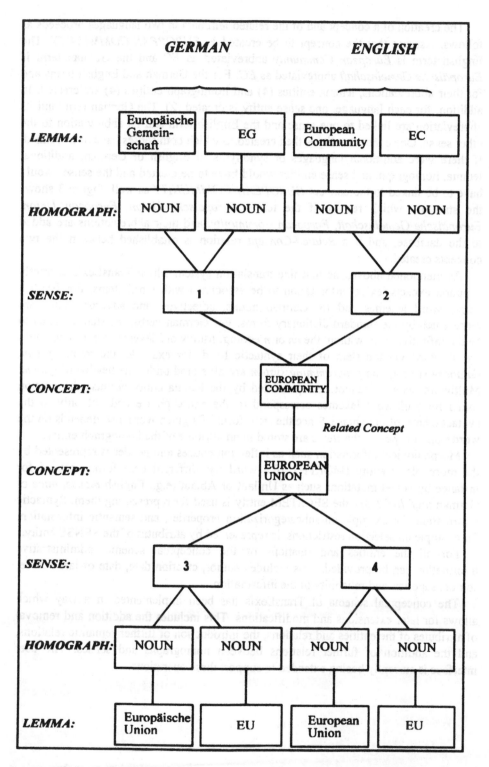

Figure 3: Example of two related concepts and their associated terms

The creation of a concept and of the related lemmata in two languages proceeds as follows. Assume that the concept to be created is *EUROPEAN-COMMUNITY*. The English term is *European Community* abbreviated as *EC* and the German term is *Europäische Gemeinschaft* abbreviated as *EG*. For the German and English terms and for their abbreviations, lemma entities (4) and homograph entities (4) are created. In addition, for each language, one sense entity is created (2). The German term and its abbreviation are linked to one sense and the English term and its abbreviation to the other sense. One concept entity is then created to which both senses have to be related. If there were additional languages or synonyms in English or German, additional lemma, homograph, and sense entities would have to be created and the senses would have to be linked to the concept *EUROPEAN-COMMUNITY* as well. Figure 3 shows the structure which results, if the terms *Europäische Union, European Union, Europäische Gemeinschaft, European Community*, and their abbreviations are added to the database, and if a *Related-Concept* relation is established between the two concepts created.

As mentioned above, the machine translation system which TransLexis currently supports expects lexical information to be associated with word stems. For English single word lexemes and for German nouns, adjectives, and adverbs, stems are represented by the standard dictionary forms. For German verbs, the stem is taken to be the infinitive form without the *en* or *n* ending. Multiword lexemes for all languages are accessed via the stem of their syntactic head; for example, the terms *system, database system*, and *programming system* are all stored under the headword *system*. Multiword lexemes cannot be represented by the lemma entity because the citation forms for multiword lexemes correspond to the entire phrase and not only to the syntactic head of the phrase. Since the stem form of a given word also depends on the word's part of speech, the stems are stored in an attribute of the homograph entity.

Morphological information such as inflection classes and gender is represented by the morphology entity (MORPH). If a word has different base forms, caused for instance by vowel mutations such as Umlaut or Ablaut (e.g., English *mouse, mice* or German *lauf, lief, läuf*), the SECSTEM entity is used for representing them. Syntactic information, for example on subcategorization properties, and semantic information, for example on selection restrictions, is represented by attributes of the SENSE entity.

For all the entities and relations of the conceptual schema, administrative information can be provided. This includes author, creation date, date of last update, source, supplier, and reliability of the information.

The conceptual schema of TransLexis has been implemented in a way which allows for later extensions and modifications. This includes the addition and removal of attributes of the entities and relations, the introduction of further semantic relations, and the addition of further relations between homographs and senses. The user interface is currently beeing extended to support these operations.

4. The User Interface of the TransLexis System

The user interface of TransLexis provides the following functionality:
- creating new entries
- updating existing entries
- searching for entries
- defining search filters
- displaying entries according to a given user profile
- defining user profiles

Assuming that the system will also be employed in larger work groups whose members have different needs for accessing the data, TransLexis permits to assign different access rights to different users. The access rights determine to which subset of the lexical/terminological data the user has access and how the data may be used (e.g., read-only, create, update, etc.). Authorization checking is performed when a user logs on to the system.

For searching the database, the user enters a search pattern, which may possibly contain wildcards, and chooses a language. The default search algorithm is case-insensitive and ignores special characters such as brackets, dots, and commas which may appear in the search pattern. Accented characters are treated like their corresponding base characters. The user can choose exact search to override the default. The system also offers the possibility to define search filters. For example, search filters can be defined which take into consideration administrative properties such as the author of a term, its source, and its creation date, syntactic properties such as the part of speech, and pragmatic properties such as the subject area, regional, and stylistic variation. Search filters may be defined by browsing through a notebook and by making the appropriate selections (see Figure 4).

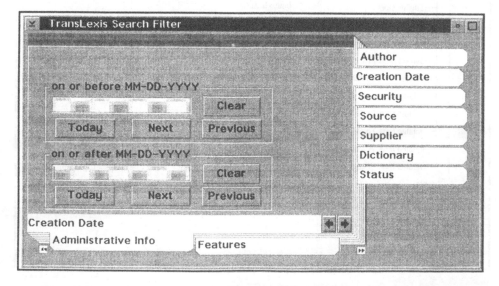

Figure 4: Search filter of TransLexis

There are two ways to display entries: the lemma-oriented view (see Figure 5) and the concept-oriented view (see Figure 6), both of which are hierarchically structured. In the lemma-oriented view, the lemma is the top node. Below the lemma, its homograph nodes are shown, and below the homograph nodes, their senses are displayed. If a sense is associated with a concept, the concept is displayed below the sense. In the concept-oriented view, the concept is the top node. Below the concept node, the terms linked to the concept are displayed. If these terms have several senses, only those senses actually associated with the concept and only the homographs associated with these senses are shown. The system also allows the user to navigate through the entries of the database: if an entry contains a reference to another lemma or concept, clicking on this reference will cause the referenced entry to be opened. As shown in Figure 5 and 6, the data can be displayed in a split screen mode. The left part of the screen serves mainly navigation purposes and the right part provides the user with the entire information associated with an entry.

Figure 5: Lemma-oriented view

Different users may have different information needs at different times. For example, while for a translator it may not be interesting to know who created a certain term and when it was created, for the chief terminologist deciding on the entry's validity this can be important; similarly, for the developmenmt of MT relevant lexical data, information needed by terminologists (e.g., definitions and source information) may not be relevant. The amount of information that is displayed can, therefore, be controlled by defining appropriate user profiles. For every user, up to 10 user profiles can be defined.

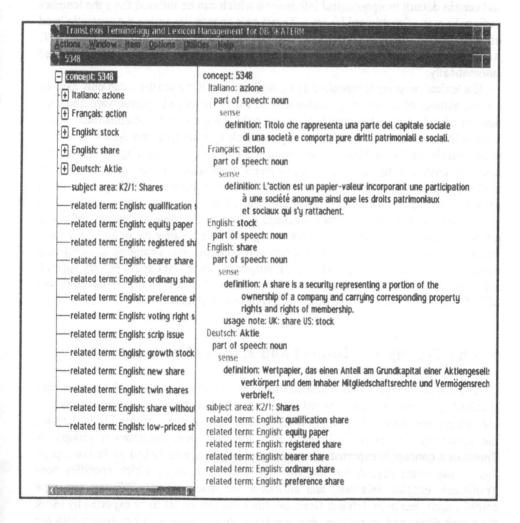

Figure 6: Concept-oriented view

Entry creation proceeds according to the view which has been chosen. In case of the lemma-oriented view, the user specifies the new lemma, the language, and the part of speech. The system then checks whether the lemma already exists and, if so, displays the lemma; otherwise, a new entry for the lemma is created. If a new concept is to be created, the system prompts the user to provide all the terms belonging to the concept and their parts of speech. For each of the terms, the system checks whether an entry for it already exists, and if so, displays the entry. Otherwise, entries for these terms are created and are linked to the new concept. The resulting concept entry is then displayed. For already existing terms, the user can decide whether to link one of its senses to the new concept or whether to create a new sense.

During creation of a lemma, certain types of information are automatically generated and proposed to the user. This comprises the stem form needed for LMT and certain default morphological information which can be inferred from the lemma's ending. In case of multiword lexemes, TransLexis tries to determine the syntactic head of the phrase which is considered as the head of the construction by LMT. Administrative information such as author and creation date is also provided automatically.

If a lexical property is modelled by an attribute and if the attribute can only assume a fixed number of values (as probably desired for regional and stylistic variation), the domain of values may be specified, for example, by the system administrator. Apart from using the domain definitions for type checking purposes, the system also uses these definitions for facilitating the interactive creation and updating of entries: the user may change or update an attribute of an entry by selecting from a list of possible attribute values, which is displayed by the system. For those lexical properties which cannot be represented by a fixed set of attribute values, free text input is expected as, for example, in the case of natural language definitions, sample sentences, and usage notes. In addition, the system provides a drag-and-drop facility for defining relations among, e.g., senses and concepts, concepts and concepts, etc. Dragging and dropping may also be used for moving and copying purposes. Since LMT requires very specific information of a word's morphological and syntactic characteristics, the development of LMT entries is supported by example-driven user dialogues.

5. The TransLexis Import and Export Facilities

TransLexis supports four different formats for the exchange of lexicons and terminologies, two of them SGML applications. For terminology interchange, a preliminary version of TIF [11, 12] is supported. Basic notions of this TIF variant are the *termEntry* (terminological entry) and the *tig* (term information group). A TransLexis concept is exported as a termEntry and the senses linked to the concept as tigs of the termEntry. A template for TIF-based exchange, which specifies how TransLexis entities, relations, and attributes are mapped onto TIF tag and type combinations, has been defined. Users can filter out the entries to be exported by using the search filters and, in addition, they can filter out the types of information which are to be exported.

TransLexis also supports a lemma-oriented exchange format based on the standard SGML dictionary exchange format of IBM Translation Manager/2 [17], which is a hierarchical structure corresponding to the structure of traditional bilingual dictionary entries. Alternatively to IBM Translation Manager/2, TransLexis entries can also be exported into the MAT system Keck MemCat. In both cases, as for TIF exchange, the user can filter out the entries and the types of information to be exported. In addition, entries of the MT system LMT can be imported into and exported from TransLexis. The export of lexical entries into IBM Translation Manager/2, Keck MemCat and LMT has been automated in the following way: each time an entry is created or updated in TransLexis, it is checked whether this has an impact on the lexical data of any of the three systems. If so, the new or revised entry will automatically be exported into the dictionaries of the three systems.

Importing lexical and terminological entries into existing dictionaries or term banks involves the problem of merging new information with already existing (parts of) entries. TransLexis supports the merging of entries in two ways: first, terminologies can be imported into TransLexis in batch import mode. In this case, merging is done automatically by a statistically based algorithm [see 6, 7]. Terminologies can also be imported interactively, which means that the system requires the user to make appropriate decisions in case of a potential conflict. By setting certain defaults, the user can control the extent to which merging is performed automatically. For example, he or she may decide to have existing definitions automatically overwritten by the definitions of the imported entries or else to have the new definitions added to the existing ones. Lexical and terminological data from different sources have been imported into TransLexis, e.g., the Collins dictionaries for English-German and German-English, a computer terminology collection, and the terminological resources of a pilot user.

6. Summary and Conclusion

In this paper, I described the lexicon and terminology management system TransLexis. In particular, I provided an overview of the different components of TransLexis, namely, the conceptual schema of its database, its user interface, and its facilities for importing and exporting lexical and terminological data. TransLexis was developed in response to the need for an integrated solution to the problem of developing and maintaining lexical and terminological data as required both by M(A)T systems and by human users.

TransLexis subscribes to the reuse idea [10] in that it strives for a theory-neutral description of multilingual lexical and terminological data and includes export facilities to derive lexicons for both human and computer use. In addition, programs have been developed to import lexical and terminological data from existing sources. Another aspect worth mentioning in the context of reusability is the fact that TransLexis can be employed both in a single-user environment and in a larger organisational framework, that is, in a multi-user environment.

From the very beginning, the design and development of TransLexis has been driven by the requirements and experience of a pilot users, in particular the terminologists at Crédit Suisse, Zürich and the developers of LMT lexicons at IBM. Through repetitive testing of preliminary versions in real-life working environments, many desiderata came to light and could be added to the system.

Currently, TransLexis is marketed as part of the IBM MT solution package Logic-Programming Based Machine Translation, but can also be purchased and employed as a stand-alone terminology management system.

7. Acknowledgements

The following persons contributed to the design, development, and testing of TransLexis:
P. Fach, B. Keck, A. Laube, Dr. H. Lehmann, Dr. S. McCormick, N. Ott, Dr. U. Quasthof, M. Rosenpflanzer, R. Reinau, Dr. P. Shann, Dr. A. Storrer, C. Sturm, and Dr. M. Zoeppritz.
For this, I wish to thank them.

8. References

1. E. Knops, G. Thurmair: Design of a multifunctional lexicon. In: H.B. Sonneveld, K.L. Loening (eds.): Terminology - applications in interdisciplinary communication. pp. 87-110, John Benjamins Publishing Company, Amsterdam/Philadelphia 1993.

2. K.-D. Schmitz: Rechnergestützte Terminologieverwaltung am Übersetzerarbeitsplatz. Proceedings of the Symposium Terminologie als Qualitätsfaktor, Deutscher Terminologietag, pp. 89-106, Köln 1991.

3. K.-D. Schmitz, G. Budin (eds.): Empfehlungen für Planung und Einrichtung von Terminologiedatenbanken. Report, Gesellschaft für Terminologie und Wissenstransfer 1994.

4. R. Arntz, H. Picht: Einführung in die Terminologiearbeit. Georg Olms Verlag, Hildesheim, Zürich, New York 1991.

5. B. Bläser, A. Storrer, U. Schwall: A reusable lexical database tool for machine translation. Proceedings of Coling 1992, pp. 510-516, Nantes 1992.

6. A. Laube: Syntaktische Kontrolle von zu importtierenden terminologischen Daten. Studienarbeit, University of Dresden 1994.

7. L. Rosenpflanzer: Import von terminologischen Daten in eine bestehende Terminologiedatenbank. Studienarbeit, University of Dresden 1994.

8. M. McCord: A new Version of the Machine Translation System LMT. Journal of Literary and Linguistic Computing 4, pp. 218-229, 1989.

9. M. Rimon, M. McCord, U. Schwall, P. Martinez: Advances in Machine Translation Research and Development in IBM. Proceedings of MT-Summit III, pp. 11-18, Washington D.C. 1991.

10. U. Heid: A short Report on the EUROTRA-7 Study. Research Report, University of Stuttgart 1991.

11. A. Melby, S.E. Wright: TEI-Term: An SGML-based InterchangeFormat for Terminology Files. Proceedings of PreCOLING-92 Tutorials, pp. 164-192, Nantes 1992.

12. ISO WD 12200: Computational Aids in Terminology - Terminology Interchange Format (TIF) - An SGML Application. ISO/TC 37/SC 3/WG 3/N7, 1992.

13. C. Brace: Bonjour, Eurolang Optimizer. Language Industry Monitor, No. 20, pp. 1-3, March-April 1994.

14. C. Brace: Trados: Ten Years On. Language Industry Monitor, No. 22, pp. 2-6, July-August 1994.

15. W.J. Hutchins, H.L. Somers: An Introduction to Machine Translation. Academic Press. London, San Diego, New York, Boston, Sydney, Tokio, Toronto 1992.

16. B. Keck: TermCat/MemCat User's Guide. Keck Software 1993.

17. IBM Translation Manager/2, Version 1.0 User Manual. IBM Deutschland Entwicklung GmbH, Information Development, Böblingen 1994.

The Use of Terminological Knowledge Bases in Software Localisation

E.A. Karkaletsis, C.D. Spyropoulos, G. Vouros

Institute of Informatics & Telecommunications, N.C.S.R. "Demokritos",
15310 Aghia Paraskevi, Athens, Greece

Abstract. This paper describes the work that was undertaken in the Glossasoft[1] project in the area of terminology management. Some of the drawbacks of existing terminology management systems are outlined and an alternative approach to maintaining terminological data is proposed. The approach which we advocate relies on knowledge-based representation techniques. These are used to model conceptual knowledge about the terms included in the database, general knowledge about the subject domain, application-specific knowledge, and - of course - language-specific terminological knowledge. We consider the multifunctionality of the proposed architecture to be one of its major advantages. To illustrate this, we outline how the knowledge representation scheme, which we suggest, could be drawn upon in message generation and machine-assisted translation.

1 Introduction

The process of isolating the culture and language-specific parts of a software product is called internationalisation. Localisation is the opposite process, since it takes a previously internationalised software product, adding features and elements that better match the target culture and marketplace [10].

Internationalisation and localisation are becoming dominant tasks in the process of software engineering. This is particularly true for general purpose software products oriented at international markets. A recent study [13] characterises localisation as the fastest growing area of the software manufacturing market. The crucial commercial requirements that software managers have to face in software internationalisation and localisation are how to improve quality, get faster times-to-market, and reduce the localisation costs of a software product [6]. Although large companies have already established methodologies to respond to these requirements, they are still seeking a more professional and systematic solution.

---

[1]Glossasoft is partially supported by the EU under the contract LRE-61003 together with Open University (GB), N.C.S.R. "Demokritos" (GR), Claris (IR), HP Hellas (GR), VTT (Fi), and BULL (Fr).

Glossasoft is a Linguistic Research and Engineering (LRE) project, which aims at producing guidelines and methods for software internationalisation and localisation which help companies to reduce localisation costs and times-to-market and to improve the quality of their localised products.

During internationalisation and localisation, a company faces a variety of language relevant problems, such as the inconsistent use of terms, the lack of uniformity in writing and translation style, spelling and syntax errors, or the retranslation of certain language-specific parts from old localised versions when new ones are created [8]. Language technology tools, such as writing and proof-reading tools, translation tools and machine translation systems, may provide solutions to these problems.

One of the Glossasoft objectives is to provide guidelines for the selection and use of the appropriate language technology tools in software internationalisation and localisation [7,8]. Writing and proof-reading tools include controlled languages, spelling and syntax checkers, and multilingual editors. Translation tools and workbenches include terminology, lexica, translation memories and translation workbenches. For each type of tool in each category, Glossasoft [8]
- identifies requirements for its efficient application in software internationalisation and localisation,
- provides evaluation criteria and guidelines to help with the selection of the appropriate tool, and
- provides guidelines for efficiently using the selected tools.

The results of our terminology work in Glossasoft are discussed in Section 2. The use of existing terminology management systems considerably assisted our work, but also had some undesirable effects. These effects motivated us to seek alternative approaches to the representation and management of terminological knowledge. Based on experience in the area of knowledge representation and processing [2,4,11,14,15,16,19,21,22,23], we examined the use of terminological knowledge bases in software localisation.

We discuss the benefits and drawbacks of knowledge-based techniques in Section 3. Our own knowledge-based architecture for the organisation of terminological data is analysed in Section 4. Our intention was to organise the terms in an interlingual terminological knowledge base that could also be used for other localisation activities, such as message generation and machine-assisted translation. The exploitation of the proposed architecture in those localisation activities is discussed in Section 5. The concluding remarks of Section 6 summarise our work and outline some areas of future research.

2 Experiences with Existing Terminology Management Systems

The use of monolingual and multilingual terminological databases in software localisation may improve terminological consistency and preserve uniformity in writing and translation style. The set-up and the management of the terminological databases is facilitated by the use of terminology management systems. Some of the

aspects that should be considered when selecting an appropriate terminology management system for software localisation are:
- the types of terminological information that the system allows to specify,
- the languages supported,
- the facilities provided for term collection and maintenance,
- the retrieval facilities,
- the support of interchange formats,
- the maximum number of terms,
- the ease-of-use of the user interface.

Glossasoft investigates the use of terminology management systems in the context of software localisation. More specifically, it provides:
- guidelines for the acquisition, normalisation, translation, and maintenance of terms,
- evaluation criteria for the selection of the appropriate terminology management systems,
- guidelines for the efficient use of terminological databases in software localisation.

Glossasoft also performs software localisation case studies, in which some widely used terminology management systems are examined according to the evaluation criteria that have been specified. In these case studies, we aim at
- identifying the domain- and application-specific terms,
- preparing alphabetical lists of terms,
- standardising the terminological record format,
- describing and formulating the scientific and technical knowledge that these terms mediate,
- storing the terms in terminological databases.

This work led to the creation of a terminological database rich in knowledge that contains four types of data [1]:
- acquisition data, which provide information on the term's origin with regard to the domain, subject, language, country, etc.;
- linguistically relevant data such as part of speech, gender, number, type of lexeme (e.g., collocation or multiword), etc.;
- explicatory data, such as the term's definition, an example of a possible context, and comments;
- deployment data, which provide conceptually related terms such as synonyms, superordinate and subordinate terms, and terms which refer to parts of the term to be described.

Some of these types of data are exemplified in the terminological records given in Figure 1. Although the terminology management systems which have been examined provided many facilities that supported the creation of the terminological database, we encountered several problems which had to do with the amount of information collected and its formulation:

(a) *Redundancy.* Often several terms have common characteristics. The terminology management systems which we examined, however, did not provide any facilities to share information between terminological entries. Instead, the same information had to be repeated for every term. For example, let us consider the records for the terms "control" and "button", shown in Figure 1. Their fields "subject", "domain", and "part-of" contain exactly the same information. This is also the case for the records for "field", "menu", "push-button", and "slider".

Entry	control		Entry	button
Subject	HP product help		Subject	HP product help
Domain	HP Manager-A		Domain	HP Manager-A
Superordinate	item		Superordinate	control
Subordinate	button, field, menu		Subordinate	push-button, slider
Part-of	dialog, window		Part-of	dialog, window

Fig. 1. Example of two terminological records

(b) *Maintenance.* Sometimes, the change of a term characteristic also affects the terms which are conceptually related to it - something for which no adequate support is provided by most of the existing terminology management systems. For example, the replacement of "window" by "front-panel" in the "part-of" field of "control" affects all the records denoted by the value of the "subordinate" field. Furthermore, the addition of a new characteristic or the change to an existing one may contradict the information provided for the conceptually related terms. For example, "item" is a superordinate term for "button" since it was defined as "superordinate" for "control" and "control" was defined as "superordinate" for "button". Therefore, the addition of "item" in the "subordinate" field of "button" would cause a contradiction. When a new terminological record is created, usually it is related to some of the existing ones. This can be a complex task for large terminological databases with a complex structure. For example, a new record for "field" must be related to the record for "control" as well as to the records for "window" and "dialog" through its "superordinate" and "part-of" fields respectively. Also, the deletion of a terminological record can cause problems which cannot be easily detected by most of the existing terminology management systems. For example, let us consider the records for "push-button" and "slider", which contain only the term "button" in their "superordinate" fields. In that case, the deletion of "button" would cut the links of "push-button" and "slider" with "control". This can be avoided if, for example, the "superordinate" field contained all the superordinate terms of "button" and not only the immediately superordinate ones. However, this solution would add to the redundancy problem.

(c) *Presentation of information.* An explicit representation of conceptual relations facilitates the graphical representation of terminological information. This is a crucial aspect since graphical representations aid learning, providing the kind of conceptual "map" advocated by numerous educational psychologists [15]. The terminology management systems which we examined, however, did not support the explicit representation of conceptual relations and the graphical representation of information. In these systems, conceptual information was encoded implicitly in the form of definitions, contexts, indications of domain, etc. This makes difficult the inspection and comprehension of knowledge contained in large terminological databases with a complex structure and many conceptual relations.

3 Benefits and Drawbacks of Terminological Knowledge Bases in Software Localisation

The identification of the above-described problems motivated us to examine other ways of organising and managing terms in terminological databases. Since, in our view, the lack of classification support was one of the main deficiencies of existing terminology management systems, we aimed at designing a framework for representing and managing terminological data which allowed us to organise terms in classes and thus helped us to avoid redundancy. For example, the terms "field", "button", and "menu" are all specific cases of "control". If a class concept was defined for the term "control", all other terms could inherit properties from that class, thus eliminating the need for specifying the corresponding properties for every term.

Such a class-based treatment would also facilitate the maintenance of the terminological data. A change to the characteristics of one class is automatically inherited by all the terms belonging to that class. A change in the characteristics of a term that is inconsistent with the information specified for the classes from which it inherits can be automatically detected. A new term can be classified according to its characteristics. If this definition is inconsistent with the characteristics of the existing classes, then either the term is not added to the base or, if it is possible, a new class is created for this term. In this way, the consistency of the terminological database is assured. The classification of terms may also be useful for the presentation of the terminological information to the users. A graphical presentation of the classes and their relations provides the user with a better view of the terminological database.

Some of the existing terminology management systems provide facilities for classifying terms [20]. However, they do not fully exploit the advantages of such an organisation, because the database technology on which they are based can only partially support a class-based approach. Knowledge-based representation techniques, on the other hand, allow for an organisation of the domain entities into class concepts according to their characteristics. Moreover, the use of knowledge representation and reasoning techniques in terminology for software localisation inherently supports

(a) *Multilinguality*. Interlingual knowledge bases can be used to represent the language independent characteristics of terms. Local knowledge bases can be attached to the interlingual one through the classification facilities provided [9,12].

(b) *Multifunctionality*. Knowledge bases facilitate the knowledge intensive tasks of software localisation, such as the multilingual generation of on-line messages [8,18], the maintenance of software systems [5], as well as the translation of software and documentation [12].

(c) *Multidimensionality*. The use of knowledge bases supports the classification of concepts in more than one way according to the conceptual characteristic that is used as the basis of classification. This is most desirable in the area of software localisation, where a term can be classified either according to the function it represents within a given software application or according to its other, for example, linguistic characteristics. Moreover, a multidimensional understanding of a domain is more substantial than a unidimensional one, and produces higher quality definitions and multilingual equivalencies [3,15,16].

However, the use of knowledge-based technology in terminology management also presents several problems that concern the following aspects:

(a) *Set-up of the knowledge base.* The creation of large terminological knowledge bases that can support a software application in practice is a complex task. It requires the knowledge engineer to have a detailed understanding of the software functions, the application domain, and of the terms' definitions [4,15,18,19].

(b) *Management of large knowledge bases.* Automatic classification, update, and inconsistency checking are complex tasks in the case of large knowledge bases [2,4,14,23].

(c) *Expressiveness of the knowledge representation language.* A very expressive language with many conceptual relations may cause problems both in terms of system performance and management. It can also complicate the presentation of information to the users [2,14,23].

4 A Knowledge-Based Architecture for the Organisation of Terminological Data in Software Localisation

In order to account for the above-described problems inherent to the knowledge-based approach while, at the same time, maintaining its advantages, we propose a new approach to organising terminological knowledge bases. The proposed architecture is depicted in Figure 2.

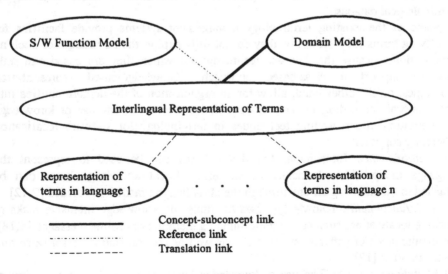

Fig. 2. The knowledge-based architecture

The main components of this architecture have the following characteristics:

- The *Domain Model* contains terminological knowledge of the domain, or subject field, and not of the given application. Domain entities are represented as concepts.
- The *Software Function Model* describes the procedures of the software user interface which is to be localised. Each procedure is described by its purpose and by the steps that have to be taken in order to achieve it. This description can assist the knowledge engineer to understand the meaning of the application-specific terms and also the functions to which they refer in specific contexts.
- The *Interlingual Representation of Terms* contains application-specific terminological knowledge. Application-specific aspects are represented as interlingual concepts that are classified under the concepts of the domain model. Those concepts that correspond to a specific procedure of the user interface or that correspond to an entity referred by such a procedure contain a reference to the corresponding procedure. This reference is the procedure's label. The link between the software function model and the interlingual representation in Figure 2 expresses this reference.
- The *Local Representation of Terms* contains language-specific terminological knowledge. This includes language-specific peculiarities that cannot be expressed by the interlingual concepts. Such peculiarities are the following [17]:
  (a) Lexical gaps: a given language has not lexicalised an interlingual concept.
  (b) Differences in taxonomic levels: two languages lexicalise the same interlingual concepts, but the conceptual relations between the lexicalisations in one language may be different than the conceptual relations that hold between the corresponding lexicalisations in the other language.
  (c) One-to-Many matches: one language has more than one lexicalisation for an interlingual concept and another has just one.
  (d) One-to-One mismatches: two languages lexicalise the same interlingual concept but the corresponding terms do not share all the same contexts, stylistic connotations, or subcategorisation features.
  We use local concepts to express these language-specific peculiarities. More specifically, the interlingual concepts are linked, through the translation links, to the corresponding local concepts. The local terms, that is, the language-specific lexicalisations, are represented as attribute values of the local concepts. The local terminological knowledge bases do not only contain the local concepts and the local terms. They may also contain language-specific grammatical and semantic information.

A prototypical terminological knowledge base, that is organised in the proposed way, is currently under development. It is based on the knowledge representation language PHOS [21,22]. Prolog is used for the implementation of the prototype. The terminological knowledge base involves three kinds of the formal objects that PHOS is able to support:

- *Concepts*. Three types of concepts are used in our representation: domain concepts for the domain-specific and language-independent aspects, interlingual

concepts for the application-specific and language-independent aspects, and local concepts for the language-specific aspects.
- *Attributes.* They correspond to properties of the concepts. An attribute value may be filled by another concept or by an individual.
- *Individuals.* They correspond to specific objects of the domain, i.e., numbers, text strings, or graphical symbols.

The knowledge management system supports the following types of inference:
- *Inheritance:* properties of a concept are inherited by its subconcepts.
- *Inconsistency detection:* a change in a concept or its attributes, or the addition of a new concept, may be inconsistent with already existing knowledge. The system detects such an inconsistency and does not permit the user to make the requested change or addition.
- *Concept classification:* all concepts that are more general or more specific than a given concept are found.
- *Subsumption:* questions about whether or not one concept is more general than another concept are answered. This type of inference is important for concept classification.

Using as an example the functionality of a module of a Hewlett-Packard software product and the terminological information collected in one of the Glossasoft localisation case studies, the proposed architecture will be the one given in Figure 3. In this example, we represent the terminological knowledge that is relevant to the user interface procedure "Modify a palette". This procedure is described in the software function model as a sequence of steps. Labels X, Y, Z are used to denote three of the procedure's steps.

The software product considered in our example is a window management system. The domain model, therefore, contains conceptual knowledge on the domain of window management systems. More specifically, the domain model contains the concepts "Dialog", "Button", and its sub-concept "Push-button".

The interlingual terminological knowledge base contains the concept "HP dialog" and its subconcepts "Color dialog" and "Modify dialog". It also contains the concept "HP button" and its subconcepts "Color button", "Color OK button", "Modify button", and "Modify OK button". A "dialog" has a "label" and one or more "tasks", which are performed by it. These tasks refer to the procedure steps described in the software function model. The reference labels specified in the software function model are used to denote explicitly the tasks a concept performs or is used in. For example, "color dialog" performs tasks X and Y, whereas "palette-list" is "used-in" task X. There are also tasks denoted implicitly through the conceptual links. For example, the task "open the Color dialog" is represented through the attribute "activates" of the concept "Color button" which has value "Color dialog". That is, to open (activate) the color dialog, the user must push the color button. The software function model can also be used as a resource for providing information on application-specific concepts. For example, if the user asks for information on the concept "select a palette", the knowledge management system will be able to provide the following information: "select a palette is a task performed by the Color dialog, it uses the palettes list, and is also one of the necessary steps to modify a palette".

183

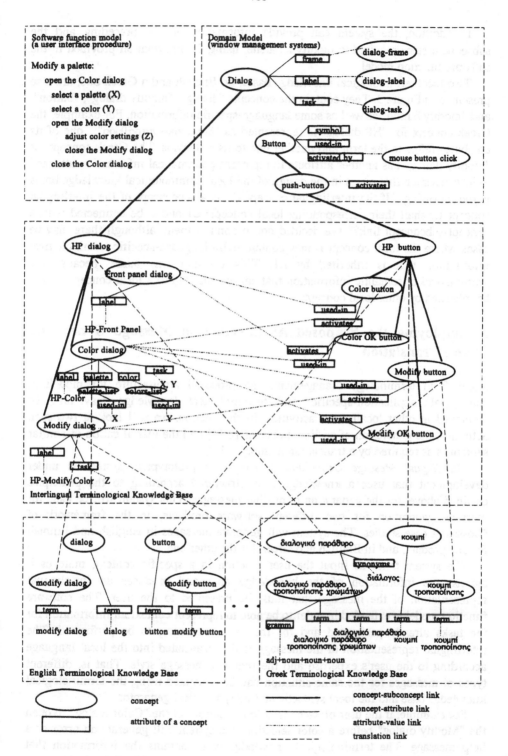

Fig. 3. An example of the proposed architecture

In addition, the system can provide information on the preceding and the subsequent steps required to modify a palette, using the information provided in the software function model.

Two local terminological knowledge bases, an English and a Greek one, are also presented in Figure 3. They contain the concepts "dialog", "modify dialog", "button", and "modify button" as well as some language-specific information. For example, the Greek concept for "HP dialog" is represented as "διαλογικό παράθυρο"; one of its attributes refers to the term and another one to its synonyms. The Greek concept for "modify dialog" has another attribute to represent grammatical information attached to it. A question that arises in the design of the local terminological knowledge bases is the following: "If the interlingual concept C1 is a subconcept of the interlingual concept C, shall their corresponding local concepts L1 and L be connected with a concept-subconcept link?" We decided not to connect them, although there may be cases where the local concept L may contain extra language-specific terminological information that is inherited by L1. This decision was made, because the grammatical or semantic information that can be attached to a local concept cannot be inherited by other local concepts.

5 Employing the Proposed Architecture in Message Generation and Translation

Apart from terminology management, the proposed architecture for modelling conceptual, application-specific, and terminological knowledge may also be employed in other localisation activities. In this section, we will look at two such activities, the generation of on-line messages [8,18] and the identification of similar sentences as required by a translation memory [8].

Multilingual Message Generation. Currently, a prototypical system is under development that uses a knowledge base structured according to the principles outlined above, for the generation of on-line messages. This system will be used for message generation for two different software products, in the framework of Glossasoft case studies. The system will generate messages in English and Finnish for one product, and in English and Greek for the other one.

The system takes as input the user reaction in a specific context, matches it against the information of the knowledge base and produces an interlingual representation of the message that must be presented to the user. The software function model is extended in order to be able to represent contextual information for the tasks already performed and for the ones remaining to be performed. The interlingual representation of the message is then translated into the local language according to the user's expertise and the required message style. That is, different types of messages for the same situation can be generated using the terminological knowledge base and the local syntactic and morphological generator.

For example, if the user presses the "Modify button" of the "Color dialog" to open the "Modify dialog" before a color selection, the system will generate an error or a help message. The terminological knowledge base contains the information that "Modify button" is used in "Color dialog" to open the "Modify dialog". Also, the information that to perform the task "open the modify dialog" the task "select a color" must be performed first, can be retrieved from the software function model. The system uses this information to produce an interlingual representation of the current task status. This is presented, in a Prolog notation, in Figure 4.

The last two predicates in Figure 4 are parts of the contextual information provided in the software function model. The interlingual representation of the error message to be generated will be:

precondition("open the Modify dialog",Y).

Different types of messages can be generated from the message and the task status representation according to the user's expertise. Some possible messages and the predicates used to generate them are:

"Select a color", from to-be-done (see Figure 4).

"Select a color from the colors list", from to-be-done and colors-list (see Figure 4).

"Select a color and then push the modify button", from to-be-done, color-dialog, and modify-button (see Interlingual Terminological Knowledge Base).

"Select a color from the colors list, and then activate the modify dialog", from to-be-done, colors-list, color-dialog, and modify-button.

By providing appropriate style rules, different styles of messages may also be enforced. For example:

"You have to select a color first",

"You didn't select a color first",

"A color must be selected first",

"To open Modify Dialog, you have to select a color first".

```
/*Interlingual Terminological Knowledge Base*/
color-dialog((task, (X,Y)),(palette, palettes-list), (color, colors-list)). /*the "color-
dialog" performs the tasks "select a palette" and "select a color" and contains the
"palettes-list" and the "colors-list"*/
modify-button((used-in, color-dialog), (activates, modify-dialog)). /*the "modify-
button" is used in (belongs to) the "color-dialog" and performs the task "open the
Modify dialog"*/
palettes-list((used-in, X)). /*the "palettes-list" is used in the task "select a palette"*/
colors-list(used-in, Y)). /*the "colors-list" is used in the task "select a color"*/

/*Software Function Model*/
done(X). /*the task "select a palette" has already been performed*/
to-be-done(Y). /*the task "select a color" is the next task to be done*/
```

Fig. 4. Task status in a Prolog notation

Machine-Assisted Translation: The proposed representation framework can also be applied to the task of matching similar sentences, a function required for the development of a translation memory. Here, our intention is to improve the accuracy of matching, when there are differences in a few terms. In that case, the knowledge base can be consulted to find out about the relation that holds between the differing terms. If a conceptual relation between the differing terms exists, the similarity between the two given sentences increases and a translation can be retrieved via the interlingual base from the target local base. On the other hand, the lack of a relation reduces the degree of similarity. For example, the translation memory entry "Choose Modify in the Color dialog." and the input sentence "Choose Color in the Front panel." differ in three words out of seven. However, "Modify" and "Color" are buttons "activating" the dialogs "Color dialog" and "Front panel" respectively, and thus the similarity between the two sentences increases. The source sentence can then be translated using the already translated part from the translation memory and the corresponding relations of the source and the target local base.

6 Conclusion

In the Glossasoft project, we examined several existing terminology management systems. We found that most of these systems present some severe drawbacks which are mainly due to the fact that they do not adequately support the definition of term classes and that they do not provide mechanisms for property inheritance. As an alternative approach to terminology management, we look at knowledge-based techniques, discuss their benefits and drawbacks, and propose our own knowledge-based architecture for the organisation of terminological data. The architecture not only includes a representation layer for the language-specific terminological knowledge, but also layers for modelling conceptual knowledge both about the subject domain and about the terms included in the terminological database as well as a layer for representing application-specific knowledge. Currently, a prototypical system is under development, which is based on the proposed architecture and which is implemented in the PHOS knowledge representation language.

A crucial issue of the proposed approach is its multifunctionality which is currently investigated in the area of multilingual message generation for software applications. The results of this work will be published in the next few months as part of the deliverables of the last phase of the Glossasoft project.

The use of terminological knowledge bases to improve the accuracy of matching by a translation memory is another research issue that we intend to investigate. We also plan to examine the problem of the knowledge base set-up, mentioned in Section 3. In addition, the use of controlled language text for the software function description as a source for knowledge acquisition as well as the exploitation of existing terminological databases are among the aspects that we intend to investigate.

Acknowledgements

We would like to thank Hewlett-Packard Hellas and also our colleagues in the Glossasoft project, Ray Hudson from Open University and Timo Honkela from VTT. Particular thanks are due to the editor of the present volume Mrs Petra Steffens, whose comments improved considerably the quality of this paper.

187

References

1. Ahmad, K., Davies, A., 1992. Terminology Management: A corpus-based approach to eliciting and elaborating specialist terms. Computing Series Report CS-92-05, University of Surrey.
2. Borgida, A., 1992. Description Logics are not just for the Flightless-Birds: A new Look at the Utility and Foundations of Description Logics. Rutgers University, June 1992.
3. Bowker, L., Meyer, I., 1993. Beyond "Textbook" Concept Systems: Handling Multidimensionality in a New Generation of Term Banks. In Proceedings of Third International Congress on Terminology and Knowledge Engineering (TKE'93), Indeks Verlag 1993, pp. 123-137.
4. Brachman, R.J. et al., 1991. Living with Classic: When and How to Use a KL-ONE-like language. Principles of Semantic Networks-Explorations in the Representation of Knowledge, ed. J. Sowa, 1991, pp. 401-456.
5. Devandu, P. et al., 1989. A Knowledge-based Software Information System. In Proceedings of the 11th IJCAI, pp.110-115.
6. Glossasoft: Deliverable 1.1 "Commercial Requirements for Localisation", v1.0, 30 June 1993. Demokritos participation: C.D. Spyropoulos, E. Karkaletsis.
7. Glossasoft: Deliverable 2.1 "Current State of Linguistics Applicable to Software Interlinguality", v1.1, 15 December 1993. Demokritos participation: E. Karkaletsis, C.D. Spyropoulos, P. Stamatopoulos, G. Vouros.
8. Glossasoft, Deliverable 4.1 "Guidelines for Linguistics for Interaction Inter-linguality", v1.0, 22 December 1993. Demokritos participation: C.D. Spyropoulos, E. Karkaletsis, G. Vouros.
9. Hovy, E., Nirenburg, S., 1992. Approximating an Interlingua in a Principled Way. In Proceedings of the DARPA Speech and Natural Language Workshop, Arden House, Feb. 1992.
10. Karkaletsis, E., Spyropoulos, C., 1993. Software Internationalisation and Local-isation. In Proceedings of the 4th Panhellenic Conference of the Greek Computer Society (EΠY), Patra 16-18 December 1993.
11. Karkaletsis, E., Fecos, N., Spyropoulos, C., 1992. System for exploiting knowledge from natural language texts. Technical report of the Research Programme ΠABE-88 (BE 224), January 1992. (in Greek)
12. Knight, K., 1993. Building a Large Ontology for Machine Translation. In Proceedings of DARPA Human Language Conference, March 1993.
13. LISA, Software Localisation in Europe, Findings from an Ovum Study. In The LISA Forum Newsletter, Vol. II, July 1993.
14. MacGregor, R., 1991. The evolving technology of classification-based Knowledge Representation Systems. Principles of Semantic Networks-Explorations in the Representation of Knowledge, ed. J. Sowa, 1991, pp. 385-400.

15. Meyer, I., Skuce, D., Bowker, L., Eck, K., 1992. Towards a New Generation of Terminological Resources: An Experiment in Building a Terminological Knowledge Base. In Proceedings of COLING'92, Nantes.
16. Meyer, I., 1991. Knowledge Management for Terminology-Intensive Applications: Needs and Tools. In Proceedings of 1st SIGLEX Workshop, June 1991, Lecture Notes in Artificial Intelligence, vol. 627, pp. 21-37.
17. Miller, G.A., Fellbaum, C., 1990. WordNet and the Organization of Lexical Memory. In Proceedings of the NATO Advanced Research Workshop "The Bridge to International Communication: Intelligent Tutoring Systems for Foreign Language Learning", Washington, September 1990, NATO ASI Series, Springer-Verlag 1992, pp. 89-102.
18. Reiter, E., Mellish, C., 1993. Optimising the Costs and Benefits of Natural Language Generation. In Proceedings of IJCAI 1993, pp. 1164-1169.
19. Skuce, D., 1993. A System for Managing Knowledge and Terminology for Technical Documentation. In Proceedings of Third International Congress on Terminology and Knowledge Engineering (TKE'93), Indeks Verlag 1993, pp. 428-441.
20. TRANSIT TermStar, 1993. Product Information on TRANSIT for Windows, November 1993, pp. 17-25.
21. Vouros, G., 1992. Structure and organisation of concepts. An epistemological approach. Ph.D. dissertation, 1992. (in Greek)
22. Vouros, G., Spyropoulos, C., 1991. The PHOS conceptual language for knowledge representation. Engineering Systems with Intelligence: Concepts, Tools and Applications, ed. S.G.Tzafestas, Kluwer Academic Publ., 1991, pp. 43-50.
23. Woods, W.A., 1991. Understanding Subsumption and Taxonomy: A Framework for Progress. Principles of Semantic Networks-Explorations in the Representation of Knowledge, ed. J. Sowa, 1991, pp. 45-94.

Navigation through Terminological Databases

Renate Mayer

Fraunhofer Institut für Arbeitswirtschaft und Organisation
Nobelstr. 12; 70659 Stuttgart

Abstract. Translating technical texts may cause many problems concerning terminology, even for the professional technical translator. For this reason, tools such as terminological databases or termbanks have been introduced to support the user in finding the most suitable translation. Termbanks are a type of machine-readable dictionary and contain extensive information on technical terms. But a termbank offers more possibilities than providing users with the electronic version of a printed dictionary. This paper describes a multilingual termbank, which was developed within the ESPRIT project Translator's Workbench. The termbank allows the user to create, maintain, and retrieve specialised vocabulary. In addition, it offers the user the possibility to look up definitions, foreign language equivalents, and background knowledge. In this paper, an introduction to the database underlying the termbank and the user interface is given with the emphasis lying on those functions which initiate the user into a new subject by allowing him or her to navigate through a terminology field. It will be shown how, by clustering the term explanation texts and by linking them to a type of semantic network, such functions can be implemented.

1.   Introduction

Most professional translators have studied a foreign language and are therefore familiar with the language for general purposes (LGP). The problems translators must overcome lie in dealing with language for special purposes (LSP). Considering that even experts do not always know all the details of their subject area, it is not surprising that translators are faced with problems in dealing with specialised vocabulary. Due to this problem, there is a clear need for supporting translators in dealing with special-language vocabulary. When looking up specialised vocabulary, translators traditionally use printed media such as lexica, thesauri, encyclopaedia and glossaries. Only recently, electronic media have come into use, especially word processors, as well as other tools which support terminology work. Also, despite much useful research and development in the field of machine translation, the fact remains that most translation is still carried out by human translators.

Section 2 of this paper introduces the ESPRIT project Translator's Workbench (TWB) and describes user requirements concerning terminology support. Section 3 contains a description of the TWB termbank; it explains the types of information accounted for by the termbank, its conceptual database schema and describes how explanation texts are linked and clustered in order to provide background knowledge for a specific subject. In Section 4, the user interface, the retrieval component, and the navigation component of the TWB termbank are described. Within the TWB project, the termbank was evaluated through user and system testing. Section 5 summarises the results of these tests. The final section contains a summary and a conclusion.

2. Requirements

This section introduces the ESPRIT project Translator's Workbench and the requirements analysis which was performed at the beginning of the project.

The ESPRIT project 2315 TRANSLATOR'S WORKBENCH (TWB) was established in order to find a means by which to support professional translators using specialised vocabulary. This support was to be in the form of simple tools to assist human translators, as opposed to elaborate translation by machine. The two-phased project was partially funded by the CEC (Commission of the European Communities). The first project phase, TWB I, began in April 1989 and was completed in March 1992. The second phase is scheduled to finish in October 1994. The participants of TWB I and II comprise three groups: (i) users, (ii) industrial partners, and (iii) research partners. The translation department at Mercedes Benz in Stuttgart, the French company SITE, and the translation departments of the European Commission make up the user group. The industrial partners include SNI Germany and Spain, EP electronic publishing (formerly TA Triumph Adler AG), and L-Cube (Greek software house). The research partners are the Universities of Catalunya, Surrey, Heidelberg, and Stuttgart as well as the Austrian terminology association TermNet and the German research institute Fraunhofer-IAO.

A user requirements study was carried out at the beginning of the project in order to investigate current translation practices and to assess how translators can benefit from advances in Information Technology. The study [3] comprised (i) a questionnaire survey of European professional translators, both freelance and in-house, as well as of students of translation, (ii) an observation study of six translators at work, (iii) in-depth interviews with ten translators. The study was performed by the TWB partners Mercedes Benz and the University of Surrey. The results of the survey showed that there is a real need for computer-based tools among professional translators such as "smart" editors, termbanks, and remote access possibilities to machine translation systems. It was also found that the three different user groups basically have similar needs with regard to their working practices. In particular, translators would welcome tools which relieve them of the laborious task of determining vocabulary and the usage of a given word.

The survey also gave some information concerning minimum requirements for termbanks. Thus, all translators agreed that the most important types of information in terminology collections are foreign language equivalents and grammatical information. In addition, most translators considered contextual examples to be as important as definitions.

The Department of Translation Studies of the University of Heidelberg provided additional requirements for the design of termbanks. Translators often find terms difficult to translate because, first, they do not understand their meaning and, second, they do not know their proper usage. This led to the conclusion that translators need two types of knowledge to be able to both understand the source text and to produce an adequate target text, namely, general knowledge of the given subject and linguistic knowledge [1]. Text comprehension is only possible if both types of knowledge interact. The textual clues are interpreted on the basis of linguistic knowledge and checked against the available general knowledge. Since translators cannot know all the details of the subject which a text covers, they also need more specific knowledge, which completes their general knowledge on the subject. A termbank can be a valuable aid for acquiring this knowledge. The next section will introduce a termbank which provides such subject-specific knowledge.

3.   The TWB Termbank

Terminological databases or, in short, termbanks have been developed in order to support translators and experts in their daily work. They help translators in that they contain terminological up-to-date data on several subjects and integrate several dictionaries. Their dynamic organisation allows very efficient processing. Apart from the terms themselves, a termbank entry often contains additional information such as definitions, contexts, and usage. Also, relationships between the entries, e.g., "is-translation-of", "is-synonym-to", "is-broader-than", etc. are given. Both retrieval and modification components allow the user to access and modify the terminology. A user interface provides the user with a quick and easy way of retrieving and modifying terminology.

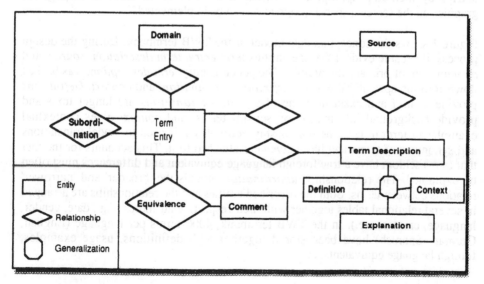

Figure 1: Conceptual data model of the TWB termbank

Within the TWB project, a termbank was designed and implemented which contains terminology on automotive engineering in three European languages (English, German, Spanish). Besides storing linguistic information about a term (e.g., morphological and syntactic properties) and relationships between terms (e.g., translation equivalence, synonymy, hyperonymy), the termbank also stores definitions and explanatory texts. Because translators often need more background knowledge in order to decide how to translate a given term or expression, the TWB termbank provides facilities for linking terms, term definitions, and explanatory texts. The TWB termbank allows its users to navigate through the resulting network. The terminology included in the TWB termbank has been compiled by the Universities of Surrey and Heidelberg.

3.1 Database Design

Although generally robust and adequate for many applications, the use of a commercially available relational database system (RDB) for terminology management has some disadvantages. For example, terminological data often include long texts which have variable lengths depending on the importance of the term entry; however, neither long texts, which are needed for definitions and explanations, nor graphics are supported by today's relational database systems. Multilingual terminology causes additional problems due to its enlarged character set. Even the 8-Bit ASCII character set is not sufficient for some European languages such as Greek or Russian. Special characters which cannot be handled by the system must be transcribed for the database. Despite such problems, a relational database system was chosen as the basis for the TWB termbank because of its capabilities for database management. This system has been adapted to the special requirements of terminology processing. For example, graphics were scanned and related to their term entries by including appropriate pointers in the entries. In order to display the graphics on the screen a special program had to be implemented.

Figure 1 shows the conceptual data model of the TWB termbank. During the design process, it became evident that the entities *term entry, term description, source,* and *domain* were of primary importance. The general entity *term description.* was broken down into the specialised entities *definition, explanation,* and *context. Definitions* provide a short and exact meaning of a term, *explanations* are longer texts and provide background information on several terms, and *context* gives contextual examples of term usage. The relationship *equivalence* is used to model translations and synonyms of terms and has a *comment* attached to it. This accounts for the fact that terms seldom have a true foreign language equivalent and differences must often be explained. The relationship *subordination* models the 'broader' and 'narrower' relations between terms. Both the described entities and the relationships are arranged in several relational tables together with their respective attributes (e.g., date, gender, language, creator, etc.). In the TWB termbank, 4000 terms per language (English, German, Spanish) have been stored together with definitions, usage examples, foreign language equivalents, etc.

3.2 Text Linking and Clustering

There are two main differences between traditional termbanks and the termbank designed within the TWB project. The first difference concerns the links which have been established between the different explanation texts; the second difference concerns the clustering of the explanation texts into semantic groups.

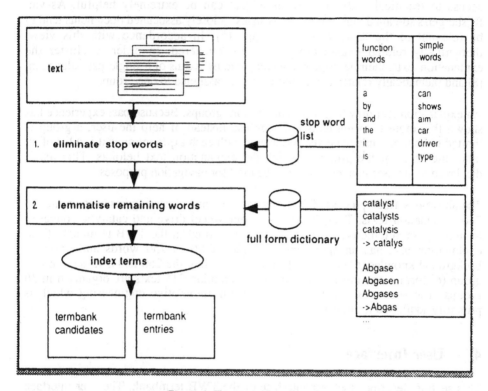

Figure 2: Text indexing process

In order to set up links between the explanation texts, a descriptor must be created for each text which establishes links between the *explanations* and assigns similar texts to one group. The descriptor represents the text content and is created by an indexing process which comprises the following two steps [6].

1. The first step of text indexing is to eliminate stop words. Stop words are function words, simple words, and numbers (see Fig. 2). Function words have a grammatical but no lexical meaning. They comprise, for instance, articles, prepositions, and conjunctions, and form up to 50% of a text. Simple words consist of adjectives, verbs, and nouns and form up to 45% of a text. For the identification of stop words, a lexicon consisting of common vocabulary is used.

2. In the second step, the remaining words are lemmatised. The result of the lemmatisation is a set of stems called index terms which represent the text content. The index terms consist of specialised vocabulary for which an entry may or may not exist in the termbank. If an entry does not exist in the termbank, the index term is called a termbank candidate. The index terms make up the so-called term list (or text descriptor) which is associated with the text.

For a translator who must become familiar with the terminology of a new domain, access to technical texts on a given subject can be extremely helpful. As van Rijsbergen's so-called cluster hypothesis states: "closely associated documents tend to be relevant to the same request" [8, pg. 45]. In accordance with this view, thematically related explanation texts were clustered. In order to cluster the explanation texts, their descriptors are compared by means of a single-pass-algorithm [8] and thematically related explanation texts are assigned to one group.

An explanation text may be part of one or more groups. Because past experience has shown that more than ten texts may confuse instead of help the user, a group is limited to no more than ten texts. Associated with each *explanation* text is a list of all other members of the group to which the explanation text belongs. This list is displayed to the user in a menu and can be used for navigation purposes.

The above-described process of indexing and semantic clustering has been applied to 260 explanation texts. These texts cover four wheel drive and catalytic converter technology in automotive engineering and are stored in the TWB termbank. Each explanation text has an approximate length of 80 to 750 words and provides background knowledge on several LSP terms. Among the 260 texts, 45 are not in a group (or form a one-member group). The remaining 215 texts are organised in 36 groups. The source of the texts is a book on automotive engineering which is primarily addressed to students.

4. User Interface

This section describes the user interface of the TWB termbank. The user interface was designed in close co-operation with the TWB project partner Mercedes Benz, whose role in the project was to specify requirements for a translator's workbench as well as to use and evaluate the system that was developed within the project. At the beginning of the project, the technical writers and translators at Mercedes-Benz were not familiar with computer use, thus the user interface of the termbank had to be extremely user-friendly. For this reason, direct manipulative interaction techniques were applied which allow the user to directly manipulate window objects with a mouse (e.g., opening, closing, moving objects, etc.) [2]. In addition to reduce training time and error possibilities, menu selection was included where appropriate.

The user interface of the TWB termbank, which was implemented on a Sun Workstation using OSF/Motif, serves two purposes: it allows the user to access the entries of the TWB termbank and it provides functions for navigating through the network of term definitions and explanatory texts. In Section 4.1, the user interface of the retrieval component is discussed; Section 4.2 contains a description of the navigation component.

4.1 The Retrieval Component

Database management systems include a formal query language (e.g., SQL) to create, access, and modify database entries. When working with a terminological database, users should not be required to use such a query language, nor should it be necessary for them to know how the termbank is organised. To relieve the user of this task, the TWB termbank interacts with the user by means of different forms. These forms offer all possible search options and allow the user to select the types of information to be retrieved as well as to define source and target languages. For example, at the beginning of a working session, a user may define the source language as English, and the target language as German. Similarly, the types of information which, the user is interested in such as 'translation equivalent', 'definition', 'explanation', 'broader term', and 'contextual example' have to be defined. For subsequent queries, the user receives exactly these types of information. The query specification form can be stored as a user profile so that it can be used in later sessions.

After having defined the desired types of information, the user enters the term and starts the search process. The retrieved information is shown in a result window. If the entered term is not a term entry, the termbank *candidate* list comes into use. Users researching a term can receive valuable information when they access a text where the term occurs even if the translation or exact definition is not given. The context of the term in question can be extremely helpful in many situations. The user, therefore, receives explanation texts in which the candidate term was used.

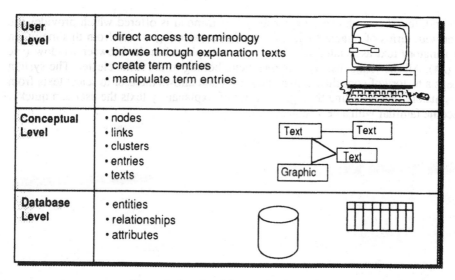

Figure 3: Levels of the termbank system

To facilitate the search, the following features were implemented:

- Search with wild cards: the user does not have to type in the whole term; instead, it can be abbreviated by a pattern, the wild card, which matches all terms of the same structure.
- Ignore spelling variation: technical terms often vary in spelling, because most of them are 'multiword terms', which may be spelled together, separately, or which are connected with hyphens.
- List search: the system searches for all relevant terms in one step and prints the results in a window or a file.

4.2   The Navigation Interface

A subject expert or translator who wants to become familiar with a new subject field tends to consult closely associated texts to gain the necessary background knowledge. The time-consuming task of becoming familiar with a new subject field can be accelerated by making available relevant information on a computer and by introducing a browsing facility. A browser is a navigation aid which guides users through linked information. Browsing is an exploratory, information-seeking strategy that depends on serendipity [5].

The TWB termbank browser visualises the interconnection between explanation texts and offers two navigation modes. First, there is direct navigation through indicated terms. For example, in a typical session, browsing through the TWB termbank starts at a technical term. The retrieved explanatory texts for this term may contain technical vocabulary, which in turn leads to additional information on the given subject. The terms for which additional information exists are displayed in boldface.

Second, together with every explanatory text a menu is offered which provides the user with terms of related subject fields. When selecting a term from this menu, an explanatory text associated with this term is displayed in the browser window (see Fig. 4). All the terms displayed in one menu belong to the same cluster. The system keeps a history of consulted explanatory texts and allows the user to select texts from this history. By browsing through a cluster of explanatory texts the user can quickly become familiar with a new subject area.

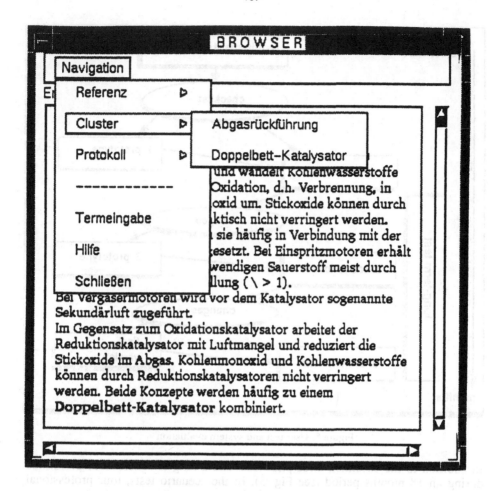

Figure 4: Termbank browser interface

5. User Involvement

In order to reach high user acceptance, early user involvement is necessary [7]. Therefore, one of our goals was the early integration of future users in the design and evaluation process. Users participated throughout the entire project and during software development in order to (i) understand and implement user requirements, (ii) test the prototypes and final tools, and (iii) evaluate the performance and functionality of the tools.

At the beginning of the project, the user requirements were established through interviews and questionnaire surveys. A checklist was developed comprising all features of the future software product. This checklist was distributed to all designers and programmers involved. The implementation of various features was checked at several points [4].

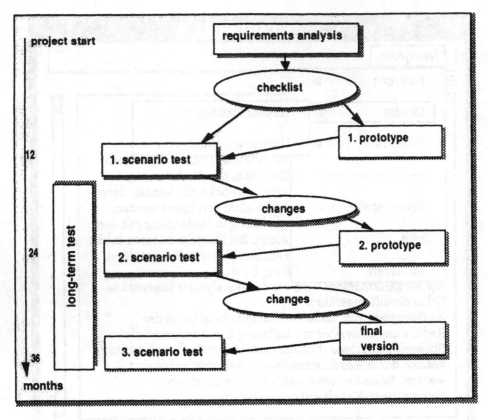

Figure 5: User test and system evaluation

In addition to the checklist, three pilot tests and a long-term test were performed during an 18 months period (see Fig. 5). In the scenario tests, four professional translators had to solve a "real-life" problem (translating a text, looking up terminology, etc.) in a given amount of time. Their comments and complaints were given back to the designers, who updated the system accordingly. At the beginning of the project, the four subjects were quite sceptical, but could see improvements in the next test and are now, at the end of the project, satisfied users of the workbench.

The results of the scenario tests show that translators who are not familiar with a given subject use the browser more often than expert translators who are content with context examples or a short technical definition.

6. Summary and Conclusion

In this paper, a navigation tool was introduced which offers terminological information for translators and other professionals dealing with terminology. Within this system, explanation texts are indexed, linked, and clustered by means of a clustering algorithm. The semantic net which is created through the links and clusters is accessed by the user through a user-friendly interface. The system was evaluated in several tests by professional translators and achieved a high level of user acceptance.

Additional multi-media tools such as video, animation, sound, pictures, etc. are presently being investigated in connection with the development of user interfaces. The TWB termbank can be enhanced by adding multi-media features. Interpreters, for example, may be interested in the correct pronunciation of a term. Technical writers can be supported through an animation component which explains the function of a module or machine.

The goals of corporate identity and enhanced inter-company communication may lead to integrated workbenches, which allow engineers, technical writers, and translators to work together. Computer supported co-operative work (CSCW) and hypertext and hypermedia systems can boost performance and help to produce improved products.

References

[1]   Albl, Michaela; Kohn, Kurt; Pooth, Stefan; Zabel, Renate: Specification of Terminological Knowledge for Translation Purposes: report on workpackage 1.4 of the ESPRIT project 2315 (TWB), March 1990.
[2]   Bullinger, Hans-Jörg: User Interface Management - The strategic view. *Bullinger, H.-J. (ed.) Human Aspects in Computing: Design and Use of Interactive Systems and Information Management.* Amsterdam: Elsevier, 1991, pp. 27-38.
[3]   Fulford, Heather; Höge, Monika; Ahmad, Khurshid: User Requriements Study: Final report on workpackage 3.3 of ESPRIT project 2315 (TWB), March 1990.
[4]   Höge, Monika; Kroupa, Edith: Towards the Design of a Translator´s Workstation - Organisational Background and User Implications. *Bullinger, H.-J. (ed.) Human Aspects in Computing: Design and Use of Interactive Systems and Information Management,* 1-6 September, Stuttgart, Amsterdam: Elsevier, 1991, pp. 1036-1040.
[5]   Marchionini, Gary; Shneiderman, Ben: Finding Facts vs. Browsing Knowledge. Hypertext Systems, IEEE Computer Vol. 21 (1988) No. 1, pp. 70-80.
[6]   Mayer, Renate: Rechnerunterstützte Systeme für die technische Dokumentation und Übersetzung. Heidelberg, Berlin: Springer, 1993.
[7]   Peschke, Helmut; Wittstock, Marion: Benutzerbeteiligung im Software-Entwicklungsprozeß. *Fähnrich, K.-P. (ed.): Software Ergonomie.* München, Wien: Oldenbourg, 1987, pp. 81-94.
[8]   Rijsbergen, C. J. van: Information Retrieval. 2nd ed., London Boston: Butterworths, 1979.

Acknowledgement. All tools have been developed at the Fraunhofer Institute IAO partly within the ESPRIT project Translator's Workbench, which is partially funded by the Commission of the European Communities and Industry. The participants in the TWB projects are: EP Electronic Publishing, SNI, Mercedes-Benz, SITE, Translation Department of the European Communities, L-Cube, the FhG-IAO, TermNet, the Universities of Catalunya, Heidelberg, Stuttgart and Surrey.

Part III

Describing Lexical Data

Types of Lexical Co–occurrences: Descriptive Parameters

Folker Caroli

IAI, Martin–Luther–Straße 14, D–66111 Saarbrücken

Abstract. In this article, I will discuss different types of lexical co–occurrences and examine the requirements for representing them in a reusable lexical resource. I will focus the discussion on the delimitation of a limited set of descriptive parameters rather than on an exhaustive classification of idioms or multiword units. Descriptive parameters will be derived from a detailed discussion of the problem of how to determine adequate translations for such units. Criteria for determining translation equivalences between multiword units of two languages will be: the syntactic and the semantic structure as well as functional, pragmatic, and stylistic properties.

1 Introduction

Expressions like idioms, multiword units, phraseological units, collocations, and support verb constructions encompass a broad range of various linguistic units which have the following common properties:

- they are composed of at least two distinct lexical elements,
- their syntactic function and/or their meaning is, if at all, only partially captured by a compositional analysis,
- their components are subject to lexical restrictions, i.e., the presence of one specific lexical element requires the occurrence of the other lexical element in order to form the whole unit.

The treatment of these units is a problem within NLP systems. A purely compositional analysis is not possible because of the lexically determined co–occurrence conditions which hold for their components. On the other hand, listing all possible cases of lexical co–occurrences for each lexical item does not seem an appropriate solution either — at least not for a large–scale NLP system. Various strategies for a semi–compositional treatment have been elaborated for some types of lexical co–occurrences within different NLP approaches (e.g., for fixed verbal expressions in Tree Adjoining Grammar (Abeillé et al. [1990]), for support verb constructions in EUROTRA (Danlos et al. [1990]) and in CAT2 (Mesli [1991]), and for some types of collocations in HPSG (Erbach and Krenn [1993])).

In this paper, I will discuss different types of lexical co–occurrences and examine the requirements for representing them in a reusable lexical resource. I will focus the discussion on the delimitation of a limited set of descriptive parameters rather than on the exhaustive classification of idioms or multiword units. As a result of this discussion, I will specify the types of lexical information which are required for a computational treatment of lexical co–occurrences.

2   Descriptive Dimensions

The definition of lexical co–occurrences stated above covers a broad range of phenomena addressed by various terms. For terminological clarity, we will use the general term *phraseological unit* to refer to any linguistic data of lexical co–occurrence; to refer to particular instances of lexical co–occurrences, more specific terms like *collocation, idiom, etc.* will be used. In this paper, I will neither discuss problems of terminology in any detail, nor will I give an overview of all the possible definitions for the different types of lexical co–occurrences[1]. It is well known that linguists working in this field are far from a convergent terminology and from commonly agreed definitions.

The lack of a commonly accepted nomenclature for lexical co–occurrences reveals a general problem of linguistic description pertaining to multiword units: we have to distinguish a broad range of various but interrelated linguistic data and we have to delimit a complex bundle of descriptive dimensions for their classification. In a first atttempt, such descriptive parameters can be derived from some common defining elements:

- the syntactic function of the phraseological unit,
- syntactic properties which refer to the degree of fixedness of the phraseological unit and to the combinatorial restrictions that hold for its components,
- semantic properties which can be described as degrees of restricted compositionality or opaqueness,
- stylistic and pragmatic properties which have to do with the metaphorical status of a phraseological unit and with its capacity for register marking.

In the following, I will discuss each of these descriptive parameters and I will show how they help us to determine types of linguistic information which allow for an appropriate representation of phraseological units in a reusable lexical resource.

3   Functional Aspects

Functional aspects of phraseological units are related to their status in the context in which they occur. A basic distinction has been made between phraseological units which are constituents of sentences and phraseological units which are sentences or even larger pieces of texts within a textual context. This distinction is depicted in Figure 1, which generalises over some of the defining conditions given in Pilz [1981], p.27.

---

[1] An overview on definitions and terminological variation can be found in Pilz [1981] and in Burger et al. [1982].

Phraseological Unit (PU) = Phraseologism

Phraseological Word = Phraseolexeme (PL)	Phraseological Sentence (PS)
Adverbial PL	**Elliptic PS**
ab und zu (occasionally) hinten und vorn (nothing like; at all)	Ab nach Kassel (to disappear)
Nominal PL	**Complete PS**
das Auf und Ab (ups and downs) das Weiße Haus (the White House)	Da liegt der Hund begraben. (Therein lies the rup.)
Verbal PL	**Sentence**
schief gehen (not to work out) ins gras beißen (to kick the bucket)	Aller Anfang ist schwer. (All beginnings are difficult.)
	Proverb
	Morgenstund hat Gold im Mund. (The early bird catches the worm.)
	Stereotype
	Herzlichen Glückwunsch (Congratulations; Happy Birthday)
	Quote
	Nun wächst zusammen, was zusammen gehöhrt. (That which belongs together is now growing together.)

Fig.1 Functional classification of phraseological units

Phraseoloexemes are considered to behave like simple or non–composite lexemes within a sentence. This, however, leads to a problem concerning their syntactic description, which will be discussed below: although phraseolexemes are considered as lexemes, they have an internal syntactic structure which must be accounted for.

Phraseological sentences are units which cannot be described as terminal nodes or as phrasal constituents, even if they are ellipses or other types of incomplete sentences. They have a clear textual function indicating, e.g., common sense judgements, a specific cultural background, a specific ideological context, etc. Because of these textual aspects, they are a serious challenge for text understanding and translation. In general, the description of phraseological units is not just a purely lexicographic task; rather, it has to account for the background knowledge required for their understanding. Translation must reproduce the textual function of these units by introducing corresponding units which carry approximately the same background knowledge and which evoke similar connotations. This is a content–related problem and not so much a question of establishing lexical equivalences between source language and target language units. Since, in this paper, I want to look at phraseological units from the perspective of contrastive lexicographic description, the focus of the following discussion will be on phraseolexemes rather than on phraseological sentences.

4 Syntactic Properties of Phraseolexemes

As was stated above, phraseological lexemes are considered to behave in a sentence like simple lexemes. At the same time, however, they are subject to combinatorial restrictions which can be described in terms of syntactic regularities. Thus, we have to distinguish two layers of syntactic properties for phraseological lexemes: external and internal syntactic properties. External syntactic properties are related to the syntactic function of the phraseological lexeme in the sentence in which it occurs. Internal syntactic properties are related to the combinatorial regularities governing its internal structure.

The basic external property of a phraseolexeme is the syntactic category allocated to the unit as a whole. A phraseolexeme may behave like a noun, a verb, an adjective, etc. For an exhaustive description, additional syntactic information, e.g., on subcategorisation properties, selectional restrictions, etc. may be necessary, depending on the phraseolexeme's external syntactic category. This type of information is determined by replacing the phraseolexeme by a paraphrase consisting of a simple lexeme which has the same syntactic category and the same meaning as the phraseolexeme itself.

This procedure is not problematic, if the unit is completely fixed. For example, the phraseloexeme *ab und zu (sometimes)* can be considered as an adverb which has the same meaning and the same syntactic properties as the simple lexeme *manchmal*. This is the simplest case of what is generally referred to as *multiword unit*. For NLP systems, multiword units pose the problem of identifying their components and of providing an adequate syntactic and semantic

analysis of the entire unit; however, they do not pose specific problems for translation. A multiword unit may be translated in the target language either by a
multiword unit or by a simple lexeme. In both cases, the same equivalence criteria hold which also hold for the translation of simple lexemes.

The internal syntactic structure of many multiword units exhibits specific
combinatorial regularities which define series of multiword units with specific
external syntactic functions. For example in German, coordinations of two nouns
like *Mann und Maus, Kind und Kegel, Sack und Pack, Heller und Pfennig* are
instances of a type of multiword unit which has the following properties:

1. the coordinating conjunction is fixed (*und*);
2. the order of the nouns cannot be inverted: *Maus und Mann, Pack und Sack,
   Pfennig und Heller* are not multiword units;
3. both nouns have no determiner and cannot be modified: *jeder gute Mann und
   jede kleine Maus, groß Sack und kleines Pack, der Heller und der Pfennig*
   aren't multiword units either;
4. the multiword unit behaves like a noun and its occurrence is limited to
   prepositional phrases modifying a sentence.

These properties are illustrated by the following examples:

(1) a. Das Schiff sank mit Mann und Maus.
       (The ship sunk with all hands on board.)
    b. Er verließ die Stadt mit Sack und Pack.
       (He left the town with bag and baggage.)
    c. Die Kosten können noch nicht auf Heller und Pfennig berechnet werden.
       (The costs cannot yet be calculated to the last farthing.)

Such combinatorial properties of the internal structure of multiword units
and the interaction between their internal structure and their external syntactic function can be used within NLP systems for identifying multiword units.
Further investigations are required to establish the complete inventory of combinatorial patterns for multiword units in each language. From such an inventory,
one could derive the syntactic information which has to be represented in a
reusable lexical resource for each lexeme that can occur in a multiword unit.

The description of phraseolexemes becomes more complicated, if their internal syntactic structure is not completely fixed. In this case, internal and external
syntactic properties interact in a complex way. The most complex cases are verbal phraseolexemes. A tentative range of fixedness of verbal phraseolexemes is
given in Figure 2.

Highest level of compositionality/lowest level of fixedness

SELECTIONAL RESTRICTIONS
Der Hund bellt.
(The dog barks.)

COLLOCATIONS
den Hut aufsetzen (*anziehen)
(to put the hat on)
das Hemd anziehen (*aufsetzen)
(to put the shirt on)

LEXICALIZED METAPHORS
eine Behauptung angreifen/verteidigen
(to attack/defend an assertion)

STRICT SUPPORT VERB CONSTRUCTIONS
Die Kommission ergreift Maßnahmen gegen den
Subventionsschwindel.
(The commission takes measures against the fraud of subsidy.)

SUPPORT VERB CONSTRUCTIONS WITH
FIXED PREDICATIVE NOUN
Das Gesetz ist seit Anfang des Jahres in Kraft.
(The law is in force since the beginning of the year.)

FIXED POLYLEXICAL UNITS WITH ALTERNATING
COMPOSITIONAL MEANING
Die Regierung faßt eine Steuererhöhung ins Auge.
(The government envisages a tax increase.)
Das Kind faßt seinem Vater ins Auge.
(The child touches the eye of his father.)

COMPLETELY FIXED POLYLEXICAL UNITS
Der Fuchs macht dem Hasen den Garaus.
(The fox finishes the rabbit.)

Lowest level of compositionality/highest level of fixedness

Fig.2 Degrees of fixedness and of compositionality of phraseological units

It is worth noting that the degree of fixedness is not only related to syntactic properties; this holds especially for the first three items in the list, for which the degree of fixedness can be described by semantic rather than by syntactic properties. More on semantic aspects of fixedness will be said below.

The fourth item in the list refers to *strict support verb constructions.* Support verb constructions are characterised by the co–occurrence of a noun and a verb, which together form the predicative kernel of a sentence. The noun semantically determines the predicative meaning of the sentence, whereas the verb loses its normal meaning and only determines such general properties of the predication as person, number, tense, and aspect. Thus, nouns occurring in a support verb construction have an argument structure which determines the argument structure of the construction as a whole.

(2) a. Der Aufsichtsrat faßt den Beschluß, in den Tarifverhandlungen ein neues Angebot vorzulegen.
    (The board of directors takes the decision to make a new offer in the collective bargaining.)

  b. Der Beschluß des Aufsichtsrats, in den Tarifverhandlungen ein neues Angebot vorzulegen, hat einen Streik abgewendet.
    (The decisison of the board of directors to make a new offer in the collective bargaining averted a strike.)

  c. Der Aufsichtsrat beschließt, in den Tarifverhandlungen ein neues Angebot vorzulegen.
    (The board of directors decides to make a new offer in the collective bargaining.)

(3) a. Lea hat den Mut, ihrem Chef zu widersprechen.
    (Lea has the courage to contradict her boss.)

  b. Der Mut Leas, ihrem Chef zu widersprechen, hat alle erstaunt.
    (Lea's courage to contradict her boss astonished everyone.)

  c. Lea wagte es, ihrem Chef zu widersprechen.
    (Lea dared to contradict her boss.)

In these examples, the first sentence illustrates the occurrence of a predicative noun in a support verb construction, the second sentence illustrates the occurrence of the predicative noun in another syntactic context with the same arguments, and the third sentence shows how the support verb construction can be paraphrased by a simple verb.

According to the definition stated above, support verb constructions are types of lexical co–occurrences of a noun and a verb, with the verb being lexically determined by the noun. Here are some examples:

(4) a. einen Spaziergang machen
    (to take a walk)

  b. einen Mittagsschlaf halten
    (to have an afternoon nap)

  c. Krieg führen
    (to make war)

d. einen Beschluß fassen
(to take a decision)

e. Angst haben
(to be afraid)

In this type of construction, the interaction between internal and external syntactic properties is very complex. Therefore, rather than providing an exhaustive description of support verb constructions[2], we will take a closer look at the relationship between internal and external syntactic properties and enumerate some aspects characteristic of their interaction:

1. The argument structure of a support verb construction is semantically determined by the argument structure of the noun. The surface realisation of the arguments is determined by the subcategorisation frame of the support verb, in which the predicative noun occupies one position. Thus, the argument structure of the whole construction is related in a complex way to the argument structure of the noun and the subcategorisation frame of the verb, as is shown by the following example:

(5) a. Der Arzt gibt dem Patienten den Rat, das Rauchen aufzugeben.
(The doctor advises the patient to stop smoking.)

b. Der Rat des Arztes an den Patienten, das Rauchen aufzugeben, wurde von diesem nicht befolgt.
(The doctor's advice to the patient to stop smoking was not followed by the latter.)

c. Der Arzt rät dem Patienten, das Rauchen aufzugeben.
(The doctor advises the patient to stop smoking.)

d. Der Arzt gibt dem Patienten ein neues Medikament.
(The doctor gives the patient a new medicine.)

2. Although the predicative noun occurs in a support verb construction with its normal meaning and with its normal argument structure, it may be subject to many restrictions concerning determination (as shown in (6)) and modification (as shown in (7)).

(6) a. Max hat (0 + *den + *einen + *seinen) Mut.
(Max has courage.)

b. Max verliert (*0 + den + *einen + ?seinen) Mut.
(Max loses courage.)

c. Max hat (*0 + den + *einen + *seinen) Mut, seinem Vorgesetzten zu widersprechen.
(Max has courage to contradict his superior.)

d. Max bekommt (0 + *den + *einen + *seinen) Mut, seinem Vorgesetzten zu widersprechen.
(Max gains courage to contradict his superior.)

---

[2] For a general overview see Danlos et al [1990], Caroli [1994], Mesli [1991], and G. Gross [1986].

   e. Max verliert (*0 + den + *einen + ?seinen) Mut, seinem Vorgesetzten zu widersprechen.
      (Max loses courage to contradict his superior.)

(7) a. Max hat (starken + *schwachen) Haß auf seinen Kollegen.
      (Max has a (strong ?weak) hatred for his colleague.)
      [polarised graduation of the predicative noun]

   b. Das Bild kommt zur (*schnellen + *erfolgreichen + *bedauerlichen) Versteigerung.
      (The picture is put up for (*quick + *successful + *regrettable) auction.)
      [no modification allowed]

   c. Max hat (*0 + leichtes + *schweres) Spiel mit seinem Gegener.
      (Max has no difficulty with his opponent.)
      [fixed use of a specific adjective]

Both the restrictions on determination and the restrictions on modification are lexicalised. Detailed information describing these restrictions has, therefore, to be provided in the lexicon for each predicative noun occurring in a support verb construction (see also Rothkegel [1989] and Caroli [1994]).

3. Although the support verb loses its original meaning in a support verb construction, it determines person, number, and tense of the construction and contributes aspectual information. Thus, a support verb can focus on the beginning, the termination, or the continuation of the process designated by the predicative noun. In German linguistic literature, these variants are addressed by the concept of *Aktionsart* (see Anderson [1972] and the discussion in Mesli [1991]). Some predicative nouns form series of support verb constructions which differ from each other only with regard to the Aktionsart they denote.

(8) a. den Eindruck haben *(aktionsart: unmarked)*
      (have the impression)

   b. den Eindruck gewinnen *(aktionsart: inchoative)*
      (get the impression)

   c. den Eindruck behalten *(aktionsart: continuative)*
      (retain the impression)

(9) a. in Wut sein *(aktionsart: unmarked)*
      (be enraged)

   b. in Wut geraten *(aktionsart: inchoative)*
      (become enraged)

(10)a. einen Rückstand haben *(aktionsart: unmarked)*
      (be in arrears)

   b. in Rückstand geraten *(aktionsart: inchoative)*
      (get into arrears)

(11)a. die Fassung bewahren *(aktionsart: continuative)*
      (keep one's composure)

   b. aus der Fassung geraten *(aktionsart: inchoative)*
      (lose one's composure)

Although the selection of a verb for the designation of a specific variant
of Aktionsart depends partially on the verb's inherent aspectual character,
which may denote a transformational or a stative process, the selection of
the support verb is lexically determined by the predicative noun. In the
examples above, different verbs are selected by different predicative nouns
for the same variant of Aktionsart.

The syntactic information that has to be coded for predicative nouns which
occur in support verb constructions is summarised in Figure 3.

Support verb constructions are the most complex lexical co–occurrences because of their semi–compositional nature. Departing from them, syntactic fixedness of verbal phraseolexemes can be defined in terms of restrictions on the
internal syntactic structure. Completely fixed verbal phraseolexemes vary only
with regard to the arguments which are subcategorised by the phraseolexeme:

(12)a. Der Hund/der Wolf macht dem Fuchs/dem Schaf den Garaus.
        (The dog/the wolf finishes the fox/the sheep.)
        [den Garaus machen = kill]
    b. Der Cowboy/der Mafia–Boss hat ins Gras gebissen.
        (The cowboy/the mafia boss kicked the bucket.)
        [ins Gras beißen = die]

Between support verb constructions which exhibit complex variation of their
internal syntactic structure and completely fixed verbal phraseolexemes, there
is a broad range of semi–fixed verbal phraseolexemes. The internal syntactic
structure of such units may vary on different syntactic dimensions as shown by
the following examples:

(13)a. Max macht um seinen Erfolg (viel + großes) Aufhebens.
        (Max made a great fuss about his success.)
    b. Max machte um seinen Erfolg kein Aufhebens.
        (Max didn't make a fuss about his success.)
        [Alternation of an obligatory graduating adjective and negation]
(14)a. Max ist ins Fettnäpfchen getreten.
        (Max put his foot in it.)
    b. Max ist mitten ins Fettnäpfchen getreten.
        (Max really put his foot in it.)
    c. Max tritt in jedes Fettnäpfchen.
        (Max always put his foot in it.)
        [Variation of preposition and quantification]

These examples show that for verbal phraseolexemes, we have to account for
the degree of syntactic fixedness, which can also be described by the properties
listed in Figure 3.

Combinatory Restrictions								Complements		
SV	AKT	Case	Prep	Number	Det	Mod	Neg	Compl1	Compl2	Compl2
< Verb >	Neuter	Acc	< Prep >	free	free	free	free	NP	E	E
	Incho	Dat		sing	Def	Grad	neg	PP	NP	NP
	Cont			plu	Indef	Illoc	no-neg	S	PP	PP
	Term				Pos	< adj >		Inf	S	S
					E	E			Inf	Inf

Legend

SV	Support Verb
< Verb >	Lexical value of the support verb
AKT	Aktionsart of the support verb construction
Neuter	Aktionsart of the support verb construction is not marked
Incho	Aktionsart of the support verb construction is inchoative
Cont	Aktionsart of the support verb construction is continuative
Term	Aktionsart of the support verb construction is terminative
Case	Case of the predicative noun
Acc	Accusative
Dat	Dative
Prep	Preposition of the predicative noun
< Prep >	Lexical value of the preposition
Number	Number of the predicative noun
free	No restrictions
sing	Only the singular of the predicative noun is allowed
plu	Only the plural of the predicative noun is allowed
Det	Restrictions on the determiner of the predicative noun
Def	Definite determiner
Indef	Indefinite determiner
Pos	Possessive determiner
E	The slot is empty
Mod	Restrictions on modification of the predicative noun
Grad	Graduating adjective
Illoc	illocutary adjective
< adj >	Lexical value of a fixed adjective
Neg	Restriction on negation of the support verb construction
neg	The support verb construction is always negated
no-neg	The support verb construction cannot be negated
Compl1	First complement of the support verb construction
Compl2	Second complement of the support verb construction
Compl3	Third complement of the support verb construction
NP	The complement is a nominal phrase
PP	The complement is a prepositional phrase
S	The complement is a sentence
Inf	The complement is an infinitive

Fig.3 Types of syntactic information for support verb constructions

5 Semantic Properties of Phraseolexemes

One of the most frequently discussed characteristics of phraseological units is their non–compositional or opaque semantics. It is generally assumed that the meaning of phraseological units can be derived only partially or not at all from the meaning of their components by a compositional analysis.

However, there exist degrees of compositionality as is illustrated by Figure 2, in which the phraseolexemes are arranged in order of decreasing composition-ality. The co–occurrence of lexemes in the topmost example is determined by semantic selectional criteria only. Since semantic selection is part of the gram-mar, examples like this mark the pole of absolute compositionality without lex-ically determined criteria of co–occurrence of lexemes. The other examples in Figure 2 illustrate different types of lexical co–occurrences with increasing non–compositional meaning.

5.1 Collocations

The second example in Figure 2 marks the lowest level of lexically determined co–occurrence. Both elements occur with their normal meaning and the meaning of the unit can be derived by a compositional analysis. However, it is difficult to identify semantic criteria which would determine why *Hut* can only co–occur with *aufsetzen* whereas *Hemd* can only co–occur with *anziehen*. The co–occurrence of these lexemes has, thus, to be considered as lexically determined.

In the linguistic discussion, multiword units of the described nature are gen-erally referred to as *collocations*. Collocations are types of lexical co–occurrences with the following characteristics:

1. Their syntax is not fixed at all and their components behave like terminal nodes of the syntactic structure.
2. Their meaning can be derived by compositional analysis.
3. The co–occurrence of the lexemes is lexically determined, i.e., it is a kind of conventional preference for one of several lexemes fulfilling the given semantic selectional criteria.

According to these characteristics, collocations are not phraseolexemes. The unit as a whole behaves like a phrase, not like a terminal node and both com-ponents appear in their normal syntactic and semantic function. This raises the well–known question of how to determine and how to describe collocations, for which several factors have to be taken into account:

1. There is a broad area of transition between co–occurrences determined by simple semantic selectional criteria and co–occurrences which exhibit a strong preference for only one of several possible lexemes. In this area of transition, the co–occurrence of the lexemes may be more or less usual (see Heid and Martin [1991]).

2. Lexically determined co–occurrence implies that there is one lexeme of the collocation which determines the co–occurrence of the other lexeme (see Hausmann [1985]). This is unproblematic in collocations like:

(15)a. eingefleischter Junggeselle
   (confirmed bachelor)

But this is not evident in the example shown in Figure 2. In this case, one can argue that *Hut* taken as a garment which can be put on determines the co–occurrence of *aufsetzen* and that, vice versa, *aufsetzen* taken in the reading of *put on some clothes* determines the co–occurrence of *Hut*.

3. Lexical co–occurrence in collocations is determined with regard to an inherent syntactic or semantic function of the collocational phrase. In example (15), the adjective *eingefleischt* designates an intensifying modification of *Junggeselle*. Only this type of modification is restricted to a single adjective; other dimensions of modifications are free.

5.2   Lexicalised Metaphors

Lexicalised metaphors, as illustrated by the example in Figure 2, are types of lexical co–occurrences, of which one element is used in a non–literal, metaphorical sense. The distinction between literal and metaphorical use addresses one of the basic intuitions about the meaning of lexemes in natural language, although it is difficult to give this distinction an operational definition. For our purpose, it is interesting to note that lexicalised metaphors can be interpreted by language–specific general principles determining various metaphorical uses. For our example, we can assume a principle like *arguing can be considered to be a fight*. Such general principles provide the basis for a series of related metaphorical uses of lexemes belonging to a common semantic field.

Lexicalised metaphors have a low level of syntactic fixedness. The elements can be modified and they can also be referred to by a pronoun. In both cases, the metaphoric meaning is retained:

(16)a. Max zerbricht sich den Kopf über das Problem.
   (Max racks his brains over the problem.)

   b. Max zerbrach sich seinen schönen aber nicht sehr klugen Kopf über das Problem, aber er kam zu keiner Lösung.
   ('Max racked his pretty but not very clever brains over the problem, but he reached no solution.')

   c. Max hat sich den ganzen Tag den Kopf über das Problem zerbrochen, und er wird ihn sich weiter zermartern, bis er eine Lösung gefunden hat.
   (Max has racked his brains the whole day over the problem, and he will continue to do so until he has found a solution.)

The general metaphorical principle underlying these examples may be something like *thinking is a (painful) strain to the head*. Such general principles can, however, interact with other language–specific stereotypes such as *schön aber dumm (beautiful but stupid* (example 16(b)), yielding effects which do not lend themselves to a lexical treatment. Since the restrictions governing such cases are not associated with individual lexemes but with principles of a more general nature, lexemes belonging to the same semantic field are interchangeable.

Similar to collocations, lexicalised metaphors are not phraseolexemes but phrases. For translation purposes, it would be an interesting field of investigation to explore the inventory of conventional general metaphorical principles for a given language and to compare them to the corresponding inventory in other languages. Equivalence criteria for metaphorical uses of lexemes could then be defined in a more general way.

5.3 Semantically Fixed Phraseological Units

On the topmost level of semantic fixedness, we find phraseological units whose meaning cannot at all be derived by a compositional analysis from their constituents. Phraseological units of this type are phraseolexemes with a global meaning which must be coded for the unit as a whole. Here are some examples:

(17)a. X faßt Y ins Auge.
   [X envisages Y.]
   b. X beißt ins Gras.
   [X dies.]
   c. X liest Y die Leviten.
   [X blames Y.]

There is, however, also a class of semantically fixed phraseolexemes which have a compositional reading in addition to their phraseological meaning:

(18)a. Der Cowboy hat ins Gras gebissen.
   (The cowboy kicked the bucket.)
   b. Der Torwart hat vor Wut über seinen Fehler ins Gras des Spielfeldes gebissen.
   (The goalkeeper, angry about his mistake, bit the grass of the pitch.)
(19)a. Die Regierung faßt eine Steuererhöhung ins Auge.
   (The government envisages a tax increase.)
   b. Das Kind faßt seinem Vater versehentlich ins Auge.
   (The child grabs unintentionally the eye of his father.)

These examples show that, for activating the compositional meaning of phraseological units, there have to be obvious syntactic and/or semantic anchors in the context of the unit. As Burger (Burger et al. [1982], p. 27) remarks, it is a central property of phraseological units that their phraseological meaning is decoded first, even if their compositional meaning were also a possible reading within the given context.

In a diachronic perspective, most fixed phraseolexemes can be considered as frozen lexicalised metaphors (information on the history of phraseological units can, for example, be found in phraseological collections). Native speakers are more or less conscious of this diachronic perspective. Even if they don't know the exact origin of a fixed phraseolexeme, they are aware of its metaphoric character. This fact has a pragmatic impact on the use of fixed phraseological units: such expressions are not completely frozen; instead, it is always possible to revive their metaphorical use.

In German, for example, the phraseological unit *jemanden drückt der Schuh* has approximately the meaning *someone has a problem*. Normally, this unit is syntactically and semantically fixed. However, by investigating text corpora of newspapers, we find examples like this:

(20) Die Lufthansa drückt der Schuh gleich an mehreren Stellen:
hohe Kosten ....., wachsende Zinsbelastungen, und Gehälter für Piloten und Bordpersonal, die international an der Spitze liegen.
('Lufthansa has several problems at the same time:...')

In this example, the adjunct *an mehreren Stellen* is added to the frozen unit *jemanden drückt der Schuh*. Usually, this would activate a literal interpretation of the unit. But in this case, the metaphoric meaning of the unit (*problems are like uncomfortable shoes*) is retained, permitting the analogy *multiple discomfort = multiple problems*.

Revival of frozen metaphors is a familiar stylistic effect. We can even envisage examples like (21), in which the literal meaning of the phraseological unit outlines an impressive scenario where the process designated by the frozen metaphor takes place.

(21) Nach seinem letzten Showdown biß Little Joe in das fahle Gras der glühend heißen Prärie.
(After his last showdown, Little Joe bit the faded grass of the glowing hot prairie)

6 Textlinguistic and Pragmatic Aspects

The stylistic aspects outlined in the last section relate to the more general topic of the pragmatics of lexical co–occurrences.

One pragmatic factor to be accounted for in a lexical resource pertains to register. Phraseological units may be marked for a specific linguistic register. For example, some phraseolexemes, such as German *Widerspruch einlegen* as in *Er legte gegen das Urteil Widerspruch ein* (*He contested the verdict*) may be restricted to being used in formal juridical communication. In general, we may say that information on register marking is an important information type for establishing equivalence criteria for translating lexical co–occurrences.

A second type of pragmatic information is related to the information structure of a sentence. For example, the use of a support verb construction instead of a simple verb may be motivated by the desire to topicalise certain elements of a sentence or to make them available for intersentential processes that establish text coherence. G. Gross (G. Gross [1986]) has examined French support verb constructions with regard to this kind of pragmatic property. Further investigations are required for defining general equivalence criteria within this domain.

The use of a phraseological unit instead of a simple lexeme may introduce some additional connotations. By their metaphorical potential, phraseological units refer to a common inventory of images and stereotypes. Thus, the use of phraseolexemes can have a specific rhetorical function. Defining equivalence criteria in this field is a difficult task which must take into account context and co–text conditions. The description of the rhetorics of phraseolexemes can thus be said to belong to the domain of stylistics rather than to the domain of lexicography.

References

[1990] Abeillé, A., Shabes, Y., Joshi A. K.: Using Lexicalized Tags for Machine Translation. In: *Proceedings of Coling 1990*, vol 3, Helsinki 1990, p. 1–6.

[1972] Anderson, S.-G.: Aktionalität im Deutschen. Eine Untersuchung unter Vergleich mit dem russischen Aspektsystem. Bd 1: Die Kategorien Aspekt und Aktionsart im Russischen und im Deutschen. Uppsala 1972. (= Acta Universitatis Upsalensis, Studia Germanistica Upsaliensia 10).

[1982] Burger, H., Buhofer, A., Sialm, A.: Handbuch der Phraseologie. Berlin: de Gruyter 1982.

[1994] Caroli, F.: Funktionsverbgefüge in der Maschinellen Übersetzung. In: Dahmen W. (ed.): *Konvergenz und Divergenz in der Romania. Romanisitisches Kolloquium VIII*. Tübingen: Narr (forthcoming).

[1990] Danlos, L., Caroli, F., Bech, A.: Support Verb Constructions. EUROTRA Reference Manual 7.0. Luxembourg (CEC, DG XIII) 1990.

[1993] Erbach, G. and B. Krenn: Idioms and Support Verb Constructions in HPSG. Saarbrücken 1993 (= Computational Linguistics at the University of the Saarland 28).

[1986] Gross, G.: Etudes syntaxiques de constructions converses. Geneva: Droz 1986.

[1985] Hausmann, F. J.: Kollokationen im deutschen Wörterbuch. Ein Beitrag zur Theorie des lexikographischen Beispiels. In: H. Bergenholtz and J. Mugdan (eds.): *Lexikographie und Grammatik. Akten des Essener Kolloquiums zur Grammatik im Wörterbuch*. 1985. (Lexicographica. Series Maior 3) p. 118-129.

[1991] Heid, U. and W. Martin: Feasibility of Standards for Collocational Description of Lexical Items. (=EUROTRA-7 Study, Document 9.4) CEC-DG XIII Luxembourg 1991.

[1991] Heid, U. and J. McNaught: EUROTRA-7 -Study: Feasibility and Project Definition Study on the Reusability of Lexical and Terminological Resources in Computerised Applications. Final Report. CEC-DG XIII Luxembourg 1991.

[1991] Mesli. N.: Funktionsverbgefüge in der maschinellen Analyse und Übersetzung: linguisitische Beschreibung und Implementierung im CAT2 Formalismus. Saarbrücken 1991 (EUROTRA-D Working Papers 19).

[1981] Pilz, K. - D.: Phraseologie. Stuttgart: Metzler 1981.

[1989] Rothkegel, A.: Polylexikalität. Verb–Nomen Verbindungen und ihre Behandlung in EUROTRA. Saarbrücken 1989. (EUROTRA-D Working Papers 17).

Perception Vocabulary in Five Languages - Towards an Analysis Using Frame Elements

Nicholas Ostler

Linguacubun Ltd
17 Oakley Road, London N1 3LL

e-mail: n_ostler@eurokom.ie   tel. & fax: +44-71-704-1481

Abstract. This essay introduces the first linguistic task of the DELIS project[1]: to undertake a corpus-based examination of the syntactic and semantic properties of perception vocabulary in five languages, English, Danish, Dutch, French and Italian. The theoretical background is Fillmore's Frame Semantics. The paper reviews some of the variety of facts to be accounted for, particularly in the specialization of sense associated with some collocations, and the pervasive phenomenon of Intensionality. Through this review, we aim to focus our understanding of cross-linguistic variation in this one domain, both by noting specific differences in word-sense correlation, and by exhibiting a general means of representation.

1 The Enormity of Cross-Linguistic Semantics

Language, especially when conveying real people's thoughts to other people[2], enlists a host of presumptions and implications that are there to back up its simplest words. The unseen presence of this background army means that our utterances can be startlingly terse ("I saw that!" "You promised me." or the Italian "Senta!"[3]); but it also means that it is very difficult to extract from such ordinary language a full report of what is going on, what is present in the discourse or the text, in the explicit "no-nonsense" way that might be generated by a report from a computer database system, or indeed a house-purchase contract[4].

The task of lexical semantics is to put these unruly forces on parade, to review the members of all the detachments that stand behind the thin line of explicit words, and show the contributions they make to its fire-power.

---

[1]"Descriptive Linguistic Specifications", LRE 61.034, co-funded by the European Union and participating companies, Feb. 1993 - Jan. 1995. The project includes dictionary publishers (Oxford UP, Van Dale) and language technology companies (Linguacubun, SITE), as well as universities (Stuttgart, Pisa, Copenhagen, VU Amsterdam). The project is about new, more nearly adequate lexical representations validated partially through systematic search of corpus evidence, and the development of a suite of tools to facilitate their use.

[2]and not, say, operating instructions or corporate pronouncements

[3]"Listen!" - but literally an appeal to use any sense but vision.

[4]and it is already clear that there can be no machine translation without the ability to generate such reports.

The scope for difference is vast. Among a few early examples[5] of the profusion that greets us in just the domain of perception vocabulary, consider first lexical specialization. Since it is often triggered by technological change, it is in principle unpredictable. We find, for instance, that in English the verb *watch*, but in Dutch the non-synonym *kijken* (which would correspond more closely to *look*), have a specialized sub-meaning of viewing a screen-based performance, which contrasts with the use of the plain verb see or *zien*.

NL1.   *Ik hab gisteravond Carmen gezien/gekeken*
EN1.   *I saw/watched Carmen last night*

In these examples, both versions are quite natural, but the second verb quoted would often be interpreted to mean that the performance was an electronic one. All this without any use of neologisms, but by re-defining our inherited Germanic vocabulary.

Other cases specialize not a simple verb, but a collocation of it. This is the case with

NL2.   *gaan zien*:   "go see"

in Dutch, which requires a form of entertainment as its object.

These were lexically-specific facts, that it is hard to expect any theory to imply. Others, although idiosyncratic, seem to be more general. For example, there is one type of pragmatic exclusion present in all the languages we are looking at which have neutral "descriptive" verbs for perceptual modalities (i.e. verbs where the percept appears as subject, while the perceiver himself is only optionally expressed). In such languages (English is one, but French is not), sight and hearing verbs may not co-occur with a predicate that connotes the modality; all the others may. So for instance:

EN2.   *feels soft/ tastes salty/ smells fragrant/ ??looks red~bright / ??sounds loud*

Another seemingly arbitrary, but rather systematic effect, is the use of the modal *can* in English to exclude metaphorical senses. The simple sensory verbs take on a non-literal sense when they have a propositional complement, but not if the verb is governed by *can*. For example,

EN3.	*I hear that the gears are slipping.*	(Information - by report)
vs.	*I can hear that the gears are slipping.*	(Auditory)

EN4.	*I feel that he will not come now.*	(Intuition)
vs.	*I can feel that the engine is disengaged.*	(Sensory)

When the verb has no metaphorical sense, it is only possible to use it propositionally if governed by *can*:

---

[5]The Dutch facts noted here were pointed out to me by Maurice Vliegen; the English ones by Charles Fillmore.

EN5.   *I smell/taste that there is trouble ahead.
and   *I smell/taste that the soup is burnt.   (Olfactory/Gustatory)
vs.   I can smell/taste that the soup is burnt.   (Olfactory/Gustatory)

This is an encouraging sub-regularity, but discouragingly, it does not seem to apply to the visual modality, where the simple form, and the modal form with *can*, are fairly indistinguishable (although the modalized form may be slightly happier in the literal sense).

EN6.   I (can) see that there is trouble ahead.   (Understanding)
        I (can) see that the piece doesn't fit.   (Visual)

In another curiosity, we note an isolated semantic constraint on the passive of *hear* sentences, when they have a NP+VP complement. E.g.,

EN7.   They saw the music have its effect on him.
                    The music was seen to have its effect on him.
EN8.   They heard the cymbals crash at bar 1223.
                    The cymbals were heard to crash at bar 1223.[6]

So far so good. But consider:

EN9.   They heard Toscanini conduct the orchestra.
                    *Toscanini was heard to conduct the orchestra.

In fact, for a passive to be possible, we must not only hear Toscanini conduct: we must hear Toscanini himself. Quite out of the blue, we discover that the clausal subject of passivized *hear*-complement must itself be heard.

This restriction is strangely gratuitous: EN7 shows that there is no comparable restriction on passivizing a *see*-complement: the music is not visible.

Confronting the task of organizing this immense body of semantic fact, which often seems arbitrarily various, it is easy to be discouraged. Yet the task is not hopeless. We can, in fact, assume that there is a fair degree of comparability among the units engaged by each language, just as there is a fair degree of similarity between the features of the human condition that they describe. We all have the same sense-organs, live in modern Western societies with other human beings, confront the same tasks of providing food, clothing and shelter for ourselves and our families, are confronted or aided by much the same degree of technical progress, and so on[7]. Translation is possible, after all.

---

[6]It is well-known that when NP+VP constructions are passivized, the VP acquires a more or less obligatory prefixed *to*.

[7]Not all of these assumptions can presently be made for all languages, of course; and we shall be intellectually the poorer if they ever can. But the assumptions hold true for a comparative study of Danish, Dutch, English, French and Italian, such as is attempted here.

In practice, lexicographers have already done well enough to give most laymen the impression that the task is completed. The lexicographers themselves know better. The DELIS project now undertakes to make a significantly deeper exploration of important parts of the lexicon, those referring (at least literally) to perception, and to speech-acts. Looking at corpus evidence in five languages, the project is to build up a picture of the use of the central words in these areas.[8]

The project has an explicit theoretical basis in the Frame Semantics of Charles Fillmore and others (e.g., Fillmore 1982, 1985). As such, it starts from characterizations of the semantic architecture of the domains: frames, whose elements are semantic roles. From this, it goes on to see to what extent, and how, the frame's relations between elements get expressed (systematically or otherwise) in particular languages. In brief, then, we ask:

(a)   What distinctions are available universally?
(b)   Which of these are discernible in particular languages?
(c)   How are the semantic distinctions conveyed in the forms of a language?

This paper concerns only some early results in the field of Perception. First the descriptive framework of Modalities, Elements and Patterns is introduced. Then some particular phenomena are discussed: those associated with generalised perception verbs, with nouns, and with the intrinsic distinction of extensionality versus intensionality.

2   The Perception Frame: Modalities, Elements, Patterns

2.1   Modalities

We distinguish the five conventional senses, together with a sixth (neutral, i.e. unspecified) mode of sense perception, and call these the sensory Modalities. They are abbreviated as follows, together with some of the English lexemes (verbs and nouns) whose properties are within our sphere.

Vision	V	*see, look, glance, stare, aspect ...*
Audition	A	*hear, listen, sound, ring, chime ...*
Touch	T	*feel, touch, grope ...*
Olfaction	O	*smell, sniff, odour, whiff, aroma ...*
Gustation	G	*taste, sip, flavour ...*
Neutral	N	*sense, intuit, perceive, seem, appear ...*

---

[8]The project also aims to develop tools which are well-adapted to promoting this sort of analysis.

2.2 Elements

The next part of the analysis is to set out the semantic roles which can be discerned in a perceptual proposition, or the "Perception Frame". These we call the Frame Elements:

The animate element will be the Experiencer who has the perception. This may be an involuntary experience (in which case we call the Experiencer passive), or actively sought (in which case we call the Experiencer active).

experiencer   (E)

    subtypes of E

        passive   (E: pas)
            I feel faint; it tastes funny TO ME

        active (also "Agent")   (E: act)
            THE DOG sniffed the air

What is presented to the Experiencer is the Percept. Evidently, there is considerable philosophical doubt on quite what that is. Language (at least the Western European languages) may be less discriminating than philosophers on this point, but still we have made a fair number of distinctions in this category.

First of all, we may distinguish the source of the percept, from the event (the stimulus) which is perceived. Less crudely, we may distinguish, within the full stimulus, a particular feature picked out (the discriminatum) from the background (the locus). Where the Experiencer is active, a potential source may be actively sought when not immediately evident (the target), or attended to constantly (the aim) in the hope for a desired percept.

The percept may be represented not as an object, but as a proposition. If so, we call it an interpretation. This interpretation may be presupposed true (i.e. factive) or not; and it may be presented without inference (i.e. direct) or not.

Finally, for convenience, we accept two frame elements which are transitional to the Frame of speech-acts and communication. If the interpretation is received linguistically, we call it a message. And if the message is not summarized, but simply assigned an area of import, we call this the topic.

percept   (P)

  subtypes of P

        source   (P: src)
           hear A DOG

stimulus   (P: stm)
hear A BANG

discriminatum   (P: dis)
hear THE FALSE NOTE in the music

locus   (P: loc)
hear the false note IN THE MUSIC

target   (P: tgt)
grope FOR THE LIGHT-SWITCH; sniff FOR DRUGS

aim   (P: aim)
stare AT THE CLOCK; sniff AT THE BAG

interpretation   (P: int)
hear A DOG ENTER THE ROOM

            [+/- factive]   *I sensed THAT HE WAS LYING*
                                   vs I felt THAT HE WAS LYING.

            [+/- direct]   *I felt HER MOVE*
                                   vs I felt THAT SHE MOVED.

message   (P: mes)
hear from John THAT SUSAN HAD ARRIVED

topic   (P: top)
hear ABOUT THE NEW BABY

In many perceptual sentences, there is a third element which is part of the frame. This is the Judgment, which gives the aspect under which the percept was presented to the experiencer.

This element appears linguistically to be of only four kinds: the eval uative judgment, which contains a goodness-rating of the percept; the ascription of a perceptual quality (pqual) which is characteristic of the modality (e.g., loudness to sounds, acidity to tastes); the sim ile, which compares the percept to something else; and the inference, which ascribes to the percept some property which is not, strictly speaking, accessible to that sense.

judgment _____ (J)

     subtypes of J

            evaluative   (J: eval)
                 sounds AWFUL

domain-specific quality   (J: pqual)
        sounds DEAFENING

simile   (J: sim)
        sounds LIKE A TRUMPET, tastes OF ALMONDS

inference   (J: inf)
        sounds HOLLOW

2.3 Patterns

Rogers 1970 distinguishes three patterns of correlation of grammatical functions with semantic roles: Cognitive, Active and Descriptive. In the last of these the Percept appears as subject, and the verb is intransitive. In both the former two, the Experiencer is the subject and the Percept the object. They, however, are distinguished by whether the Experiencer is passive or active.

Some examples from our corpus illustrate these Patterns in the V, T and G modalities (vision, touch and taste):

Cognitive:
Not exactly, miss, but once I SAW a shadow and FELT a presence...
In another dream, he was window-shopping when he FELT a hand in his pocket.
I can TASTE blood running down the back of my throat...

Active:
There is a "zoom" facility for users wishing to LOOK at graphs in more detail.
...rubbing thumb and finger together, as if FEELING a piece of cloth.
There is no better way of buying cheese than from a specialist cheese shop, where you will be encouraged to TASTE before buying...

Descriptive:
The French economy is beginning to LOOK attractive to smaller companies ...
I'm a great believer in doing what FEELS natural.
after reading her descriptions of dishes, and... how they are meant to TASTE.

In our early work in DELIS, Charles Fillmore added a fourth, really a subtype of the first, in which the Percept is differentiated into a Discriminatum (marked as the direct object) and a Locus (in some prepositional phrase). This may be called Cognitive (Discriminative):

Cognitive (Discriminative):
In the works of Bacon, Richier, de Kooning and Golub we SEE ugly and disturbed people...[9]

---

[9]Despite the intuitive availability of such expressions as "feel the quality in the cloth", "taste the salt in the stew", these are actually very rare in the English corpus we have.

To some extent, there are differences in lexical representation between these different patterns. Hence if we consider the most salient word in each modality in English:

1.	Cognitive	*see, hear, feel, smell, taste, perceive*
2.	Cognitive (Discriminative)	*see, hear, feel, smell, taste, detect*
3.	Active	*look, listen, feel, smell, taste, try*
4.	Descriptive	*look, sound, feel, smell, taste, seem*

These patterns are primarily distinguished semantically, each giving a different nuance to the perceptual modality. But there is also a characteristic pattern of linking semantic role with grammatical function; and not all roles can co-occur with each type. Considering the English facts for the auditory modality:

1.   Cognitive   E   *hears*   P

2.   Cognitive (Discriminative)   E   *hears*   P:dis   *in*   P:loc

        (or [10]   J   *in*   P

)

3.   Active   E:act   *listens to*   P:aim

4.   Descriptive   P   *sounds* J   (*to* E:pas)

However, these patterns of linking and co-occurrence are not universal:

IT1.   *sebbene sentisse la collana calda ...*
          (lit. "though she felt the necklace warm")

This example shows that, in Italian, it is possible to include a Judgment in a Cognitive or Cognitive (Discriminative) sentence.

3 Non-specific Modality

The simple words in English are all fairly explicit as to perceptual modality, but this is not true in all languages. Notably, in Italian, *sentire* is ambiguous as between all the modalities except for vision, and is often distinguished only by context. The direct object expression often contains an explicit noun marking the modality:

---

[10]This equivalence (or equivocation) draws attention to the close conceptual status of the Discriminatum and the Judgment. Linguistically, though, the former will usually be represented by a noun, the latter by an adjective.

IT2.   *sentire*   *l'odore dell'erba*   (the smell of the grass)
                    il rumore della macchina   (the noise of the engine)
                    il gusto dei fichi   (the taste of the figs)
                    il tocco leggero della sua mano   (his hand's light touch)
                    il bisogno di riforme   (the need for reforms)

As the last example shows, however, the modality may also not be marked in any way, leaving the sense neutral.

In fact in all the languages, more complex perceptual meanings are usually non-specific re modality. English provides plenty of examples:

> *attend to, witness, notice, recognize, identify, discern, search for, find, survey, nspect, scrutinize, scan, discover, explore, ...*

4 Nouns·

Very little work has been done as yet on perception nouns (and none on adjectives). Once this begins [11], variety and disparity emerges.

What are the nouns, and what is their range of meaning? We find that there is, for many modalities, a three-way distinction available among the Experiencer's faculty of perception in that modality; his subjective experience; and a quasi-objective word for the external stimulus (the sensible quality of an object).

	Faculty	Internal Experience	External Quality
V	*sight*	*sight*	*look*
A	*hearing*	*hearing*	*sound*
T	*touch*	*touch, feel*	*touch, feel*
O	*smell*	*scent*	*smell, scent, odour*
G	*taste*	*taste*	*taste, flavour*

Discriminating contexts for these three would be something like:

Faculty: *he has lost the power of _____*
Internal Experience: *my _____ of it disturbed me greatly*
External Quality: *the _____ of it pervaded the place*

Only *taste* has all three aspects to its meaning, but there is no consistency about the aspects which are united in a single term for the other modalities. Besides this, metaphorical uses are exceedingly various: e.g., for *taste*:

---

[11] The preliminary results reported here are largely due to Charles Fillmore and B.T.S. Atkins.

Faculty	F	*touch, taste, smell, hearing and sight*
Internal experience	E	*a first taste of life in the fast lane*
External quality	Q	*what a strange taste in this omelette*
Discrimination	D	*a man of taste and refinement*
Preference	P	*I cannot abide his taste for loud ties*

Although the same frame-elements are at issue with most of these nouns, the actual mapping of semantic roles onto constituents of the sentence is much more varied. [12]

5 Extensionality and Intensionality

This distinction pervades discourse about perception, and is not restricted to complement clauses. However, such sentences intrinsically involve both the narrator's (Extensional), and the experiencer's (Intensional), view. Extensional arguments will be referential or factive, intensional ones not even necessarily present (or true) in the speaker's realm of discourse.

Considering the range of frame elements' semantic roles from this viewpoint, we can classify them as follows.

Types of Percept:			(Extens.)	(Intens.)
source	hear A DOG		-	+
stimulus	hear A BANG		-	+
discrim.	hear A FALSE NOTE in the music		-	+
locus	hear a false note IN THE MUSIC		+	±
target	grope FOR THE SWITCH; sniff FOR DRUGS		-	+
aim	stare AT THE CLOCK; sniff AT THE BAG		+	±
interpretation	[+factive]	You sensed HE WAS LYING	+	+
	[- factive]	You felt HE WAS LYING	-	+
	[+ direct]	You felt HER MOVE	-	+
	[- direct]	You felt SHE MOVED	-	+
message	hear from John THAT SUSAN HAD ARRIVED		-	+
topic	hear ABOUT THE NEW BABY		+	+

Typically, what is extensional is also intensional. But not always: for example, the aim (marked by *at* in *look at*) may mark an item absent from the perceiver's view: blind people can learn to look at their interlocutors; and it makes good sense to say, for instance, *Hamlet was looking right at Polonius when he said this, although he had no idea Polonius was behind the arras.*

---

[12]See Fillmore, to appear for some early analysis.

Judgments (J) of whatever kind are necessarily intensional.

Intensional arguments typically become extensional when made definite. For example:

EN10.   *He smelt (the) smoke.*

NL 3.   *Karel luistert naar de vogels.*
K. listened to the birds.

NL 4.   *De componist luisterde nauwlettend naar fouten in de uitvoering van zijn werk.*
The composer listened intently for mistakes in the performance of his work.

There is a further degree of inwardness ("subjectivity") which can be distinguished from intensionality, but only apparently in the case of the modality N. This is where the object of the perception is essentially private to the perceiver, a psychic state in itself, rather than the perceiver's personal perception of something which is in principle intersubjective. Consider, for example, the three-way contrast in English:

Extensional:
EN11.   *He feels the pressure from them (*but they are not pressing him at all.)*

Intensional:
EN12.   *He feels pressure from them (but they are not pressing him at all.)*

Subjective:
EN13.   *He feels worry about them (*but they do not worry him at all).*

In the first case, the sentence records the experiencer's perception of a fact accepted by the narrator. In the second, the fact that the narrator can deny the truth of the perception, means that it must be a recording of the experiencer's intensional point of view. In the third, the fact is in principle not distinct from the experiencer's perception of it.

Another means, besides Definiteness, of distinguishing Intensional and Extensional is the use of the modal *can*. Compare with EN12:

Extensional:
EN14.   *He can feel pressure from them (*but they are not pressing him at all.)*

The quality, and indeed the possibility of, machine translation depends partly on detecting objectively recognisable signs of this kind of latent meaning difference. What needs to be transmitted from a version in one language to a version in another is precisely this extensionality or intentionality, not whether the perceptual verb was modalized, or an ambiguous preposition used (such as *naar* in Dutch). But this can only be discerned by noting which surface phenomena correlate with it in which languages.

Clear facts about extensionality are not limited to such constructions as are shared by all languages in our survey. For example, *lugte* "smell" in Danish can take a sentential complement, but presupposes its truth.

Extensional (because factive):
DK1.   *Mor kunne lugte på miles afstand at jeg var ked af det.*
       Mother could smell from miles away that I was sad.

6 Conclusion

These are preliminary results, prolegomena to DELIS, rather than even its early fruits. We have set out the proposed set of constructs for perceptual vocabulary (Modalities, Elements, Patterns), and drawn attention to some of the semantic variation that needs representation.

As a means of mapping all the distinctions made by a language within a semantic domain, the DELIS framework alone will not be fully adequate. This type of incompleteness is inevitable, and other resources of semantic theory will have to be called on if a full map of a semantic domain is needed.

However, DELIS's application of Frame Semantics to perception language has provided a framework in which a variety of different aspects of this field can be represented and compared. As such, it should have brought a little nearer the day when the definition, as well as the syntactic information in a dictionary entry, can be usefully analysed.

References

Fillmore, C.J. : Frame semantics. In: Linguistics in the Morning Calm. Seoul: Hanshin 1982, pp. 113-137.

Fillmore, C.J. : Frames and the Semantics of Understanding. In: Quaderni di Semantica 6.2, 222-254 (1985).

Fillmore, C.J. : The Hard Road from Verb to Nouns. MS, UC Berkeley (to appear).

Rogers, A.: Three Kinds of Physical Perception Verbs. In: Proceedings of the Chicago Linguistic Society, 7.Chicago: CLS 1971: pp. 206-223.

Relating Parallel Monolingual Lexicon Fragments for Translation Purposes

Ulrich Heid

Universität Stuttgart
Institut für maschinelle Sprachverarbeitung, Computerlinguistik
D 70174 Stuttgart, Germany

Abstract. In this paper, we introduce the methodology for the construction of dictionary fragments under development in DELIS. The approach advocated is corpus-based, computationally supported, and aimed at the construction of parallel monolingual dictionary fragments which can be linked to form translation dictionaries without many problems.

The parallelism of the monolingual fragments is achieved through the use of a shared inventory of descriptive devices, one common representation formalism (typed feature structures) for linguistic information from all levels, as well as a working methodology inspired by onomasiology: treating all elements of a given lexical semantic field consistently with common descriptive devices at the same time.

It is claimed that such monolingual dictionaries are particularly easy to relate in a machine translation application. The principles of such a combination of dictionary fragments are illustrated with examples from an experimental HPSG-based interlingua-oriented machine translation prototype.

1 Introduction

1.1 Framework and Context

The DELIS project[1] deals with the construction of tools to support corpus-based dictionary building. The advantages of corpus-based lexicography are widely rec-

---

[1] DELIS stands for "Descriptive Lexical Specifications and tools for corpus-based lexicon building". DELIS (February 1993 through April 1995) is a shared-cost project partly funded by the DG XIII E of the Commission of the European Community, Luxembourg, under its LRE programme (Linguistic Research and Engineering project 61.034). The project brings together expertise from system builders (Sonovision ITEP Technologies (Paris), Lingsoft (Helsinki)), from (computational) linguists (Universities of Amsterdam (VUA), Clermont-Ferrand, Copenhagen, Pisa, and Stuttgart), Linguacubun Ltd. (London) and from dictionary publishing (Den Danske Ordbog (Copenhagen), Oxford University Press and Van Dale Lexicografie (Utrecht)).

ognized since the COBUILD dictionary, one of the first general-language dictionaries mostly built on the basis of corpus material, was published and made a major impact. The fact that lexical descriptions can be illustrated with material from actual text rather than with made-up examples, as well as the possibilities, for the lexicographer, of capturing in the dictionary the usage of lexical items as they occur in texts, are commonly accepted as the most important advantages of corpus-based dictionary compilation. Given that there are not many tools to support the process of corpus-based lexicography, the DELIS tools are aimed at supporting a methodology of lexicographic work which takes full advantage of corpus material.

Along with this, the tools support lexical modeling, as it is known from the creation of NLP dictionaries and becoming more and more widespread in non-NLP lexicography as well. Definition templates as used in COBUILD, or types of dictionary article microstructures as supported by syntactic consistency control functions in data entry tools, or templates for the description of lexical items: these can all be seen as, albeit weak, models of lexical description; of course, they are not linguistic "models" in the strict, formal sense of the term. Usually, we can ensure the syntactic consistency of dictionary articles, i.e., the sequencing of item types in the microstructure: for example, we can state that the entry word is followed by a grammatical category annotation, a sense number, a definition and then an example. Once such a "syntactic structure" of the dictionary article is defined, computational tools can be used to ensure that it is followed by all articles. This task is commonly performed by tools based on a document type definition (DTD) of SGML which is used to define the "syntax" and layout of dictionary articles. What cannot be ensured by a DTD, is the way in which the individual items are internally structured and worded. In a recent paper at the EURALEX International Congress, Henk VERKUYL (see [Verkuyl 1994]) has given the example of chess pieces and their treatment in a major monolingual dictionary of Dutch: for some pieces, the form, the movement, and the importance of the piece has been described, for others not all of these properties have been indicated in the definition. However, being part of the same system, in that case the chess game, there is no reason why to exclude some of the relevant properties from the description of some of the pieces, while including such descriptions in the definitions of others. More generally speaking, what is necessary, is *consistency* of the description of elements of a domain; to support (semi-)automatic checking of this consistency, a content model, as it is, for example, embodied in typed feature based representation languages, is needed. We claim that the availability of controlled content models is also a prerequisite for the efficient construction of parallel fragments in a machine translation scenario: if we can ensure consistency across monolingual descriptions of a given domain, it is much easier to build well-organized translation dictionaries which cover the relevant fragments and facts more homogeneously than this is often the case.

The second main goal of the DELIS project, along with tool support for corpus-based lexicography, is thus to make a step towards tools for the control of consistency of lexicographic content models. This goal goes well together with the corpus-based approach: evidently, the corpus material does not readily furnish any interpretation in itself. On the contrary, acquisition of evidence for lexical descriptions only makes sense if there is a target model which can be filled with analyses of corpus material. However, the relationship between corpus and lexicon is not one-way. Of course, an initial model needs to be filled by analysis of corpus data, but the corpus usually makes material available for which there is no description in the initial model the lexicographer has started out with. And often, the analysis of corpus data leads the lexicographer to a much more detailed description than just introspection. For that reason, "model evolution"[2] is seen as an essential component of lexicon building, and tools to support this are in the process of being designed in DELIS. The process of creating dictionary entries is indeed seen, in parallel to grammar engineering in NLP, as a spiral-wise process, similar to the prototyping cycle in software engineering. The DELIS tools support a methodology of work where the lexicographer constructs a first "prototypical" dictionary entry, verifies it by comparison with the corpus data at hand (using support tools to do this semi-automatically[3]), modifies his lexicon entry by inclusion of new descriptions and/or modification of the existing ones, checks his new version of the entry again against corpus data, possibly still enhances his dictionary entry, etc. The three main components of the dictionary building process are schematized in Figure 1 below: corpus and (upcoming) content model in their two-way interaction, as well as the exportation of data from a given state of the model, towards applications.

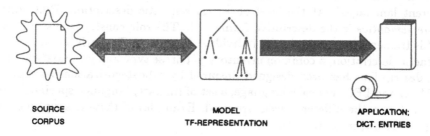

SOURCE   MODEL   APPLICATION:

CORPUS   TF-REPRESENTATION   DICT. ENTRIES

Fig. 1. The basic components of DELIS: corpus sources, lexical model, and applications

1.2 A Proposal for a Methodology of Dictionary Building

The work procedure which DELIS is in the process of elaborating is influenced by what has come to be known in lexicography as the onomasiological approach.

---

[2] The term is used in database technology, for example in the development of object-oriented databases, to denote the fact that schemata underlying the content model of a database, may be updated over the life cycle of the database. The main technical challenge, in this context, is control of data integrity and consistency.

[3] See [Linden 1994] and [Emele 1994] for a description and examples.

First, lexical semantic descriptions and rough classifications (according to FILL-MORE's *frame semantics*) are worked out for prominent items of a lexical field. These are then refined and linked with syntactic and morphosyntactic descriptions. At the lexical semantic level, information contained in predicate-argument structures, as well as a description in terms of roles as proposed in FILLMORE's *frame semantics* (cf. [Fillmore 1993a], [Fillmore 1993b]), but also structural information (selectional constraints, linking statements giving the relation between semantic roles and grammatical functions) are given. Syntactic information, including a description of the complement structure of verbs and the distribution of adjuncts, as well as morphosyntactic information indicating the phrase types by which verb complements are realized, complete the description. The onomasiological point of view implies that on the one hand a decent coverage of related meanings from one lexical semantic field is aimed at (in DELIS, fragments covering the verbs of perception and the main speech act verbs are being described), and that on the other hand not all "readings" of a given verb are worked on at a time: for example, many verbs of visual perception can be used metaphorically in meanings close to 'mental processes' or 'considering', 'awareness', 'testing', etc. These readings are not (fully) described in the first place, since the 'perception' readings are the focus of interest.

The DELIS approach also has commonalities with ongoing work in view of the standardization of lexical descriptions. The DELIS fragments, intended to cover five European languages (English, French, Italian, Danish, and Dutch), are being built with one and the same inventory of descriptive devices in mind for the different languages[4]. At the level of lexical semantic description, FILLMORE's *frame semantics* is the descriptive framework. The role constellations proposed in this framework are used in the individual fragments. Similarly, at the level of syntactic description, a common inventory of phrase type and grammatical function descriptions has been designed, inspired by subcategorization descriptions in HPSG and LFG. For each language, a set of (in part) language-specific linking rules between the different levels are used. Examples of these descriptions will be given below, in Section 2.4.

The monolingual lexicon fragments provided by DELIS are constructed according to a shared methodology, and on the basis of a shared set of descriptive devices. The use of "content models" embodied in the encoding of the language specific classes in typed feature structures enhances the consistency of the descriptions, with respect to the classification criteria used. This is in our view a good starting point for the construction of contrastive dictionaries for machine translation. The lack of transparency and of generalizations in such dictionaries has often beeen deplored: a recent example is the discussion of grooming verbs and their treatment in METAL, by Thierry FONTENELLE and others: they

---

[4] See CALZOLARI's article in this volume, concerning the EAGLES initiative for the standardization, among others, of lexical descriptions. DELIS has contributed to and, in part, integrated EAGLES proposals for morphosyntactic description in computational lexicons.

show that much could be gained from a systematic and consistent description
of similar phenomena belonging to the same field, by similar (or identical, but
parameterized) rules.

The DELIS work on the first, still preliminary, results of which we report in
this article, aims at making such sharable translation rules available for a few
domains, on the basis of linked parallel dictionary fragments.

1.3 Structure of this Article

The purpose of the present article is to investigate the usefulness of the DELIS
approach for the construction of parallel monolingual lexical fragments for different languages and for relating these fragments in view of bilingual translation
dictionaries. The linking should be made easier and more straightforward by
the fact that a common descriptive vocabulary is used. The onomasiological approach to the description of lexical fields should as well support the contrastive
use of the individual lexical descriptions in the construction of a translation dictionary which would be similar to KAMEYAMA's proposal of using a "multilingual
lattice" as a common conceptual or lexical semantic information structure for
source and target language (cf. [Kameyama/Ochitani/Peters 1991]).

The DELIS claim about contrastive dictionaries is that if monolingual lexicons have been worked out according to a parallel working methodology and
for the same fragment, and if these lexicon fragments are represented in the
same (constraint-based) formalism, the monolingual descriptions should easily
be linkable to make up contrastive dictionary entries for a translation dictionary. In addition, DELIS is assessing the usefulness of a meta-classification on
the level of types of contrastive problems for the purpose of further structuring
the contrastive dictionaries[5].

In this article, we first outline the descriptive devices used in the DELIS modeling of perception verbs, as well as a few relevant properties of the encoding in
the typed feature structure format used in the project. We then investigate the
possibilities of linking monolingual descriptions constructed according to these
principles and we give a few examples, also from work on HPSG-based machine
translation; finally, we illustrate the possibilities of linking monolingual descriptions to build contrastive descriptions.

---

[5] See [Barnett/Mani/Rich 1991] on such meta-classifications, and [Heid 1994] on the
notion of "contrastive classes." In the present context, we cannot go into details
about constrastive classifications.

2 Constructing Parallel Monolingual Dictionary Fragments

2.1 Framework and Purpose

The DELIS project has chosen the domain of perception verbs as a field for experimentation: the working methodology and the descriptions under development in the project are being tried out on this dictionary fragment[6]. By "parallel dictionary fragments" we mean lexical specifications which, together with the appropriate grammars, describe a set of sentences which can be accepted as translations of each other.

A detailed description of the main lines of the description, according to *frame semantics*, has been given by [Ostler (Coord.) 1994], as well as in OSTLER's contribution to this volume. We thus need not repeat the main facts and the details of the descriptive approach here. We limit ourselves to an overview which allows to situate the encoding work.

The choice of *frame semantics* is not arbitrary, but also not the only possible one. As pointed out by OSTLER (this volume), *frame semantics* inherently supports onomasiological work. In the context of the DELIS tool building work, *frame semantics* is seen as a prominent example of a framework for lexical semantic description by which a lexicographer may be led in his/her corpus exploration in view of the construction of dictionary entries. *Frame semantics* is interested in a description of "scenarios" (frames), by means of roles; but it also contains a component which is aimed at making explicit statements about which (possibly cross-linguistically observable) lexical semantic distinctions are expressed in a given language and by which syntactic means. An explicit and detailed description of the syntax-semantics interface is thus inherent to a *frame semantics* approach.

For the practical work of the lexicographer, the "semantics-first" approach in corpus exploration is quite attractive (a preliminary grouping of sentences illustrating the same "reading" of the keyword is not too hard; ideally, it is then supported by a more theoretically informed approach to the grouping of the material, as furnished by frame semantics). A formalization of corpus exploration according to this principle is however only possible by "indirect" means, given that (semi-)automatic corpus query is essentially based on the retrieval of sentences according to the syntactic properties of the lexemes they contain.

Although *frame semantics* is a prototypical example of the kind of approach supported by the DELIS tools and methods, it is yet seen as an *example* of a theory guiding lexicographic corpus exploration; another approach which would provide an explicit syntax-semantics interface, for example at the level of predicate-argument structures, could in principle be supported as well. In all cases, the goal

---

[6] A second domain is that of speech act verbs; first results are expected there for end 1994.

is to make the interrelationships between partial syntactic and partial semantic descriptions explicit, and to use such interrelationships in corpus exploration. Thereby, we can as well make a step forward towards better reproducibility of lexical semantic classifications in dictionaries[7]. The assumption is that by making both lexical semantic and syntactic descriptions more explicit and by linking them, a better means of reproducing the classification used by the lexicographer should become available[8]. The lexical semantic classifications in DELIS are documented in different ways: at the level of individual instances, the lexicographer can give examples of corpus sentences; at the level of lexical classes, the relationship between different descriptive levels also serves as documentation: by stating the relations between a lexical semantic description in role constellations, a syntactic one in terms of grammatical functions and finally one in terms of phrase structural constructs, a way of binding the lexical semantic classifications to observable (i.e., corpus-retrievable) phenomena is given; this "cascade" of relations accross the different descriptive levels is of course only a very rough approximation, and applying it automatically to extract relevant corpus lines leads in general to some noise. A trained lexicographer would in many cases perform better, but the lexicographer would use much of the available work time to first read through the corpus lines, in order to select the relevant ones; the advantage of a semi-automatic device is that it allows to reduce considerably the amount of corpus lines from which the lexicographer has to select the relevant ones[9].

2.2 Representing Lexical Descriptions in a <u>Typed Feature Structure</u> Format

The *Typed Feature Structure* (TFS) System (cf. [Emele 1994], [Emele 1993], [Zajac 1992]) is used as a lexical representation language in DELIS. The system belongs to the same "family" of typed feature logic based formalisms as

---

[7] One of the intriguing observations of [Fillmore/Atkins 1991] is the fact that only very few of the "reading distinctions" used to describe the English noun and verb *risk* are shared by the major definition dictionaries of English. If there is no agreement, how can we find out at least about the *criteria* used to classify the readings or to divide a polysemous item up into different readings?

[8] A minimal requirement for "reuse" of lexical descriptions is their "reinterpretability". This task of understanding which set of data is covered by a given description is somewhat easier if there is documentation. DELIS descriptions are not meant to be more original or in any other way preferable over other descriptive linguistic work, but the intention is to make them better documented (or documentable), and thus easier to reuse.

[9] In an 18 million word corpus used by Oxford University Press for the purposes of DELIS work, 1359 occurences of the word form *taste* were found; out of these, 959 contain the noun, 365 the verb. Out of these verb readings, only 23 illustrate the construction *sth tastes like...*, another 17 *sth tastes of...*, some 50 the construction *sth tastes* ap *(nice, bitter, awful,etc.)*. The DELIS search tool (cf. [Linden 1994]) retrieves them in a few seconds. The lexicographer using such a tool can concentrate on a more "fine-grained" analysis.

the one described by KRIEGER in this volume, although there are differences of detail.

The TFS system is based on typed feature logics, and its formal and computational properties are well understood. Combining aspects of object-oriented programming and knowledge representation with properties of constraint logic formalisms, the TFS system can be used for both the representation of partial linguistic descriptions and the evaluation of queries. Other than in many databases, there is just one data structure (typed feature structures) used as data description language, data manipulation language, and query language. This reduces the interface problem: lexical descriptions of each linguistic level are represented as TFS types, and the interrelationships between the levels are encoded as relational constraints or as recursive mapping statements, again in TFS[10].

Although it is most likely not necessary to have recursive types within a lexical representation language (other than in grammar encoding, except for very few cases of derivational morphology, no natural use of recursion in the dictionary is envisageable), the usefulness of such devices for mapping rules, exportation tools, lexicon converters, etc. should not be underestimated; also for the use of these tools, no interface problems arise.

The constraint-based properties of TFS include powerful consistency checking (e.g., through the use of appropriateness statements, typing of the feature structures used as data types, etc.). Moreover, the system provides ad-hoc-querying facilities which allow for flexible extraction of subsets of the lexical descriptions according to criteria defined by the user on the basis of his particular needs.

The object-oriented properties of TFS, which are most relevant for its use as a lexical representation language, include the notions of class and instance, and monotonic multiple inheritance along a user-defined class-hierarchy. This in turn allows to define the lexicon in terms of hierarchically structured classes of partial descriptions from the different descriptive levels, lexical items being instances of these classes.

2.3 Dictionary Architecture

DELIS dictionaries are characterized by the properties of modularity and "access neutrality", as well as by the use which is made of classificatory devices. Most of these properties are supported or made possible by the choice of the TFS formalism as a lexical representation language.

2.3.1 A Classificatory Approach to Lexical Description DELIS dictionaries are *classificatory*. Types of TFS are used to denote lexical classes. For each

---

[10] Examples of such relations are discussed in a schematic way below, in Section 2.3.2 and illustrated in Figure 4.

descriptive level, a class (or: type) hierarchy is provided: there is a hierarchy of partial lexical semantic descriptions (role configurations), a subcategorization class hierarchy, etc.

A "reading" of a lexeme is encoded as an instance of a class. To keep track, in the description of the readings, of the different descriptive levels, we follow the model of HPSG's description of the *linguistic sign* and consider a lexical instance as having a number of attributes, at least one for the applicable role configuration, one for the syntactic subcategorization properties, and one for morphosyntactic properties (if relevant). Additional ones may be added (e.g., for the purpose of a given type of dictionary). The lexical entries of a given reading are thus considered as instances of classes belonging to separate class hierarchies: information from the different levels of description "flows together" as schematized in Figure 2.

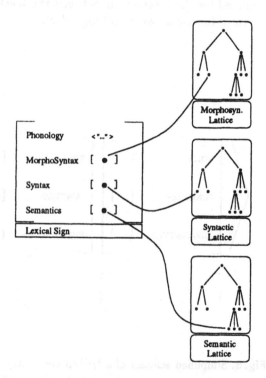

Fig. 2. Lexical entries: information flowing together from different knowledge sources

2.3.2 Modularity of the Lexicon *Modularity* is achieved by breaking lexical descriptions up according to the traditional levels of description. Thus, lexical semantic descriptions by means of role constellations, syntactic descriptions in terms of grammatical functions and phrase types, and morphosyntactic descriptions are kept in separate modules. For the purpose of contrastive description, the *frame semantics* description of the lexical predicates (roles, semantic feature constraints) is shared: not only the same descriptive devices (e.g., role names, role configurations) are used, but the monolingual descriptions are also integrated into a common hierarchy of role configuration types[11]. For the levels of functional syntax and morphosyntax, language specific modules are built.

The level-specific modules need to be related. To encode these interrelationships, sets of relational constraints have been formulated. These constraints are applied to the combination of partial descriptions from different levels. So, for a given lexical instance, the following must hold:

- the reading must be an instance of exactly one class of role-configurations and exactly one syntactic subcategorization class or a set of related ones[12];
- the combination of the classes must satisfy the product of the relational constraints formulated for the interaction between the levels (e.g., between roles and grammatical functions, as in linking rules).

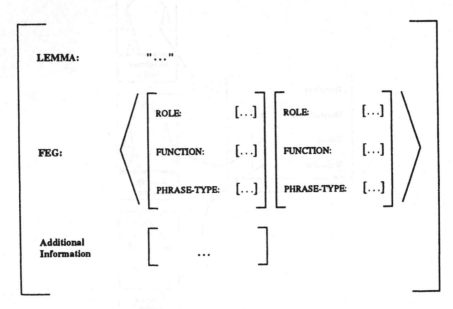

Fig. 3. Simplified schema of a DELIS verb entry

---

[11] This is not an "interlingua". We use partial lexical semantic descriptions to ease translation, but we do not make any claims about the status of these shared partial content descriptions. In particular, no attempt at constructing a meaning representation for the whole sentences to be translated is made. We consider the role constellations as approximations of some of the properties relevant for meaning description, but certainly not all.

[12] Syntactic variation without meaning change is treated by disjunctive definitions of syntactic classes. Alternative representations are possible.

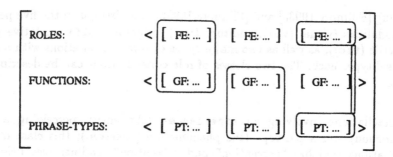

Fig. 4. Relation between levels of description

The encoding in TFS can be schematized as in the above illustration in Figure 3: along with the LEMMA, a FRAME ELEMENT GROUP (FEG) is given, which is a list of triples made up from roles, grammatical function types, and phrase types. Role constellations are expressed by the sequence of roles appearing in the triples of an FEG value; the information usually given in subcategorization lists (e.g., LFG's "predicate value") is expressed by the sequence of grammatical functions appearing in the triples of a given FEG value. Each such triple is only well-formed, if it satisfies the relational constraints. This is schematized in Figure 4, where the boxes symbolize the relational constraints.

2.3.3 Access Neutrality: Ad-hoc Query in a Modular System

The modular approach, the class-wise dictionary organization, and the inherent ad-hoc query capacity of TFS together support the access to DELIS dictionaries by any kind of underspecified query. None of the descriptive levels is considered as the primary "access key" to the lexical information contained in the dictionary. This property is called "access-neutrality" in DELIS: other than, e.g., with databases, no single access path to the relevant information is "privileged"; the ad-hoc query facility of TFS is fully exploited in the dictionary tools. As is the case with all constraint logic based formalisms, TFS can be queried with arbitrary feature structures. For example, a query in terms of the role names of the first and second argument, but without specifying the lemma name and the syntactic properties, will return all syntactically well-formed readings of all those lemmas the description of which contains the roles specified in the query. Similarly, we can ask for all verbs contained in the dictionary which have a certain role in the first argument (say an **experiencer**), and the second argument of which is realized by a certain grammatical construction, say a *wh*-clause (irrespective of the underlying role). These possiblities can evidently be used in a translation situation, when it comes to the selection of target language items.

2.4 A Few Examples

We now illustrate the descriptive work going on in DELIS with a few examples from the domain of perception verbs.

Following [Fillmore 1993a] and [Fillmore 1993b], we distinguish the five perceptive modalities (visual (vis), auditory (aud), olfactory (olf), gustative (gus)
and tactile (tac)), as well as two major types of role constellations with a number of subtypes each. The two classes of role constellations can be described as
follows:

- constellations involving an **experiencer** (the entity perceiving a phenomenon) and a **percept** (the phenomenon perceived); this class of constellations englobes "perception" and "attention" readings (see below for
  details);
- constellations involving in addition to (one or both of) the above a
  judgement role (denoting the subjective or objective evaluation which the
  perceiver may formulate on the percept, based on the perception. This class
  is called "judging", in DELIS).

Each of these two broad types of role constellations has subtypes; for example,
a major distinction concerns the intentional vs. non-intentional participation
of the **experiencer** in the event: in "perception"-events, the **experiencer** is
non-intentional, in "attention"-events, the experiencer participates intentionally.
The **percept** role can be further subdivided, according to whether it denotes an
"actual" perceived phenomenon or a "target" (as with the verb *look for*[13]).
Similarly, the **judgement** role has subtypes denoting a **veridical** judgement
(*this smells sweet*), an **evaluative** one (*this smells awful*), or an **inference**
(*she looks angry*).

The table in Figure 5 illustrates some of the topmost types of role constellations,
with English examples.

Some English perception verbs are quite polysemous within the perception domain (we disregard additional non-perceptive readings). An example of such a
verb is EN *to taste*. For the sake of illustration, we list a few, not all of the
readings identified in the corpora used in DELIS, in the table in Figure 6 below.

Readings of *taste* fall into each of the lexical semantic classes indicated in the
left column of the table in Figure 6. Each is defined by its characteristic role
configuration, some have as well particular syntactic properties or selectional
constraints.

As indicated above, there is a set of subcategorization classes for each language.
In preliminary experiments, grammatical function labels from Lexical Functional

---

[13] The case of *look for* is not a very clear-cut one; this item could also be classified as an
element of a subclass of verbs of "searching"; the visual perception is not central, in
this case. Frame semantics support the idea that different frames can be combined.
The **judgement** subclass of the perception verbs can be seen as a joint subclass of
both the basic perception class and another basic frame class, of "judging events",
which involve a person judging, an item judged and a judgement, independent of
any perception.

subclass	role constellation	examples (instances)
perception	<[ROLE: exp-nonint] [ROLE: pct-act]>	*John saw the light.* *John saw the car.*
attention	<[ROLE: exp-int] [ROLE: pct-act>	*John watched the car.* *John looked at the book.*
attention-tgt.	<[ROLE: exp-int] [ROLE: pct-tgt]>	*John looked for a pen.*
judgement-ver.	<[ROLE: pct-act] [ROLE: jud-ver]>	*The juice tastes sweet.*
judgement-eval.	<[ROLE: pct-act] [ROLE: jud-eval]>	*The juice tastes awful.*
judgement-inf.	<[ROLE: pct-act] [ROLE: jud-inf]>	*She looks tired.*

Fig. 5. Role constellations defining subclasses of the perception vocabulary

Type	Example
perception	I tasted garlic in the soup.
attention	Could you please taste this soup?
jud.-veridical	This juice tastes bitter. This soup tastes of garlic. This substance tastes like cardamom.
jud.-evaluation	This juice tastes awful. This thing looks like hell.
jud.-inferential	This food tastes rotten. She sounds happy.

Fig. 6. A few readings of the English verb *taste*

Grammar (LFG) have been used, as well as a traditional inventory of types of phrase structural constructs; given that LFG's functions are, however, to a considerable extent defined in terms of phrase structure types anyway, a less redundant formulation of the syntactic classifications is possible, if at the level of grammatical functions only distinctions between **subjects, complements, predicative** elements, and **adjuncts** are made, as is the case in HPSG. On this basis, a subcategorization classification for each of the DELIS languages is elaborated[14].

Below, we reproduce a few readings of the Dutch verb *kijken*, in the TFS encoding. The readings contain the relevant syntactic description, along with the semantic one[15].

---

[14] For English, another description, for example [Sanfilippo 1993]'s modeling, could also be used; it is mostly compatible with, e.g., HPSG.

[15] The TFS examples are taken from a preliminary encoding exercise carried out in DELIS; the TFS notation follows closely the entry scheme given above in Figure 3.

```
kijken-tgt-voor
[LEMMA:    "kijken",
 MODALITY: vis,
 FEG:    <fe
            [FE: exper-i[INTENTION: +],
             GF: subj,
             PT: np]
            fe
            [FE: p-target,
             GF: comp,
             PT: obj-pp[PREP: voor]]>].


kijken-tgt-cl
[LEMMA:    "kijken",
 MODALITY: vis,
 FEG:    <fe
            [FE: exper-i[INTENTION: +],
             GF: subj,
             PT: np]
            fe
            [FE: p-target,
             GF: comp,
             PT: wh-cl[COMPLT: wh-compl]]>].


kijken-att
[LEMMA:    "kijken",
 MODALITY: vis,
 FEG:    <fe
            [FE: exper-i[INTENTION: +],
             GF: subj,
             PT: np]
            fe
            [FE: p-actual-ent
                 [SORT: entity],
             GF: comp,
             PT: obj-pp[PREP: naar]]>].


kijken-media
[LEMMA:    "kijken",
 MODALITY: vis,
 FEG:    <fe
            [FE: exper-i[INTENTION: +],
             GF: subj,
             PT: np]
            fe
            [FE: p-actual-event
                 [SORT: event],
             GF: comp,
             PT: np]>].
```

The readings of *kijken*, above, are semantically classified as indicated in Figure 7.

Reading	Semantic class	Paraphrase EN
kijken-tgt-voor	attention-target	"look for sth"
kijken-tgt-ce	attention-target	"look whether ... +sentence"
kijken-att	attention	"look at sth"
kijken-media	attention [Sel. Restriction: percept: a media event]	"watch (TV)"

Fig. 7. A few readings of Dutch *kijken*

These few examples show what is meant by the construction of "parallel" fragments of lexicons: the lexical semantic descriptive devices are shared, and the overall layout of the lexical entries is identical across languages.

3 Relating Dictionary Fragments for Translation Purposes

The inventory of role constellations which is being set up for the domain of perception verbs of English, French, Italian, Danish, and Dutch lends itself to the contrastive description by means of sharing. The onomasiological approach underlying the construction of the monolingual fragments, as well as the claims of frame semantics support such an approach.

We have elsewhere described a similar lexicon design in the framework of an HPSG-based approach to translation (cf. [Heid/Kuhn 1994]): there, the semantic description used was provided by the value of the content-attribute of HPSG's sign definition. In Figure 8, we schematically depict the translation process as it is carried out in the HPSG experiment: a sentence is analyzed by an HPSG grammar and lexicon, and a syntactic and semantic description is built up. Given that the TFS system, which has been used for the encoding, supports queries with partial descriptions, the input which is given to the system can be formulated as a query of TFS (preceded by the question mark "?"); this notation has been used in the figure to illustrate the points in the "processing" where the two grammars receive input.

When the shared semanctic description has been produced, it is "handed over" to the target language HPSG grammar and lexicon. The source language grammar and lexicon are used to "analyze" the sentence, i.e., to identify the lexical semantic role constellations involved. The target grammar and lexicon are used ("in generation mode") to identify lexical items on the basis of the shared role constellations.

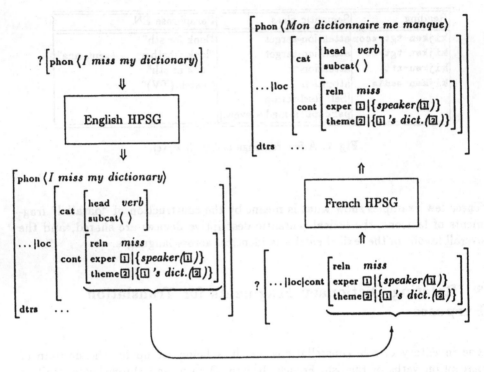

Fig. 8. Schema of translation process (from [Heid/Kuhn 1994])

3.1 A Few Data: Divergences in the Perception Field

In principle, this architecture directly supports the use of the DELIS lexical entries, because they make all of the necessary information available. Given that there are no grammars which would directly use DELIS format dictionary entries, a reformatting towards HPSG is necessary before the experiment can be run. In the HPSG approach, not only trivial cases as the ones indicated below in Figure 9 can be handled, but also more complex translation problems, such as the typical divergence cases which have frequently been discussd in the machine translation literature.

More complicated cases involve divergences (in the terminology of [Dorr 1990], [Barnett/Mani/Rich 1991], etc.), i.e., cases where different languages use syntactically different means to convey a given meaning. If such cases are described in the framework of the DELIS approach, divergences can be treated at the level

NL	luisteren	<SUBJ *naar*-OBJ>
EN	listen	<SUBJ *to*-OBJ>
FR	écouter	<SUBJ OBJ>
NL	kijken	<SUBJ *wh*-COMPL>
EN	see, look	<SUBJ *wh*-COMPL>
FR	regarder	<SUBJ *wh*-COMPL>
NL	zien	<SUBJ OBJ *als*-PREDIC>
FR	voir	<SUBJ *en*-OBJ PREDIC>

Fig. 9. A few simple cases of translation equivalence in the perception domain

of the relationships between role constellations and syntactic descriptions[16]. In [Heid/Kuhn 1994], we have shown how an HPSG-based shared-content model of a machine translation system can cater for the major types of divergences observed in the MT literature. These divergences include the following (we adopt the terminology used by [Dorr 1990], although DORR's classification would need some more discussion[17]):

- categorial divergence
  (EN *be hungry* ↔ FR *avoir faim*)
- conflational divergence
  (EN *to mispronounce sth* ↔ FR *prononcer qc de travers*)
- thematic divergence
  (EN *I miss my dictionary* ↔ FR *mon dictionnaire me manque*)
- demotional/promotional divergence
  (head switching: EN *he happened to be on the phone* ↔ DE *er telefonierte zufällig*)

Within the perception domain, a number of these cases appear quite frequently; in particular, in the translation between Germanic and Romance languages (e.g., French and Dutch), there are quite a few examples of categorial and promotional/demotional divergences. Consider the French expressions for olfactory, gustative, and tactile perception, as well as veridical and evaluative judging[18], given in the table in Figure 10; the respective English verbs (*smell, taste, feel,*

---

[16] We are aware that this implies a considerable amount of simplification, because the descriptive granularity of role configurations does not allow to keep track of a number of linguistic properties (e.g., discourse semantic, connotational, etc.) which may sometimes influence the choice of translation equivalents. The granularity used is however similar to that of other machine translation systems.

[17] We have somewhat reduced DORR's original list of divergence phenomena; those of DORR's types which we left out are covered by our "simple cases": these include, for example, **transitive** vs. **p-object** constructions, as exemplified above in Figure 9. For a discussion of contrastive problem classes, see e.g. [Heid 1994].

Type	vis	aud	olf	gus	tac
perception	voir	entendre	sentir l'odeur de np	sentir le goût de np	sentir (la sensation de) np
attention	regarder	écouter	sentir	goûter	sentir/toucher
jud.-verid.	–	–	avoir une odeur adj	avoir un goût adj	ressembler à np
					qc. est adj au toucher
jud.-eval.	qc. est adj	qc. est adj	avoir une odeur adj	avoir un goût adj	avoir un toucher adj [rare]
	à la vue	à l'oreille	qc. est adj à l'odeur	qc. est adj au goût	qc. est adj au toucher

Fig. 10. The perception field in French

etc.) are distributed as in the table in Figure 11, and there is a set of equivalent pairs EN ↔ FR which falls under the above types of divergences. The following are a few examples:

- conflational divergence ("perception class")
  - EN *he smelled a fire*
  - FR *il a senti l'odeur d'un feu*

  - EN *he tasted garlic in the soup*
  - FR *il a senti le goût de l'ail dans le soupe*
- categorial divergence ("judging-veridical" and "judging-evaluative" classes)
  - EN *This juice tastes bitter*
  - FR *Ce jus a un goût amer*

  - EN *This substance smells nice*
  - FR *Cette substance a une odeur agréable*[19]

3.2 Mismatches: Differences in Role Configurations

Along with these cases, where the role configurations in source and target language are the same, there are also a few examples in the field of perception verbs, where one language has lexicalized readings the role configurations of which are not readily lexicalized in the other language. For example, in Dutch (and German), it is possible to express the perceptive stimulus of an interpretation, whereas a similar construction would be strange in French or Italian: *Ich*

---

frequency: *avoir un goût* adj. is more frequent than *être* adj. *au goût*, but *être* adj *au toucher* is most likely more frequent than *avoir un toucher* adj. A corpus-based study of the items described in Figure 10 is under way.

[19] The cases of categorial divergence involve support verb constructions (*avoir une odeur* adj) in French. The treatment of support verb constructions in HPSG Grammar has not been completely satisfactory, so far. [Erbach/Krenn 1993] have made a few proposals on this topic, and now, [Kuhn 1994] has elaborated a more general description; this allows to integrate support verb constructions into the general proposal for the treatment of categorial divergences made in [Heid/Kuhn 1994].

Type of event	vis	aud	olf	gus	tac
perception	see	hear	smell	taste	feel
attention	look watch	listen	smell	taste	feel
jud.-verid.	–	–	smell	taste	feel
jud.-eval.	look	sound	smell	taste	feel

Fig. 11. Overview of the perception field for English

sehe an ihren Augen, daß sie glücklich ist. Similarly, the **experiencer** role can be expressed with judging-evaluative readings in English as an optional argument (*this juice tastes strange to me; to me, this sounds awful,* etc.). In German, this is possible with *schmecken* (**gus**), but not with *riechen* (**olf**): *das schmeckt mir gut; das schmeckt gut; das riecht gut; *das riecht mir gut.* In French, it is impossible to express the **experiencer** role by means of an analogous construction to the English one, and one has to use either an evaluative verb (leaving out the "perceptive" meaning component from the verb: *cela me paraît agréable,* etc.) or to use an adjunct construction (which is stylistically less preferred): *selon moi, cela a une odeur étrange,* etc.

The treatment of these cases (which is under way) will have to make sure that there are additional means available, in the target language, to express roles which are not "covered" by the lexical items: if no lexical equivalent for a given role configuration is available, the "closest natural rendition" (terminology of [Barnett/Mani/Rich 1991]) has to be identified, and additional lexical or grammatical means must be deployed to render the relevant meaning.

The DELIS lexicon encoding seems to be useful for this task as well: the comparison of potential equivalents with respect to their role configuration is an easy task, given the availability of the relevant information in the dictionaries. It should then also be possible to make lexical and grammatical means available for the translation of elements not covered in the role configurations of the lexical item of a given language.

Whether there are regularities in the way how these differences can be dealt with, and whether these regularities can be captured in rules or contrastive classes, as it is possible with divergences, remains a topic for further research. The set of parallel fragments for Germanic and Romance languages, along with the common underlying lexical semantic and syntactic description, should constitute a good descriptive starting-point for this kind of work.

4 Summary

In this article, we have presented the working methodology for the construction of parallel monolingual dictionary fragments which is under development in the DELIS project. It uses a shared lexical semantic description, in terms of role constellations of *frame semantics*, for the description of lexical items from different languages. Dictionary construction proceeds in an onomasiological way, insofar as readings of lexical items belonging to a given lexical semantic field are treated together. For each language, the syntactic properties of the lexical items described, as well as the syntax/semantics-mapping are developed separately. The separate language-specific dictionary modules can be combined to support translation along the lines of the "shared content-approach" which has been tested already in the framework of HPSG-based machine translation. In the framework of this testing, devices for the treatment of the major classes of contrastive divergences have been developed.

Although work on this topic in DELIS is still ongoing, we can already foresee that the linking of the parallel dictionary fragments is easy to carry out: no additional descriptive devices are needed with respect to the monolingual grammars and lexicons, to provide the lexical input for a machine translation application.

As we report on it, the DELIS description work is ongoing. A formal encoding, in the framework of typed feature structures, is under way for the monolingual lexicon fragments. Once all lexicon fragments for the different languages are available, it will be possible to combine them to cater for divergence cases, along the lines of the HPSG-based work discussed in this article, and to assess in more detail the usefulness of the encoding for the treatment of contrastive problems arising from the fact that not all of the role constellations identified for the different languages generalize over all of the five languages under analysis.

The methodological outcome of DELIS will allow to assess to what extent it is possible to use a shared descriptive framework and a common encoding scheme more widely for the purpose of the development of machine translation dictionaries. A field where this approach seems to be promising is the creation of parallel fragments on a common text corpus basis for sublanguage and specific text types, such as parallel corpora of translated (or separately generated) technical documentation.

References

[ACL-29 1991] Proceedings of the 29th Annual Meeting of the Association for Computational Linguistics, University of California, Berkeley, California, USA, 1991.

[Barnett/Mani/Rich 1991] James Barnett, Inderjeet Mani, Elaine Rich: "Reversible Machine Translation: What to do when the Languages don't match up", in: [Strzalkowski (Ed.) 1991] pp. 61-70.

[Dorr 1990] Bonnie Dorr: "Solving Thematic Divergences in Machine Translation", in: *Proceedings of the 28th Annual Conference of the Association for Computational Linguistics* (Pittsburgh, Pa.: University of Pittsburgh), 1990, pp. 127-134.

[Emele 1994] Martin Emele: "TFS – The Typed Feature Structure Representation Formalism", in: *Proceedings of the International Workshop on Sharable Natural Language Resources (SNLR)*, 1994.

[Emele 1993] Martin Emele: "TFS – The Typed Feature Structure Representation Formalism", in: [USZKOREIT (ED.) 1993]: *Proceedings of the EAGLES workshop on implemented formalisms*, (Saarbrücken) DFKI report, 1993.

[Erbach/Krenn 1993] Gregor Erbach, Brigitte Krenn: "Idioms and support-verb constructions in HPSG", (Saarbrücken: Universität des Saarlandes), ms. 1993, [= Computerlinguistik an der Universität des Saarlandes (CLAUS), *Report Nr. 28*].

[Fillmore/Atkins 1991] Beryl T.S. Atkins, Charles Fillmore: "Starting where the dictionaries stop – The challenge of corpus lexicography", in: Beryl T.S. Atkins, Antonio Zampolli (Eds.): *Computational Approaches to the Lexicon*, Oxford, to appear.

[Fillmore 1993a] Charles Fillmore: "A Cognitive-Frames Approach to the Vocabulary of Sensation and Perception in English", Draft, ms., 8 pp, University of California in Berkeley, 1993.

[Fillmore 1993b] Charles Fillmore: "Frame semantics and perception verbs", contribution to Dagstuhl Seminar 9313, in: Hans Kamp, James Pustejovsky (Eds.): *Universals in the Lexicon: At the Intersection of Lexical Semantic Theories*, 1993, ms., Dagstuhl.

[Heid 1994] Ulrich Heid: "Contrastive Classes – Relating Monolingual Dictionaries to Build an MT Dictionary", in: Ferenc Kiefer, Gábor Kiss and Júlia Pajzs: *Papers in Computational Lexicography, COMPLEX '94*, Budapest, 1994, pp. 115 - 126.

[Heid/Kuhn 1994] Ulrich Heid, Jonas Kuhn: "Treating structual differences in an HPSG-based approach to interlingual machine translation", in: Peter Bosch, Christopher Habel (Eds.): *Proceedings of Arbeitsgruppe AG-6 der DGfS-Jahrestagung 1994*.

[Kameyama/Ochitani/Peters 1991] Megumi Kameyama, Ryo Ochitani and Stanley Peters: "Resolving Translation Mismatches with Information Flow", in: [ACL-29 1991], 1991, pp. 193 - 200.

[Kuhn 1994] Jonas Kuhn: *Die Behandlung von Funktionsverbgefügen in einem HPSG-basierten Übersetzungsansatz*, ms., (Stuttgart: IMS-CL University of Stuttgart, Institut für maschinelle Sprachverarbeitung) 1994.

[Linden 1994] Krister Lindèn: *Specifications of the Delis Search Condition Generation tool*, Appendix to Deliverable D-V-1 of Delis (LRE 61.034), Helsinki, April 1994.

[Ostler (Coord.) 1994] Nicholas Ostler (Coord.): *A corpus-based syntactic and semantic description of lexical items: structured collection of data and exemplary description of prototypical items*, and *Towards a methodology for corpus-based lexical description leading to reusable lexical specifications, Part 1: The description of individual prototypical lexical items ("lexical analysis")*, deliverable D-II of DELIS (LRE 61.034), final version of May 3rd, 1994, (London: Linguacubun Ltd.), 1994.

[Sanfilippo 1993] Antonio Sanfilippo: "LKB Encoding of Lexical Knowledge", in: Ted Briscoe, Ann Copestake and Valerio de Paiva (Eds.): Inheritance, Defaults and the Lexicon, Cambridge, 1993.

[Strzalkowski (Ed.) 1991] Tomek Strzalkowski (Ed.): *Reversible Grammar in Natural Language Processing*, Amsterdam, 1994.

[Verkuyl 1994] Verkuyl, Henk: "Knowledge Representation in Dictionaries". Presentation at the 6th Euralex International Congress, Amsterdam 1994, ms.

[Zajac 1992] R. Zajac: "Inheritance and Constraint-Based Grammar Formalisms." *Computational Linguistics*, 18(2), 1992, pp. 159–180.

Lecture Notes in Artificial Intelligence (LNAI)

Lecture Notes in Computer Science